JOURNEY TO THE BACKWOODS

JOURNEY TO THE BACKWOODS
AUTOBIOGRAPHY OF THE OLD WOODSMAN

BY DALE FRANCIS TERRILLION

A Division of WINEPRESS PUBLISHING

© 2007 by Dale Terrillion. All rights reserved.

Pleasant Word (a division of WinePress Publishing, PO Box 428, Enumclaw, WA 98022) functions only as book publisher. As such, the ultimate design, content, editorial accuracy, and views expressed or implied in this work are those of the author.

No part of this book may be reproduced in any form, except for the inclusion of brief quotations in a review, without permission in writing from the author or publisher.

Unless otherwise noted, all Scriptures are taken from the Holy Bible, New International Version, Copyright © 1973, 1978, 1984 by the International Bible Society. Used by permission of Zondervan Publishing House. The "NIV" and "New International Version" trademarks are registered in the United States Patent and Trademark Office by International Bible Society.

Scripture references marked KJV are taken from the King James Version of the Bible.

Scripture references marked NASB are taken from the New American Standard Bible, © 1960, 1963, 1968, 1971, 1972, 1973, 1975, 1977 by The Lockman Foundation. Used by permission.

ISBN 13: 978-1-4141-0864-3
ISBN 10: 1-4141-0864-8
Library of Congress Catalog Card Number: 2006935347

DEDICATION

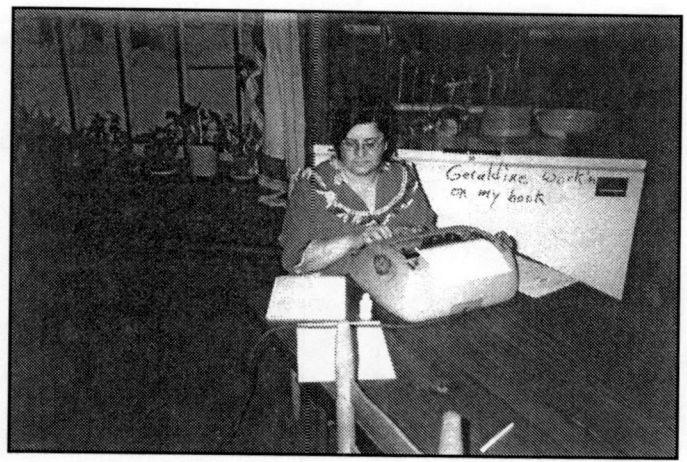

To Geraldine, who put up with me for so many years.

To our children: Tina, Troy, Tracey, and Rosemary.

To my mother and all my relatives and friends that God gave me on this trail of life.

They made this journey worth traveling.

TABLE OF CONTENTS

Preface xi
Acknowledgments xv
Stub xvii

1. Too Young to Know the Danger 21
2. Croghan the Town 26
3. Dad, Mom, and some Deviltry 35
4. Everyday Life and What Those Kids
   Won't Think of Next 46
5. Spread'n Our Wings and Run'n Away 54
6. Family Tragedies 66
7. The End of the Road – A Better Place 72
8. Winters at the Homestead 93
9. Spring Brings New Adventures 100
10. More Grow'n Up 113
11. A Backwoods Love Affair 123
12. Trap'n Massawepie – The First Years 144

13. One of the World's Best Nabors 150
14. The Other Best Nabors, and They Had Horses .. 155
15. The New House 164
16. The Dogs 173
17. Old Timers 182
18. Misfired Guns and Unusual Hunts 195
19. Hideouts and Secret Places 206
20. Further'n my Education 212
21. When Men were Men 219
22. More Education 229
23. Log'n, A Life's Destiny 235
24. An American Heritage 245
25. Big Buck and a Snowshoe Winter 252
26. The Year of Seventeen 261
27. Mr. Slayko and Murphy's Law 269
28. Old Hank 276
29. Married fer Life 284
30. Always Sawing Wood 295
31. Our Galvanized Ghetto and New Ventures 310
32. Filling In 324
33. A Pot of Black Gold 334
34. A Couple of Wood Hicks 348
35. Hang 'Er Up and Drive 364
36. Where Does Yer Stick Float? 371
37. Old Log'n Camp 379
38. Life was Better 389
39. Head'n into the Midnight Sun 405
40. To the Island of Monster Bears 414
41. The Log'n Camp 420
42. Bears Beyond Belief 430
43. Big Sky Country 441
44. Cut'n Timber 460
45. Good-bye Town – Hello Homestead 470
46. Forever Out'n the Woods 483

47. The Nitty Gritty	501
48. End of the Old Journey	520
Epilogue	530
References	532

PREFACE

I have labored on these chapters to present the feelings, emotions, and excitement of the age in which I lived them. It will be obvious to readers of this book that my schooling was limited, and that I didn't make the most of the time I spent in school. It was not because the teachers were lying down on the job. They did their best as they saw it, but did not understand a boy born to follow the ways of the creatures in the wild. If they'd have taken a poll of "who would have been the least likely to succeed," it surely would have been me. Any old timer would have observed this lad was no ordinary sponge to absorb institutional knowledge. It seems to me that society always measures a person's worth by their academic achievements or their financial status. But time and history have recorded quite another story.

JOURNEY TO THE BACKWOODS

Consider the "uneducated" Benjamin Franklin who once said, "If you would not be forgotten as soon as you are gone, either write things worth reading or do things worth writing."

I suppose people write books for all sorts of reasons: to make money, change the world, record history, influence morals, and perhaps just leave a record of their passing. All of the above had some influence on my writing this book of my backwoods journey, but I hope this to be a life-link to an almost-forgotten past or perhaps for older folks, a walk down memory lane.

My main reason for writing is that I want my journey to mean something to you personally, and inspire you to consider your own life's journey. Life is very short and, like it or not, each of us is on a journey. We are but pilgrims on this earth and the choice of which fork in the road we will take—is our very own. One way is broad and leads to destruction and many are those who travel it, while the other is narrow, and few are those who find it. After a while it resembles a path more than a road with blown-down timber and boulders to block the way. There are mud holes, and then at times the path even looks untrodden. You'll know for certain you've taken the right turn if you took along your best friend. That friend is God, the Creator of heaven and earth.

PREFACE

On my side, I require of every writer, first and last, a simple and sincere account of his own life.

> —The Hermit of Walton Pond,
> Henry David Thoreau.

I am what I am, and that's all that I am.
—The great Roy Rogers, King of the Cowboys.

A journey of a thousand miles begins with the first step.

> —Ancient proverb

ACKNOWLEDGMENTS

A special thanks to Jared Shear of Thompson Falls, Montana, for providing the cover artwork for this book. Visit his Web site at http://www.zupzup.com.

To Lloyd and Geraldine George for their part in compiling and editing.

STUB

A red-haired, freckled little boy
This fellow they call "Stub,"
He's a little scrap of mischief
With hands that need a scrub,
A shock of gold gets in his eyes
An ink splash on his cheek
And still he beams up from his desk
With face so round and pink.
No matter where I catch his eyes
Even if in mischief he's been caught
He'll smile the same wide open grin
And challenge me to call it sin.
Perhaps it's clothes upon the floor
Where I inspecting soon must pass,
Or a paper stuck beneath the door
With poetry his time he passed
Horn habit is for me to speak
To scold, even slap that freckled cheek.

JOURNEY TO THE BACKWOODS

Where in my heart, I love his fun,
And wish when all my work is done
To laugh a minute with that boy,
To share his sorrows and his joy,
To be a friend and not a foe,
To guide his footsteps as they go.
The books write all for discipline
Keep everything just so,
But could they break a little heart
With cruel words or a blow?
Won't God be always satisfied
If I turn their infant steps
To Him with gentleness and love
And sometimes miss their tricks?
For it seems to me, God made a boy
To live and laugh, to life enjoy.
And not to just an angel be, never breaking rules.
And me
How can I help but love that boy
Where oh, so plainly I can see
That 'neath the freckles and the tan
There is the making of a man.

From the *Journal and Republican* newspaper in Lowville, New York, about 1980. Author unknown, printed by permission from the *Journal*.

The first steps on the journey

CHAPTER ONE

TOO YOUNG TO KNOW THE DANGER
Circa 1949

The wind, in a rush, bore the scent of alder and beaver grass from the creek. I was held, embraced by the odor of adventure. And now, the two-toned song of a redwing blackbird floated up from the willows along the water's edge. And so I dreamed there by the back door while sitting on the steps.

I 'most died of a broken heart every time Brother James headed down to the creek to trap muskrats. Agonizing days drifted into the despairs of a crushed spirit. I'd beg, giving Mom no peace, (that is, when Dad wasn't around). "You're too young to know the danger," were her admonishing words of warning. My hopes would vanish like a spark in the wet beaver grass.

How much of this was a lad expected to endure? Who understood the exploring mind of a five-year-old born to follow the ways of the wild creatures? Who understood the yearning? Only those who belonged to the "brotherhood of the Long-hunter" understood, of whom Uncle George was a life member. Uncle was a great hunter, veteran, and carpenter who lived near the backwoods.

Ya know, mothers have inherited a tender heart. My mother was no exception. She could see my emotional suffering while I was planted on those back steps. I could hardly believe it the day she said yes! "But only if you stay close to Brother James."

"I promise!! I promise!!" I yelled as I tore off after Jimmy.

I could hear the frogs croak'n down by the creek.

If'n ever a boy was overjoyed to leave the yard, it was me. With every step and stumble I expected Mother to change her mind. I never looked back, for fear she might call out. Mothers always worry. She could see the spring runoff that left little doubt of the danger. The creek was in a wild rage. All I could see was adventure, and what was life without some hair-raisin' scrapes.

But Black Creek almost turned into black death for me.

Yes-sir-ree, this was where I belonged, sneaking through thick tag alder, jumping in the water over my boots. Ma is nowhere in sight to voice her disapproval of this trap'n endeavor. I just wanted to be as wild as the wild creatures.

TOO YOUNG TO KNOW THE DANGER

Jimmy and me meandered on up the meandering creek. By now my feet were soak'n wet but I paid no attention. I might as well been walking on air. Brother checked his traps while I stumbled along almost hypnotized. Nothing missed my notice, the freshness of spring, the smell of skunk cabbage, songbirds singing praise to the Creator.

No doubt about it, life was a great adventure. Up ahead I spied a feller coming around the bend. He appeared about Jimmy's age. "It's Kevin!" Brother said. "He's trap'n too." Brother James trapped to a certain point up the creek and Kevin came down to that point, that way each had his own territory. It was near the settlement of Croghan.

It pays to get along with your neighbors and be friends.

They commenced to talk trap'n whilst I became bored standing around in my wet boots. Glancin' about for some exciting thing that I might help happen, I spotted chunks of ice floating and bobbing along. Riding on the current they came crashing into the clumps of alders. Now this was real entertainment. I felt like a bear cub out and about for the first time. Or like a coyote pup who had just crawled out of the den for his first look at the world. I became impatient waiting for more clumps of ice. I proceeded to pack snowballs to throw into the water. There's just something about floating objects on the water that's interesting for a boy. Perhaps in a young'uns imagination they're little boats. Anyway, drifting down the creek, they commenced to pile up in the bend just below us. With childlike reasoning I concluded that if I got them all moving again, why, they'd float all the way to Beaver River.

Finding a long stick I crept close to the bank to push the snowballs into the current. But my stick wasn't quite long enough, so I held onto the alders and leaned over the creek. "Snap" went the dead tree and into the creek I plunged! The current seized me and sucked me under. Terror gripped me, and I struggled but only sucked in water. I remember looking up and seeing the surface of the water, then I remembered no more till I awoke in bed—nature had taken me to the woodshed. Mother was giving me sips of a blackberry brandy sling, a concoction of a little brandy, warm water, and ginger. My first thought was, *Will she ever let me go trap'n again?*

Decades later, I concluded that most of us would have to be trusted with the martyrdom of life.

As I learned later, Kevin saw me go under and charged past my brother to jump in and rescue me. James had his back to me and never saw me fall in. The sound of the water muffled my death dive. Kevin dove under, grabbing my coat and pulling me to the surface. Jimmy swung me up on the bank. Many times in later years I've thought how Kevin Turck had the courage to jump in and pull me out. If he hadn't, my life's journey would have ended there in the churning waters of Black Creek. Thirty-two years later someone else would reach down and draw me out of deep waters, and save my life, but that's in a much later chapter.

A boy's will is the wind's will, and the thoughts of youth are long, long thoughts.
—Henry Wadsworth Longfellow
(1807-1882)

CHAPTER TWO

CROGHAN THE TOWN
Circa 1949

Great stately maples lined that street we lived on. Their long slender limbs often intertwined and the leaves would gently brush one another. No finer canopy could ever be devised by mankind to shield the body or buildings from the hot summer sun. What else would you name it but Shady Avenue?

Croghan, New York, was a picturesque small town inhabited by about five hundred hardworking patriotic souls. It was named after "George Croghan who migrated from Ireland to America in 1741. He became a frontier trader and acquired great knowledge of Indian habits and languages. Croghan was sent into the Northwest to conduct negotiations with powerful tribes. He also became an agent and played a leading role in Indian treaties and councils."[1]

Brothers—Front left Richie, front right Jimmy, back row Wilson and Gilbert holding Dale

As an interpreter and leader of guides and scouts, Mr. Croghan was much respected by Benjamin Franklin. Franklin helped supply General Braddock with provisions for about 1,400 British troops who were to fight the French and Indians. General Braddock slighted and neglected Mr. Croghan and about one hundred guides and scouts who were with him.

JOURNEY TO THE BACKWOODS

So they left the general's company. If General Braddock had been a little more humble and listened to Croghan, it would have saved much bloodshed. For the enemy about destroyed the company of troops under Braddock.[2] From Croghan's journal dated August 15 and September 19 in 1759:

> "I cloathed the Twightwees and Cuskuskees and gave them a cannoe to carry home their sick, and Provisions for which they were very thankfull & assured me that in the fall their chiefs would come here to me, & that they would remain stedfast Friends to the English as long as the Sun & moon gave light...The Delewares delivered me up Mary Baskins and two white Boys who were Prisoners amongst them their Names unknown. The crows came over the river and delivered me up on Camble a white boy, his father lives in Conicocheque, this lad speaks the Seneca Language well."

> "The date of Croghan's departure from the service of Gen. Braddock is uncertain. However, authorities agree that he was in Bedford on May 4 of 1763.

> "Within two weeks the ill-famed uprising of Pontiac, the Ottawa Chief, broke out with savage intensity. The Army officers and Indian agents had long known that the Indians were uneasy, but the real danger had not been properly anticipated.

CROGHAN THE TOWN

"Among the frontier posts familiar to the reader of Croghan's journal, Venango, Le Boeuf, Presque Isle, Sandusky, Miami, Quiatanon, Michillinackinac and St. Joeseph's were soon captured and their garrisons and fur traders massacred or taken prisoner. Detroit and Pittsburgh endured long sieges as did several other posts fortunate enough to hold out. Untold horrors were visited on the frontiers which might have been avoided had the British followed the more liberal policy towards the Indians advocated by George Croghan."[3]

Mr. Croghan, who served so well, died in poverty.

Through the seasons of life, when I had lived enough to know what injustice was, I considered all the old woodsmen I had known and read about. He who contributed so much for the comfort of so many. He who had made so many timber barons wealthy. He who opened up the land for settlers. When he was all used up, he was cast away like an old shoe. Nuth'n left but his memories. Very few were ever appreciated till long after they died.

Perhaps George Croghan's frontier spirit still lingered there along the game trails and near the water's edge. Formed by nature's mold and the age of time. Perhaps this was the restless spirit I felt, for I too had to be a restless adventuring backwoods wanderer on a journey.

Anyhow, get'n back to the settlement. It was right out of Norman Rockwell's America. Croghan had the usual churches, bars, hotels, stores, and gas stations that it took to round out a community. Even

JOURNEY TO THE BACKWOODS

had the Beaver River Railroad that ended there just past Farney and Steiner's feed mill. Yup, the end of the line. As I remember it, the old iron horse had three or four cars behind the engine, and of course the caboose. One of my childhood dreams was riding that train, but I never got the chance. And there behind the old harness shop was the railroad station, a building of another era, the old depot. I remember go'n there with Uncle Vinny once to pick up someth'n in a crate. It was sad years later to see most of it disappear. Recently, I returned there for a graveside service for Mom and was glad to see the old depot was a museum. Trucks have made life easier no doubt, but we lost more than someth'n nostalgic.

Then there was the old Mobil gas station. Just who started it and operated it when I was a young whippersnapper, I don't recall. But years later it was run by two men whose last names were Monnat and Nortz. In fact, it became known as Monnat and Nortz's gas station. Back in the early days it had a huge red horse with wings that hung up over the doors. Every time I went by there I looked at that sign and in the imagination of a child wondered if'n there ever was such a horse. Boy oh boy, could I get a ride on that bronc!! Like I said before, when I was a boy I did a lot of dream'n.

Say, I just remembered, do you recollect the rubber-coated line that laid out near the gas pump? And it went ding-ding every time a car drove over it? Sometimes we'uns would stop there when we rode to the milk station with Uncle Vinny. Us young-uns would sneak over there and jump on that thing every chance we got, then run fer it. Kids, what the poor station attendant had to put up with! This here town about had it all, include'n the butcher, the baker, and the candlestickmaker.

One cold stormy winter night, Mother told us kids a story about the feed store in town, which became the scene of Grandfather Terrillion's unusual event. Back in Gramps's day, some men would gather at the feed store to visit quite regular like. Folks would be a-com'n and a-go'n with them wagons, bring'n grain to get ground and buy'n some also. In those days and into my childhood, feed came in 110-pound bags. Whenever someone purchased a bag, Gramps quickly made an offer to load it fer the customer: without use'n his hands! Human nature be'n what it is the customer most always wanted to know just how this feat might be accomplished. Sez Grandpa, "I'll set that there bag on your wagon grip'n it neither with my hands or my feet, but when I do it'll cost you'uns a buck. And if'n I can't manage it, I'll give you one silver dollar."

Well sir, a few folks just gathered up their reins, chuckled to their team and chuckled to themselves as they drove off. But many had to satisfy their curiosity and gave him the go-ahead. He would simply put his hands behind his back, bend over, sink his teeth into the bag, walk over to the buggy and load it! Some folks say he had no neck a-tall, his head just sat on his shoulders. Later years he died from a large goiter on his neck. Back then they didn't know

JOURNEY TO THE BACKWOODS

about our need for iodine. We should all be grateful for whoever started put'n it in table salt.

John Terrillion was the seventh of eleven children. His dad Stephen came from Alsace-Lorraine about the mid 1800s. Born in the old country in 1834, John married Mary Ortleib who was of Swiss and German descent. Anyway, Mary's grandfather owned a brewery. And it was said Mary's dad, when a young man, enjoyed the "fruits" of his labors to excess and would hide behind the barn. After quarrel'n with his father, he left home at the age of seventeen and came to America and took up farming. I guess our ancestors came here for all sorts of reasons.

Head'n back into Croghan, I remember it unique in yet another way. It boasted the only water-powered mill of its kind in the state of New York. The sturdy structure showed the craftsmanship that was so apparent in the area. The good folks there could mill you just about anything of wood; flooring, window frames, doors, boy the smell of that place! The pine, oak, cherry, and maple—who needed perfume anyway where you could inhale nature's grandeur? The mill always seemed like such a place of adventure to me because it was on an island. The building actually moved back and forth a little from all the belts and pulleys strain'n under all that water power. Stand'n there on that floor, it gave you the feel'n of nature in the raw. That mill is still there today use'n waterpower. Last I knew it was owned by the Martin family.

You know, come to think of it, that little town had about everything you needed to live a fairly comfortable life. Even the stores were neat and unusual. But still, to me it was town.

Off to the north and across the road from our place beyond Tabolt's pasture, huge smokestacks shot into the sky. They came from a place known as the Block Mill. There men labored to make bowling pins from the hard sugar maple. The early settlers once wished to make this tree a national treasure, and believed it so valuable it ought to be protected. The colonists even considered the maple syrup from this tree could be turned into an industry. But the sugar maple had many uses as lumber. Said to be the hardest dry-kilned wood in the world, to this day it remains number one wood fer bowling pins and the wood used in bowling lanes.

But what of the lumberjacks who cut those trees? That's what I wanted to know. They were the stuff of liv'n legends. These fellows really produced something. From their backbreak'n labor, mankind enjoyed the comforts of home, benefited from hundreds, yes, thousands of paper products, shelter fer his animals and countless other good and wonderful things. Deep down I knew a part of me belonged to these "Paul Bunyans of the brush." My greatest desire was to see these fellows log'n.

Every now and then a log truck would roar by the house. I'd get excited, jump up and down, wave and yell. The loggers always waved, sometimes blew their horn. I could see 'em there at the wheel, rugged look'n characters, always a big smile. Golly, it makes me sorta homesick.

When children are little they step on your feet.
When they grow up they walk on your heart.
—Old Mother's saying

CHAPTER THREE

DAD, MOM, AND SOME DEVILTRY
Circa 1950

Father was a good carpenter and built many houses. The nicest, of course, was the stone house he was a building there in Croghan. The new house was really tak'n shape, but till it was finished we lived in a three-stall garage he'd built first. It contained a huge wood furnace that to a young boy resembled a foundry. Dad used it fer such a purpose one winter.

I remember see'n him open the huge doors and thrust the iron into the glow'n embers; it was quite a sight for us kids! As he put the red hot iron to the anvil and shaped it, one might have thought this was primitive indeed. But wait. He was shape'n iron to fit the wooden runners he'd cut out of maple. It was a sled...and what a beauty!! A bobsled about four

Here I am with all the curls at about three years of age.

feet long and looked like the big log'n bobs; only this one was just for young-uns.

It turned out to be a real piece of craftsmanship. Too much of that tradition has gotten lost along the

DAD, MOM, AND SOME DEVILTRY

way of modern progress. Seems like most everything is plastic today. The old craftsmen are dying off, leav'n no one to teach the young.

Back then Dad hunted a lot; he also drank a lot. When he and a man named Jeremiah got to drink'n they usually went hunt'n—at night. There I was in peaceful dreams one night in the garage when someth'n warm and wet and sticky was laid upon my face. I bolted upright in bed to find Dad holding a bloody deer's liver on me. Mother, of course, was in near hysteria. Dad just calmly laughed and said it wouldn't hurt me any. I guess it never did, for I don't even remember crying. I just wanted to go a hunt'n.

Here's one hunt'n story that captured my youthful instincts. Dad was after a big buck once near Pine Creek. Someone had said there was spotted a "ghost buck" one moon night. He spent day after day track'n this huge footprint. Finally one morning there he was!! A huge white buck runn'n flat out! Dad shot but wounded him, so he followed him all the next day. Snow commenced to melt, and the track went cold. He came out at a place called Paul Grunet's camp. Paul asked Dad what he was track'n. Dad said matter-of-factly, "A white buck."

"Well," Paul sez, "I ain't seen no white ones, but a pink buck crossed just down the road a while back." Seems like the blood turned the white deer pink. Sad, he was never found.

It was even said Dad made his own "poison." Mom said when he and a relative named Anslem made a batch and proceeded to test it. Dad got so spaced out on the stuff that he ended up locking himself in the outhouse fer three days with a jug and a shotgun. Fer some reason, or lack of reason perhaps, he figured them there revenuers were prowl'n about. If'n anyone approached him to come out, he threatened to blow the door off.

Say, that brings to mind a little story I heard once. The white man from the Old World usually used wine and beer for social gatherings mostly. Of course, there were always some drunks. Anyway, as folks sat around to visit, they enjoyed a relaxing drink or two. Then they brought it to the New World and gave it to the red man. And ever since that day our red brother has been ruin'n himself and even kill'n himself with alcohol. On the other hand, the red man used tobacco at social gatherings. They sat around to visit and talk peace and enjoyed the pipe. They in turn gave tobacco to the white man, and he's been kill'n himself ever since.

Ain't it a strange world?

One of the few times Mom persuaded Dad to attend a church meet'n, they ended up leave'n us three youngest at home alone in the garage; me, Tom, and Sister Bonnie. Now sister had these here beautiful long bouncy blond curls that looked too long; at least that was me and Tom's assessment. So we became self-appointed barbers and proceeded to trim it just a mite. What children don't think of to get into. Yes-sir-ree, "When the cat's away the mice will play." Just what our defense was when

DAD, MOM, AND SOME DEVILTRY

everyone returned home, I don't quite remember. Mother put both hands over her face in shock when she saw her only daughter had been clipped. Father proceeded to show his disapproval in the usual fashion. I don't quite recollect where we'uns received the just punishment in that garage, but it couldn't have been as severe as in the house or I'd have remembered it.

Come to think of it, the garage was the scene of my own first haircut at the tender age of six. It was in preparation fer my first day of school. Mom cried as she snipped away, and I think she has the ringlets cached in an old cigar box somewhere still.

The photos of long ago tell it all. There I stood with those curls of a time almost forgotten. Sure hard to believe. It's true though, "A picture's worth a thousand words."

Life in the garage saw other common trials and normal grow'n pains. It was there that Brother Richard went through a longer than usual stage of no eat'n blues. Mom got some super liquid vitamins that were super-duper bitter. Whenever he refused to eat, out came the bitter guile, "Yuk." What faces he made and fits he threw.

There was a time when Richard was a baby that death clutched at his very throat. He had asthma so bad that he would wheeze, choke, and be unable to catch his breath. Mother would sit in a chair and hold him all night, so when he failed to breathe she would hear his choke'n and awake to assist him. In her despair she would often cry out to God to heal him.

JOURNEY TO THE BACKWOODS

By and by she felt compelled to take Richard and go to a place of healing, somewhere down around the Thousand Islands, I believe. Anyway, hope increased as they entered and saw wheelchairs and crutches that others had left behind: a visual testimony that their owners had left a life of pain. Fer some God chooses to completely heal. Mom prayed, "Would my Richard be one of those?" The man there with the gift of healing inquired of her, "Do you believe God can heal your son?" Mother replied that she believed so with all her heart. Soon after she returned home, Richard's breathing was normal. He never again had asthma. Long ago it was written in Matthew 17:20, "I tell you the truth, if you have faith as small as a mustard seed, you can say to this mountain, move from here to there and it will move. Nothing will be impossible for you."

There came a time when Tom and I had to explore the attic of sorts that led up behind the huge furnace in the garage. Most everything owned was kept there wait'n fer the finish of the house. Among all the boxes of treasurers there, Tom and I just happened to stumble across a big box of assorted shotgun shells. What a treasure trove. Of course, guns were kept out of our reckless hands (a good thing). So we sat and pondered just what sort of deviltry we'uns might get into with these explosive devices. You know the old say'n, "If'n you don't keep your kids busy, then the devil will."

Well, it didn't take two natural hunters long to figure out the make up of a shell. We opened up the

DAD, MOM, AND SOME DEVILTRY

end and poured the fine shot out. We really thought it was neat stuff. But we soon tired of that. So now what? With a mischievous team effort, we decided to go fer the big bang. But how to achieve this without the aid of a firearm? Com'n from a long line of woodsmen and jack of all trades, we instinctively knew fire would create the desired results. We figured all that was needed was a cannon of sorts. Our search was rewarded with an empty fifty-five gallon barrel fer our fireworks out behind the garage. After slip'n out with some matches, we soon had a toasty fire go'n. We then tossed some shells into the fire and ran fer it! We huddled behind other barrels and cringed as all hell broke loose. Then fear struck our hearts. This mayhem we had devised would again demand punishment. We kept try'n to come up with some "cock and bull story" but we knew Dad wouldn't buy it. Soon Mother came and put an end to our big-bang experiment. Later that night Father applied the rod of discipline—that was one time we deserved it. We took a real shellacking over that adventure. Good grief...it's a wonder we didn't get killed over such a stunt! Our guardian angels were work'n overtime.

Boy, life was sure boring in town.

We took note that after much hard work by Mom and Dad the house was get'n done. Like I said before, it was a house of stone. The best part I remember about it all was once in a while we got to ride in the old 1938 one-and-a-half ton green Chevy truck. It was a long ride to near the Thousand Islands, so we children drank in the scenery of every farm and

JOURNEY TO THE BACKWOODS

country vista along the way. We weren't headed to the backwoods, but at least it was a journey. Sometimes Dad would overload the old truck and have a flat tire. Too poor usually to have a good spare, he would take it off and roll it to a farmhouse and fix it with borrowed tools.

"Poor people have poor ways," they say. Father sure hauled a lot of rock fer the new house. Mother said the stones were rejects from a quarry that was cut'n 'um fer a mansion. She always said, "Waste not, want not." Most common folks usually don't like see'n things go to waste, it puts a strain on the environment.

As fer as live'n quarters go, the house was a major improvement. The house with all its individual rooms seemed confining after the one huge area in the garage. Those buildings are there to this very day, real American craftsmanship.

The new home boasted a large fireplace. It was wonderful to sit there and watch the flames dance and glow and feel the warmth. Firelight tossed shadows off the walls, and Tom and I figured this might be the only permissible way to enjoy the glow'n embers.

In this here wonderful house, Father had also built a den for his privacy. To enter this near-sacred room required a pass of sorts. A short-term one was sometimes issued if'n we maintained a refined attitude. We could usually handle it fer a few minutes.

We adjusted quickly to the new house.

DAD, MOM, AND SOME DEVILTRY

Fer sometime now we could see other young-uns up the street, and there seemed to be a lot of laughter and horseplay go'n on. We were die'n to get out of the yard and play with other kids but Father forbade us to go there. We knew, of course, he was very sincere about carrying out his threats! Disobedience meant a trip down behind the new furnace. The cellar in the house was a torture chamber in our young minds. Dad's stern voice, "Downstairs!" struck terror in our hearts, for the outcome was always certain. So our wailing and cry'n usually started at the top of the staircase and became louder and more pitiful as we neared the stove. There among the woodpile was the object of our fear, as Father's temper usually didn't permit him to choose a small switch, fer his hand was not always controlled with reason. Mother thought the spankings were a little severe and came up with a wonderful invention. The next time she feared a bad licking com'n up fer Brother Richard she inserted a very thin pillow in the seat of his pants. Dad soon discovered the pain reliever, however, and the thrashing was carried out.

Grow'n up on the edge of town, boy it was really tough, life was just too short to let it be so dull. I'm sure there were times when we needed the rod of discipline, fer the Good Book sezs, "to spare the rod is to spoil the child." But many a time a scolding would have been sufficient. Discipline that's overdone can cause children to lose spirit and sometimes become bitter. Many times I remember after the trips down behind the furnace I would stand in the driveway sobbing and look north to the mill and the cold deck of logs, and there was a voice from the forests. I knew someday I'd get out of town, and be embraced by Mother Nature and welcomed into the solitude of her bosom.

My son, do not forget my teaching but keep my commands in your heart.
For they will prolong your life many years and bring prosperity.

—Prov 3:1,2

CHAPTER FOUR

EVERYDAY LIFE AND WHAT THOSE KIDS WON'T THINK OF NEXT

Circa 1951

About this time, older Brothers Gilbert and Wilson were in the service of our country. So need'n a role model, I looked to see what Brother James was up to. 'Cuz if'n the season was right, he most always was trap'n. Now trap'n done in the most humane manner possible taught a boy a lot about wildlife and earn'n money. Sometimes it was the only income a country boy could catch. Them was the times when a quarter looked as big as a dinner plate to most of us.

Brother James had to hustle up 'fore light, real early and check his traps 'cause he had to be back to attend school.

He ran home, changed his clothes and sped off to class—hopefully on time. Most every morning I'd run out to play in the back yard. Ain't this the life

EVERYDAY LIFE AND WHAT THOSE KIDS WON'T THINK OF NEXT

The stone house in Croghan. Still standing the test of time.

of a true kid? Anyhow, a very unusual odor greeted me one morning, not really pleasant but not all that offensive to a backwoodsman. There hang'n from the clothes line was a skunk!!! Brother James didn't have time to skin it that morning and just took off fer school. About every hour throughout the day, Mother would voice her opinion of the fur trade. Come to think of it, the school marm really didn't care much fer Jimmy's enterprise either.

Boys will be boys. Or perhaps it should read, "Boys must be boys."

Brother Tom and I spent most of our time out where the land dropped off towards Black Creek. We did a considerable amount of river watch'n. From that edge of the drop-off and beyond, it became to us young-uns the forbidden zone. With the rod of discipline fresh in our minds, we agreed to make the best of it in the free area.

JOURNEY TO THE BACKWOODS

Most of this plot allotted to us had an overabundance of the goldenrod plant. Our gifted and talented minds soon made a wonderful discovery. If we'uns put the stuff into bundles and tied 'um together we could make a lean-to and camp out right here at home. Boy, it was great!! If Dad wouldn't let us leave the yard, we would just create a backwoods camp'n trip right here at home. It was Yankee ingenuity at its finest.

We soon made all the necessary improvements and were enjoy'n our view of the creek and the place called 'second rock beyond it. Brother James went over there somewhere in the fall to collect crab apples. Mom made great jam from 'um. He would come home with Dad's pack basket loaded right full. He always walked with a hint of a gimp, one leg was shorter than the other, but still, he could carry a very heavy load. Maybe I could go there someday and get apples, just maybe.

Yes-sir-ree, we'uns could almost handle liv'n on the edge of town with our newly-erected hideout. Everyone seemed to go fer the idea. This way Mom knew where we were and what we were up to—most of the time.

It wasn't much more than a New York minute 'fore we realized our childhood endeavor was turn'n into a boondoggle. The quiet life was boring us almost to tears. We had come to the conclusion that woodsmen who camp out must have a campfire. Why, to do otherwise was almost un-American. But how could we forget the last fiasco we got into

EVERYDAY LIFE AND WHAT THOSE KIDS WON'T THINK OF NEXT

with matches? Mom used to say, "What will you kids think of next?"

Was there ever a child born who never disobeyed his or her parents? History records only one. So we took a vote and decided to take a chance. Our campfire was do'n great 'cause we kept it small. Fuel, however, was in rather short supply so we kept it go'n with pieces of dry goldenrod. The stuff burned real good too, so we threw some whole bundles on that we had left over from the lean-to. Our cheerful campfire became a bonfire in no time. Did it ever!! Sure wasn't long 'fore our cozy little shelter was a blazing inferno. Sparks leaped into nearby grass that quickly caught fire. We made a beeline fer the house with the news. The same fear I felt when we exploded the shotgun shells returned: we'uns were in fer it again!

Shortly, many men appeared to put out our cheery campfire. It not only could have burned down our place, but the neighbor's house was also in danger, the one that Father had built and sold to Mr. Schlier.

Be'n an adventurous young boy sure had its drawbacks. We observed our happy campsite was now a black smoldering no-man's land. I realized we must pay for our disobedience. That particular discipline from Father, I'll never forget. We wished Dad had more free time to take us out of town and go fish'n or hunt'n or just go out'n the woods. Boredom fer us was turn'n into a weapon.

JOURNEY TO THE BACKWOODS

At our house a dog was earnestly needed, and wanted, that is by everyone 'cept Dad, of course. There was just no way he would let us have a dog liv'n there at the edge of town. Kids need a critter or two around to grow up with; animals are just plain good for children, fer anybody really.

As things sometimes happen to help such worthwhile projects get underway, an English setter appeared one day. A quick glance told us he was lost. His once-beautiful coat was all burdocks, and his ribs gave evidence to poor nutrition. I commenced to jump up and down and yell, "We really got a dog!" He was so friendly, at times his tail wagged so vigorously I feared his body would become dislocated. Soon however Dad appeared with that serious look on his face; he had other plans and "man's best friend" soon went away. We were so sad. Someday I'd have a dog, I vowed. Yes, and a horse too. Someday, I wouldn't live in town.

Memories of boyhood had many secret sorrows and longings. Everyone knows April showers bring May flowers. They were everywhere in the pastures. Like a soft beautiful carpet the Creator had rolled out over the land. Just where we got the next great brainstorm from I don't know. Sell'n May flowers was to be our first venture into capitalism. We'uns just knew we'd clean up if we sold the delicate blossoms fer, say, five cents a bunch. Our next door nabors, Mr. and Mrs. Farney, were our first customers. We approached their door with all the candor of a Fuller Brushman. Boy, what a great idea! Mrs. Farney

EVERYDAY LIFE AND WHAT THOSE KIDS WON'T THINK OF NEXT

pleasantly told us she didn't need any flowers. We couldn't figure out why she didn't need such beauty. After all, she had a flower bed by the house. But what cultivated flower could compare with God's wild bouquets? Who could arrange it all like the Creator? So our promising enterprise crashed. No one liked our bunches of pretty flowers. They just didn't see nature the way we did. We figured they were the real losers. Oh well, so much fer the best laid plans of mice and boys. Life just seemed to be full of rejection.

Father really wasn't impressed with our flowery enterprise either. He decided he must resort to hard measures to prevent these young entrepreneurs from further mischief. He then constructed a high fenced play area by the garden and locked us in most of the day. Our spirits were crushed again. The thing was like a prison compound. We plotted and screamed. We climbed the fence, but we couldn't get over the sharp wire at the top. Our cries went mostly unheeded. We were doomed. I couldn't even see the big log deck from our "pen." We were like caged wild things, pacing back and forth, talk'n about the backwoods or Uncle Vinny's farm we'd heard so much about.

Somehow we made the best of it, and after a certain time of "detention," we were released under the watchful eye of older brothers.

Sister Bonnie was the baby and Dad's favorite, so it is with a lot of families with the last child born. Having picked right up on that, Tom and I figured to use her as a scapegoat, should the need arrive to keep us from the dreaded furnace room. Certain things in life seem to be unavoidable—death, taxes, and run'n amuck of Dad's laws.

Somewhere 'bout the age of seven, I recall our first puff on a Chesterfield, or was it a Pall Mall? At any rate, this wasn't go'n to turn out to be a "Lucky Strike." Father tossed the smoke away one evening as he got out of the car in the driveway. I don't remember just who spotted it first, but we whispered a plan and waited fer Dad to go into the house. We figured once he was out of sight we'd make our move. We finally got our hands on Phillip Morris, and like a couple of hippies hunched over a joint, we passed it back and forth. But someone spotted us crouched down behind the car puff'n away. It should have been obvious to us by now that there would be no peace when you do bad things, seems like we were always in a pickle.

Someone yelled, "Dad wants to see you two in the house," but we'uns knew where we were headed. As our last plea, we screamed and cried all the way to the furnace room that "Bonnie made us do it." The ol' wack would be heard again like a beavertail on the pond. Then we put in another spell under house arrest.

Go down, Moses
Way down in Egypt land,
Tell old Pharaoh
Let my people go.

—An Old Spiritual

CHAPTER FIVE

SPREAD'N OUR WINGS AND RUN'N AWAY

Circa 1951

Back row, Kirsch boy, Jimmy
Front row, Tom, me, Richie, and Kirsh boy

SPREAD'N OUR WINGS AND RUN'N AWAY

On past our house, Shady Avenue turned into a main road, crossed Black Creek, and headed fer the village of Beaver Falls. It was a one-lane lumpy strip of blacktop, the center and sides rolled up from the heavy loads, hauled over the too-thin layer of asphalt. Look'n down the road with a heavy heart, I could see there in the distance a big mountain of granite. It was said someone fell there and cracked their head, and from that day forth it was known as "skull rock." The name, of course, added a sort of mystery to the place. As fer this young boy, there it was, just wait'n to be explored, but I dare not leave the yard.

There was a few times I had been close to this haunted outcrop of stone. I looked out at it from the truck or car window as we sped past and dreamed in a trance as I stared at that mysterious hunk of rock. I told myself someday I'd explore the pine forests near the top, I just had to. Heavenward went a childlike prayer.

Do dreams come true? It is said Benjamin Franklin never dreamed.[4] But I did. What would childhood be fer a hemmed in boy? How could his spirit survive? Never in a million years would I have guessed my dream would become a reality through a schoolhouse. A field trip at the end of the first grade helped erase some bad feelings about the classroom. It wasn't quite all boring study and confinement.

Boy oh boy. I never figured we'd get there. The good nuns, be'n the order of perfection, had to line up all the children. Make sure some mischievous

JOURNEY TO THE BACKWOODS

lad didn't disappear, or start some tomfoolery. Some moms who drove had lined up their cars to haul us down there. Thought me, "Monkey around, monkey around. Let's get this show on the road."

Finally!! We arrived and hiked near the west end 'cause it was easier to get on top. Once up there I looked back towards town. I had escaped!!! God had answered my prayer and cut me loose. "Don't get near the edge," an adult screamed! Teachers and Moms, boy do they worry so. Such freedom I had never known. It was just a few hours, but I cherished it fer months.

Many a time after that trip when I couldn't leave the yard or had to sit in a classroom, my mind went on instant replay. I could feel the soft pine needles under foot, smell the pitch and hear the breeze whispering through the treetops. I imagine the songbirds twill their joyful notes. And I remember the red squirrel with the cone stuck in his mouth, sit'n on a limb motionless, try'n to hide. The other kids hadn't seen it, but I did. I was a dreamer. Yes-sir-ree, a real dreamer. And out'n the woods, life was always an adventure.

After our short stay on top, we headed on down near the mouth of Black Creek. There my almost tomb emptied into Beaver River. And I got my first look at the train trestle. It was massive!! I remember wish'n the train would come along, so I could see it go over the top. What a day, what a day. My older brothers would get no peace now when they went fish'n unless they took me along.

SPREAD'N OUR WINGS AND RUN'N AWAY

It's been a number of years since I last saw skull rock. I was disgusted to see on it where students had told the world the year of their graduation. Heartfelt graffiti shared the names of their sweethearts, and, of course, the picture of the crossbones and skull gave evidence of the rock's name. Those young people never realized what they were do'n. That paint will be there fer decades! 'Course the rock is red granite, and they may just grind it up and haul it away, so much fer history and memories.

The next couple of summers brought the most happiness of the seven or eight years I lived in Croghan. No one enjoyed those fish'n trips down the creek more than I—no one. James and Richard were old enough to take me and Tom along, and we took full advantage of it. There in a tree one day I saw my first possum, right beside the creek. It was exciting to see this goofy critter hang'n upside down. I thought, what a strange, ugly varmint. Sure wasn't cute like a raccoon. Yup, Tom and I figured now everything was hunky-dory.

Our fish'n trips produced chubs and pickerel, but there was always a chance for a trout. One time the Fish and Game stopped near the bridge below the house. They had one of them there outfits that shocked the fish temporarily. Then any fish near this contraption turned belly up. I thought, what a great way to fish! They said it was just a test to see what kind of fish was in Black Creek. Lots of suckers they was, and they gave 'em to us. Home we ran just as proud as could be. Mother cooked 'em up, and we picked bones fer hours. Some folks call suckers poor-man trout, but we were glad to have 'em.

Like I said back-a-ways, the pasture across the road belonged to Mr. Tabolt, he was a good steward of the land, a wonderful nabor. I had seen him attending the Catholic church in Croghan. He allowed everyone to enjoy skull rock and fish Black Creek. Of course, in those days no one sued their nabors or left junk behind when they went to enjoy the great outdoors. Morals sure have changed.

Mr. Tabolt had a huge barn fer his dairy cattle. Folks said the barn once belonged to the timber baron Mr. T. B. Baslum. Mr. Baslum, at one time had many race horses, even a racetrack near the barn. The barn had a hip roof and lightning rods on the top, and the lightning rods were real fancy ones at that. It was very impressive to me. I sneaked up there one day and peeked inside. There were two real long rows of stantions. The barn smelled of cows and hay and grain, and was very clean. Just inside the doors where I stood on the right were big box stalls made from heavy timbers left over from the days when Mr. Baslum owned it and kept stud horses there. It was built with those heavy planks all the way to the ceiling.

I really needed to satisfy my curiosity and go look inside those stalls. I could hear something mov'n about in there. I stood there listening with the intensity of an Indian scout. Then I heard it heavy breathing there in the stall. Creep'n up real quiet like, I peeked through a crack in the wall. There

SPREAD'N OUR WINGS AND RUN'N AWAY

stood a massive Holstein bull with a ring in his nose. And he knew I was there!! He charged and hit the plank, WHAM!! All the while snort'n and slobber'n and foam'n from the mouth. Was I scared or was I scared?? I leaped back and high tailed 'er outta there, my heart pounding in my throat. I ran fer home like a rabbit with a fox hot on his heels.

That there same bull almost killed one of my older brothers once. The bull had a long chain that hung from the ring in his nose. The only way the bull could charge fast was hold his head high in the air so the chain was away from his front feet. 'cause bulls most always charge with their head down. And when they stepped on that chain it sorta put a pain in the old nose. Anyway, he chased Brother James (I believe it was James) to the fence. Jimmy dove through just in the nick of time, only one step ahead of ol' Ferdinand.

There was some awful mean bulls around that neck of the woods. Just about every boy that cut across some farmland was put up a tree sometime or other: if'n they was a tree that is. Or you ran fer your life. Us boys would position ourselves in a safe spot and then tease some of the bulls by mock'n 'em. We'd beller and they'd beller, back and forth. All the while Mr. Dangerous would paw the ground and throw sand in the air, show'n his anger and frustration. Some of these bulls were so bad the owners had wired an old license plate to their horns, and it covered their eyes so they could only see straight down to the ground to eat. Them there bulls really

JOURNEY TO THE BACKWOODS

did look awfully awful. Everyone grew up with the knowledge that there was this danger about. It was hiker beware. Many a Mom was worried sick wait'n fer her children to come home from a fish'n trip in farm country. Sometimes Mothers' worries are warranted.

Of course, it was town as usual fer me and Tom. But more and more the settlement of Indian River possessed us. Maybe every adventuresome boy runs away, if not in reality then at least in fantasy. Finally, one clear day with our short child memory bank block'n out scenes from down behind the furnace, we'uns cut out fer Uncle Vinny's. Our emotions helped us overcome our fears. We were on a high that few youngsters nowadays would understand.

We didn't aim to just stay in town to drown in our sorrows when we still knew how to swim.

Up through town and past the floor'n mills we ran. Every once in a while look'n back to make sure Dad didn't somehow figure out our runaway intentions. We crossed the bridge that spanned Beaver River and stopped fer a moment while I listened to the river tell me tales of beaver upstream, elusive whitetail deer, brush wolves and big trout near the headwaters. It was still talk'n to me when we pushed on.

A little farther along, rounding a corner we recognized the farm where Mom and Dad got eggs and milk. Some cows in the pasture galloped right up to us. We hurried on by fer fear the folks might somehow recognize us, and ask questions that we

SPREAD'N OUR WINGS AND RUN'N AWAY

didn't want to answer. We came over a little hill onto a flat with a meadow on the left and behind it the timber started. We recognized it as the place where Dad once shot at a deer while we were on a Sunday drive. Every once in a blue moon Mom could talk Dad into such a good family endeavor.

Anyway, we discussed this as we hiked along, and it caused us to get more excited by the minute. Yes-sir-ree, Father was shoot'n his .22 Colt woodsman pistol—and he missed. Mother was hav'n a fit for fear the game warden would come along. Us kids were all at the window of the car watch'n, expecting the deer to fall down. It was very exciting fer us. But as soon as the gun cracked, the little buck's tail went up and away he ran.

With these exciting fragments of last year in our minds, we took on fresh courage to keep on keep'n on. Indian River seemed like a long, long ways off to a pair of little boys. But this was no wild-goose chase.

Like I said before, it was a hot summer day and the tar was a-melt'n along the edge of the old cracked asphalt road. We soon discovered that it was kind of tasty to chew on, sort a like gum. I didn't think Mother would approve. And then we noticed the grasshoppers snapping and bounding along the road. We 'uns could hear the meadowlarks calling their cheerful farmland salute. Lush timothy hung over the roadway just invite'n us to pull a stem and savor its sweet juicy contents. Yes-sir-ree, we'uns were country boys.

JOURNEY TO THE BACKWOODS

The road wound back and forth ahead of us, and we could see it cut'n through the Joe hill that loomed in the distance. Seemed like it was always in the distance. We really didn't want to admit to each other we were get'n tired.

We passed a couple of homesteads and took in the daily-ness of life down on the farm. This was hay'n time. You didn't need to see it 'cause the smell gave it away. Everyone was out help'n make hay while the sun shined, moms and daughters as well as fathers and sons. Was there ever a better place to raise a family? No upper class here. In fact, the whole naborhood was perty much a classless society, hard-work'n Americans.

Soon we were thankful fer any distraction along the way that got our minds off the road ahead. Walk'n down a road that you can see so far ahead was ever so boring fer young boys. The lonely stretch of primitive blacktop seemed endless. The heat waves off the road danced and disappeared. Still in front of us was Joe hill.

About the time we might faint from thirst the trickle of a little creek reached our ears. We ran to drink and splash and cool off. Consuming enough water fer a bellyache, we retired a little while by the creek. As I lay there in the shade, timothy stem hang'n out of my mouth, I was soon in hard thought. I considered it was much farther to Uncle Vinny's than when this run-away notion was first conceived.

SPREAD'N OUR WINGS AND RUN'N AWAY

This here flight to freedom was begin'n to flutter and die. The desire was still there, but the flesh wasn't too willing. You know there's just something about brotherly love. Ecclesiastes 4:10 says: "If one falls down the other can lift him up." Tom gave me the inspiration to get up and go on. We gathered up our weary bodies and moved out. We walked along till we'uns hit the Joe hill, we finally made it! Now what? This was look'n more and more like a harebrained scheme all the while.

The day was fad'n like our enthusiasm, and we weren't even halfway to the farm. Our legs were get'n a little rubbery, and golly it was hot and there was sweat in our eyes. I reckoned we best face the inevitable. We better be backtrack'n towards home. Mother would surely worry where we were. We hadn't thought how concerned she would be. And father, well, we were in fer it again! The walk home was a solemn thing, all the excitement and anticipation gone. We'uns had failed. The closer we got to town, the lonelier I became. Why did we have to live in town? I was beside myself think'n of answers, but none came.

We turned the corner by the Miller house onto Shady Avenue. This is it, I thought. Perhaps there's still time to come up with a plan. What if we don't beat Dad home? Just as we stopped to talk this over, guess who drove by. Our hearts were flooded with the old fear and terror again. He slowed down and pointed a finger of authority towards home, and the expression on his face left little doubt of his feelings.

JOURNEY TO THE BACKWOODS

A decade of minutes dragged on. Our runaway outing would end down behind the furnace, like a final flutter to our stretching of youthful wings.

We were indeed a couple of sad young boys.

That last escapade kind a broke our spirit, so we'uns stuck pretty close to home. Father was now a boss on the great Saint Lawrence seaway project and was gone a lot. We got double warnings but were now allowed to play with the kids up across the street.

A day so sad even Mother Nature cried.
—Old Russian saying.

CHAPTER SIX

FAMILY TRAGEDIES
Circa 1951

Mom at about 14 and her brother Robert.
Two days before he died, he told Mom he was going to
heaven to be with God and the good angels.

FAMILY TRAGEDIES

Most fireplaces—and ours was no exception—had a beautiful mantle graced with pictures of the family. Brother Gilbert was there, oh so handsome in his uniform—what a smile he had. He was the oldest, serving in the armed forces in Germany at the end of World War II, a very athletic fellow. And how he loved the backwoods. Years later I learned he would take his .22 rifle, fishhook and line, sometimes a blanket and head for the forests. I wonder if'n he heard the same voice I had. I'm sure he did, fer woodsmen are born, not made, you know.

Times were tough, and a man did what he had to do. Usually the only money he got fell to his gun. Gilbert hunted a bit with a renowned foxhunter. The old hound would chase the foxes till they played out and then would hole up. Gilbert be'n young and tough would dig 'em out and his partner would dispatch them as they tried to make a getaway. Gilbert was a man of adventure, maybe that's why he became a military policeman. I only remember him from his pictures. He died in Germany.

Mother was grief-stricken. I remember her weeping fer weeks. Years later, when we visited the graves, she would kneel and cry. Of all the church services I attended as a child, the only one that stayed with me was Gilbert's funeral, the long procession of cars, the solemn people, the gravesite. The big flag that covered the coffin is still draped fresh in my memory. See'n the soldiers fold it and give it to Father, I could not at that age comprehend their loss. I was just too young to really understand sorrow, tyranny, war, and freedom.

Brother Gilbert who died in Germany.
He was a talented guy.

We have Memorial Day now and the poppies so that the rest of us never forget the sacrifices given fer freedom. On very rare occasions wars are necessary. "There's a time for peace and a time for war." This from Ecclesiastes 3:8. Not all wars are justifiable. Corrupt governments, evil people and politicians, will sometimes get common folks to fight fer wars that are not moral. In fact, I don't know if there is such a thing as a moral war. Dietrich Bonhoeffer, a young pastor in Germany when Hitler came to power, denounced such madness as Nazism and strongly opposed how some "Christians" were be'n sucked in. Being passive in his theology, more or less,

FAMILY TRAGEDIES

he still thought it right to help with a plan to assassinate Hitler. When asked how he could justify such a thing he replied: "If you saw a maniac in a runaway car heading for a group of children, wouldn't you do anything you had to that you might prevent it?"

So anyway, all the relatives came to pay respects and share the sorrow; at least as much as was possible. The Creator has a way of let'n children forget pain. Otherwise young people would carry things from their childhood to their adult life that they would be best off forgetting. Time heals most everything, at least, partly.

And how! Uncle Vinny was there and I was overjoyed to see him. He brought to mind our runaway attempt and I thought much about his little stump farm near the backwoods. Boy, Tom and I would have loved to go home with him. And Uncle George was there also. Always with that air of mystery about his trapping and hunting, like most other old woodsmen. With the passing of seasons through time, he would become our walkin', stalkin' backwoods instructor. Life seemed to return to somewhere near normal a few months after Gilbert's death. Brother Wilson was get'n married to a girl from Lowville since he completed his service in the Air Force. I was get'n old enough to see the friction between Mom and Dad. They was about as different as you can get. He was wild as the wind while she was a devout churchgoer. Sometimes I felt like the son of fire and ice—a child of the flame.

JOURNEY TO THE BACKWOODS

It could have been their rocky marriage, or Gilbert's death or maybe it was everything come to a head. I don't know just why, but, when I was eight years old Mom decided to separate from Dad. They went before the judge in Lowville. Dad gave Mom no more than he had to 'cause he was bitter about it all. I didn't understand any of it. What good would come from a home break'n up; this young boy wondered? I didn't know it then but the Good Book sezs: "God hates divorce."

So the hammer of justice fell. It was final. Dad could go on liv'n like he wanted to. Ma would get the old homestead on the Jerden Falls Road, a little cash and thirty-five dollars a month alimony. That is, when she could collect it. I just pushed it all inside like most kids do in those situations. The tragedies of childhood don't hurt so much as the memories of them years later.

All that really mattered to me now was, I was head'n fer the backwoods!!!

Sow a thought, and you reap an act;
Sow an act, and you reap a habit;
Sow a habit, and you reap a character;
Sow a character, and you reap a destiny.
—Samuel Smiles (1812-1904)
In Life and Labor

CHAPTER SEVEN

THE END OF THE ROAD – A BETTER PLACE
Circa 1952

And so we headed on up the Indian River Road I never looked back, I wanted to yell, Ya-hoo! After several miles we passed Mr. Orry Monnet's general store and hotel, then turned onto the Jerden Falls Road. I was really get'n excited now—woods on both sides of the road. We passed the small farm of Julius Brouty. Like all the rest of the farms in that area, there was no shortage of rocks and boulders. I noticed a big bull out in the pasture with the cows. I'd remember him.

Just past Brouty's farm was Ruben Kloster's place. He too had a small farm. But he worked down at the block mill in Croghan also. Where the big cold deck of logs was, that became the object of so much of my dream'n. Boob was Ruben's nickname so we'uns all called him that. Old Boob worked so hard, made

THE END OF THE ROAD – A BETTER PLACE

Grandma's Falls, where me and Husky dog
caught the many brook trout.

me think of a feller named Horace Mann. Mr. Mann once said he was rocked in the cradle of toil, and she rocked me too hard. Boob's wife's name was Nora. She was a wonderful soul, good wife and mother, kind and helpful to her nabors. As the years passed, we witnessed her big heart and selfless servanthood. It would be hard nowadays to find someone like her. They had a passel of kids too, seven I believe. I remember think'n I could play here.

Just a little farther up the road was Mr. and Mrs. Ver Schneider's. He would pick us up fer school in his old Ford "Woody" wagon. His nickname was "Uggy." He had some kind of contract with the public school system to deliver us to the one-room schoolhouse near the Texas road. We just had to learn the three R's: read'n, rite'n, 'rithmetic. Funny thing, I never learned Uggy's real name. Seems

JOURNEY TO THE BACKWOODS

like everyone in that neck of the woods went by a nickname.

After that we passed through quite a stretch of nuthin' but woods. My heart skipped a beat!! The forest had laid claim to me. I could see old stumps that were nearly rotten now. They showed of someone's struggle to build a homestead. I visualized tough men with teams of horses pull'n out the stumps. The men's shirts were wet with sweat, the horses all lather where the harness laid on their hide. But Mother Nature had claimed it back to her bosom. Mother Nature is sometimes hard, but she's always honest.

Boliver's Corners was next. That's where the mailboxes were, and we hung a right. A few hundred yards, and the timber opened up to some meadows and a homestead. It was where George Boliver lived. He was an old bachelor who was about half blind. He had a team of horses and a few cows. His brother John lived in Croghan and would come up once in a while to help him put up hay and get wood. They argued constantly, bickering and even swearing at each other. I could sometimes see'n 'em headed fer the woods with the team of horses, waving their arms at each other. Mercy, the air was just blue from all the cuss'n. It was too much fer a young boy's ears.

Just a little farther on the right was another Boliver place. A widow lived there by the name of Maggie. She had quite a bunch of boys. Let's see, there was Earl, Lyle, Herbert, and Harold. There was a girl or two also, but my memory fails me. Seems like old

THE END OF THE ROAD - A BETTER PLACE

Old Massawepie Camp and the old hunters, unknown to me.

Maggie always had gray hair, and was forever knit'n wool socks like her family depended on it. Those socks were of the finest quality.

Well, from there the road dropped off a little and after several hundred yards it was the end of the road. I knew this had to be it!! I could feel it!! Not many kids got to live on the end of a gravel road, no-sir-ree.

The old homestead didn't look like much, just kind a leftovers from someone's hopes and dreams. But it gave testimony that indeed folks had once lived and loved there. I was sure it had been full of laughter, and had welcomed a happy young bride. Children had played there under the big pine in the yard. Down below the house where the barn had stood, the walls had caved in. It was here the man had milked his cows and stabled his horses. Out back was an apple tree that supplied the family with fruit. Oh, the smell of those blossoms. There was another

JOURNEY TO THE BACKWOODS

old wall to the left of the house, must have been a shop and building fer wagons and buggies.

Yup, the old homestead was perty bleak. The roofing was shot, the chimney in need of repair, the door was ajar. Inside the plaster was fall'n off the walls exposing the wood slats—and the north wind. Down cellar the wall needed point'n up. There wasn't any table or chairs either, but Mom said we'd make do. To the folks down at the settlement, they just knew fer sure that poverty had embraced us in its ragged arms. There it stood, that old shack. Fer many seasons all it had housed was the wind. It truly was the lonely remains of someone's hard labor. But I loved every weathered board and shingle.

It wasn't long 'fore Mother had the place livable. She did the work of three people. Mom would say as she wiped sweat from her brow; "Man works from sun till sun but a woman's work is never done." I remember read'n once about a teacher tell'n her class the hardships the pilgrims faced their first winter. In the midst of her description concerning the starving conditions, one of the first-graders raised her hand and said, "I wish my mommy had been there. She always knows what to do."

One of the first jobs Jimmy had to do was clean out the well. It was a masterpiece of craftsmanship that well was, about six feet wide at the top and three feet at the bottom. The depth was about twenty-five feet. We bailed and bailed till we got the water all out, then Jimmy climbed down in and cleaned all the stones off. The well was laid up with just stones,

THE END OF THE ROAD - A BETTER PLACE

no cement or lime. That's why it was tapered in as it went down. There was even snakes in it! Tom and I thought this was a mysterious place. The two-hole outhouse was made usable with minimal labor. In summer it was a great place to sit after dark. As you did your job you could leave the door open and gaze at the moon. I don't rightly remember if we had Sears and Roebuck or Monkey Ward fer comfort.

Then they fixed up the woodshed that was along the northwest side of the house. Put tin on the roof and repaired the chimney. In the living room was a big "round oak" stove fer heat. The kitchen had a kerosene stove fer cook'n. Mom built a table off the floor like a big counter top, and built in a bench on each side too. She plastered the walls and said she wished she had some kind of insulation. I don't remember ever see'n any Fiberglass in those days.

The stairway near the round oak stove led up where us boys slept. 'Cept fer a attic off to the side, the upstairs was one large room with many iron post beds. It was summer, but winter was a-com'n.

The mice had taken over and turned the place into a nursery. They were hav'n a joyful existence till Mom declared war. They'd be no mice in her cupboards! There weren't no frills on the table there at the old homestead. When Mom went to town it was only fer necessities. She bought sugar, flour, lard, yeast, cornmeal, and kerosene. We didn't have electricity fer a couple of years. We broke the darkness with good old oil lamps. The table always had homemade bread. Mom was a cook beyond all praise. And when she had the time we'uns had blackberry and blueberry pies, m-m-m-mm-good. The one thing I remember not liking was the corn meal mush. Man, I got sick of that stuff. We could never afford milk.

Mom went once a month to Lowville where they had the county home and got "surplus food." Let's see now, there was canned pork, some flour, and cornmeal (but the cornmeal was usually wormy), powdered milk, powdered eggs, peanut butter, and I think raisins, too. There could have been other stuff but I don't remember. Anyhow, we would have gone hungry many times without it.

Many, many years later, I worked cut'n timber in Montana fer a man who grew up in North Dakota in the Great Depression. He said the crops dried up, and they had no money to live. If not fer the "surplus food" they would have perished. He recalled the grapefruit juice in the cans, sez it were like candy to him. The government ain't all bad you know. At least, in those days it weren't. Perhaps they should have stayed with that there system instead of going to food stamps. After all, so many farmers get subsidies that come from our taxes. Why not give away this bounty from the farm that received those subsidies? This food stamp thing has cost so much money and been abused so.

But get'n back to kid's stuff. Tom and I had nuthin' but outdoors to roam in. I took to the woods like a prodigal takes to vice. A old mountaineer named Buckskin Bill, who once lived on the Salmon River

THE END OF THE ROAD – A BETTER PLACE

in Idaho, said, "If you look out your window and see a house, you're a poor man; if you look out and see a lot of houses, you're a very poor man; if you can't see any at all, you're all right." Well sir, that settled it, we were all right.

They was only a few acres that went with the place, but it was bordered by state land on two sides. Back when homesteaders went broke on the land, the state bought it fer a few dollars an acre. This was one of many once-thriving homesteads that proved almost impossible to scratch out a liv'n. The state planted it with pine trees, and it made a great place to hunt and explore. When we got real bored we could climb the big white pine in the yard (when Ma wasn't look'n). I'd climb way up near the top and look all over. I could see where the dead swamp laid and the place called Oak Hills. And somewhere over there, a little north of east, through the woods was Gramps's old camp. If'n it was real early I could watch the mountaintops put on the glory of the morning sun. I loved it up in that tree. What a place to daydream! Whenever Mom discovered me up there she would rant and rave how I was go'n to fall out. Mothers just don't understand the adventure of it all.

The first summer at the end of the road stayed special. Evenings a whippoorwill would come to the old barn wall and lullaby us with his relaxing song. And if'n that weren't enough to calm your tired body, the crickets would sing you to sleep. I thought, *Who would ever trade this fer a place in town.* No orchestra in the world could hold a candle to the

JOURNEY TO THE BACKWOODS

whippoorwill's song. It was the whippoorwill that kept vigil over my dreams.

Out front near the fence the old bush road took off, winding its way into the backwoods, and Gramps's camp near the Oswegatachie River. It was just a wagon road with ruts and was a muddy quagmire. Every once in a while Uncle Vinny went that way to cut pulp and logs. Then Uncle Tony, who was kind of a hermit, would also show up, park his old car, and hoof it up to the river. He usually had on an old hat and wore a ragged hip-length denim coat; he reminded us of a sheep herder. He had such a gentle spirit and seemed so lonely. He lived up with Grandma and Uncle Vinny.

It was just a matter of time, you know, 'fore Uncle Tony would let me tag along. Down the bush road we went. I was so excited, I practically ran after Uncle. It was the same exuberance I had felt when Brother Jim took me trap'n. We crossed mud creek—it was dry in the summer. The black flies and mosquitoes were chewing on me, but I wasn't go'n to cry out fer fear Uncle would take me home. He saw me scratch'n and itch'n though, and put some strong smelly stuff on me. He called it Woodman's fly dope. It had oil of pine tar, camphor, pennyroyal, oil of citronella, and I think oil of bay. Anyway, it was full of good ol' anti-fly stuff. The road then took us up through Uncle's four-hundred-acre woods lot, the Oak Hills, and under the big high-tension power lines that cut across the property.

THE END OF THE ROAD – A BETTER PLACE

I could hear the wires hum from all the electricity passing through 'em.

We got near the far side of the lines and Uncle Tony pointed to a place just off the trail. "There's where I killed my last deer many years ago." His voice had a sorrowful tone. "Don't ya hunt, Uncle?" I asked. As we walked on he told me the story. It was late in the summer, he was heading fer camp to stay awhile and needed some meat. Be'n after dark, he had on a miner's lamp and spotted deer eyes up ahead. He was shoot'n his old Model 12 Winchester, 12-gauge with buckshot. He fired and went over to dress out his game and was confronted with a disturbing sight. The deer he'd shot was a young one with spots and it laid dead across another one the same size. He hadn't seen the eyes of the other deer and had kilt 'em both. He said it was a gloomy unfortunate thing to happen. It got kinda quiet as we walked along. I never asked him again why he didn't hunt.

We passed through a beautiful stretch of hardwood timber and just ahead I could see the object of my dreams—Gramps's old log'n camp!! I ran ahead, leap'n and jump'n. I came to the old horse barn first and peeked in through a large crack in the door. It was dim light inside, but I could see the stalls where the big log'n teams had stood many, many seasons past.

I wanted to go in and explore, but Uncle was over near the cabin, and I didn't want to miss out on be'n first inside. He opened the door, and I bounded in.

JOURNEY TO THE BACKWOODS

Surprise-surprise!! There was a big porcupine right in the middle of the room. He had chewed a hole up through the floor and was gnaw'n on anything that contained salt. He beat a hasty retreat back down under the camp. Uncle ran him out from under the building and dispatched him with an ax. We went back in and cleaned up the mess. Uncle cut open a discarded coffee can and made a neat tin patch to cover the hole.

That scene of Uncle making the quick, precise swing with the ax to do away with old porky left me thoughtful. "Uncle Tony," sez me, "what if you'd just chased that old quill pig off, then you wouldn't had to kill him?" Uncle sat there at the worn table rolling himself a smoke. In his quiet, thoughtful manner he replied: "The porcupine has a place in the great plan of things out here in the wild. They chew the ends off hemlock limbs in the winter when the snow is deep, and deer can feed on 'em. They also strip bark from some trees causing them to die, thus it opens up a area fer sunlight to come in and new plant life can grow. And if'n a person was lost with only a knife he could club one and keep from starvin'. Also the fisher feed on 'em, they'll climb up under one in a tree and rip their soft underside out. Not to forget the American Indian use the quills fer decoration.

"But let's not kid ourselves, sometimes animals cross the line and must be destroyed. Up here an ax and shovel are very important tools, yet if they can, ol' porky will eat the handles off fer the salt. They'll

THE END OF THE ROAD – A BETTER PLACE

even eat the seats out of the outhouse. It's a lot of work to replace those things. So you see, Young Lad, everything has its place." That little talk left a lasting impression on me. These are the things learned from men with hard and callused hands who have paid their dues.

Then Uncle went about tidying up the rest of the cabin while I looked it all over. Them bunk beds, hurricane lanterns, the old Home Comfort stove. Sleeping mats hung from poles near the ceiling so mice couldn't get 'em. And outside across the windows, crosscut saws were nailed. Be'n a typical kid who had to know the why of everything, I asked Uncle how come they was there? "It's time fer a bite to eat," said he, "so let's set up at the table, and I'll tell you 'bout it.

"A couple of years ago there was a great fire in Canada. The next winter was hard, and game was scarce, so brush wolves came down here in large packs. We had a big wind that blew down a lot of timber. It created a good situation fer the wolves because things was pretty wild out there'n the woods. I'd come up to camp to look over the downed timber and do a little fish'n late in the spring. I heard the wolves howl once in a while after dark but didn't pay much attention at first. I'd seen their tracks in the sand down on the river and did notice one was very large. Meanwhile, a young raccoon discovered my dump hole out back where I threw my empty cans. He was rattling around there every night 'bout dark. In no time he was up at the door sniff'n out the odors from the cabin. Once and a while I'd leave a morsel by the doorway, and he'd sneak up and grab it. He finally got so tame I could feed him from my hand. He came fer a handout every night just like clockwork. He sure was a curious cuss.

"Well, a few evenings passed just like that, I was enjoy'n the coon as company. One night though about the time he usually showed up, I heard a blood-curdling scream out by the back of the cabin. I knew in an instant something was kill'n my pet. I raced out around the corner and was met by those wolves. I jumped back in the cabin and slammed the door just in time. I could tell the big wolf was out there and had claimed the coon because I heard him snarl and fight off the others. Soon all was quiet, but I knew they hadn't gone away. I picked the lantern off the table and walked over to the window to see if I could make out anything in the darkness. I was almost there when a large wolf put his front feet on the sill and showed his teeth at me. I quickly thrust the lantern in the window and he disappeared.

"A few seconds later, in the other window another one appeared. So I gave him the light and he also vanished. I stayed up all night for fear one might break through the glass. In the morning I took those extra saws and nailed 'em there. They never came back to the cabin. The problem was, they were so plentiful that there just wasn't enough fer them to eat. They killed many of the deer. There was some strange colored ones too. Somewhere along the line

THE END OF THE ROAD - A BETTER PLACE

they may have inbred with large husky-type dogs. They sure had no fear of humans."

By this time I had quit munching on my sandwich Mother had sent. I was on the edge of the old bench wait'n to see if Uncle was to tell more. He sat there calm and just nibbling on a piece of cheese. He had a few days' growth of beard and sure looked like a mysterious hermit. It was awful quiet in the old shack. I glanced out through the open door and saw late-afternoon shadows were falling out'n the woods. I wished Uncle had shut the door. I slid a little closer to him on the bench.

"Well," he said softly. But I jumped anyway. "Let's take a hike down to the pigeon lot and do a little work on the road."

I wondered, *Ain't it too late fer that?* It was never too late fer Uncle Tony—he never came out of the woods till two hours after dark. That night on the way out I must have turned around a thousand times look'n and listening. I stayed real close to Uncle. I kept conjuring wolves sliding along like shadows in the moonlight. Disappearing among the blown-down timber, only to reappear again on one side or the other of the old wagon road.

That first summer passed so quickly. September came, and we had to go to school, I would go reluctantly. When it came to school, I guess I didn't care to be organized or supervised. We all need to know read'n, 'rite'n and rithmetic, but all I could do was think of what I was miss'n out'n the woods. Mother would get us up real early. She always made

JOURNEY TO THE BACKWOODS

sure we were squeaky clean. "Be'n poor is no excuse fer be'n dirty," was her admonishment. Uggy would pick us up in the old Ford Woody, (I think it was a '49). It had real wood trim instead of chrome. He was very protective of his car. There were army blankets on the seats. It was a station wagon.

We attended the little one-room country school above Indian River where the Texas road takes off. It was what school ought to be. There was a big blackboard up front. The teacher was on her guard fer country boys and their pranks. But we managed to pull off a few anyway.

She separated the girls from the boys as much as possible. But when she turned her back to write on the board, we whipped out our spit wad shooters (miniature blow guns made from rolled up paper) and took a shot at someone. The littlest kids had some kind of red clay to play with, and it made great ammo. Us backwoods boys were constantly up to some mischief. We had a hard time applying ourselves to learn the basics.

The bathrooms were downstairs, the stairway split about halfway, to the left the girls went and to the right was the boys. Up near the ceiling was a vent in the wall. Us boys would try and climb up to peek at the girls, but it was too high. We'd get to laugh'n, and the girls would hear us. It would get real quiet on their side.

The school was heated with wood and coal. It had a huge furnace. Mrs. Andrew Lyndaker came down every morning early and put wood on the fire.

THE END OF THE ROAD – A BETTER PLACE

They put coal in at night 'cause it lasted longer. It was always warm in there.

Outside there was a huge swing set. You could pump up and really go high. About fifteen to twenty feet away was Alvin Zehr's fence and his hay meadow. Fer us boys who needed to show off how brave we were, you got as high as you could on the swing then jumped off over the fence. If the teacher caught us at it she'd scold us, and we'd have to stay in the rest of the play time. Boys will be boys.

On the other side of the school was a big area to play softball. We had a great time choosing sides, with the old hand-over-hand style on the bat. In the winter we built snow forts and snowmen. We had great snowball battles, the forts were far enough away from each other that no one got hurt. No one could afford big gyms up there in the country, so we made our own entertainment. It didn't cost the taxpayers anything, and we got plenty of exercise.

This here school went to the sixth grade. Then we had to either go to the Catholic school in Croghan or the government school in Beaver Falls. Soon after I went to Croghan, the big shots from the school in Beaver Falls decided to close down the little country school. They said it would be cheaper, and the kids would get a better education: hogwash!! The local people said no, this was in their area, and they wanted their children to get started in this small school.

Well sir, a great debate followed, and even some heated discussion. Our good and highly-respected

JOURNEY TO THE BACKWOODS

nabor, Andrew Lyndaker just up the road, had quite a few kids who were to attend this school. There were many other children within walking distance. How could you beat that fer saving money? Anyhow, the high-arky fought the people tooth and nail. The people even hired a lawyer to press their case, but the government closed it down anyway. So much fer a government of the people, by the people, and for the people. The learning system has gone downhill since the closing of those little schools. Bigger is not always better. And parents have little control over what kind of materials their children study. We don't think this can happen in America but it can. I wouldn't even trust some of these government people with the Lord's Supper.

Enough school fer a spell. Fall in the backwoods had put on the best of autumn. Bright orange and gold sugar maple, the deepest red of the soft maple, light amber of oak and elm, and the last wedge of geese was winging its way across a late October sky. Such beauty the Creator has put here to inspire us to consider Him and His greatness that we might worship Him.

The old apple tree out back was loaded with shiny red apples, winter apples Mom called 'em. She said they were the best fer pie and applesauce. As we had no electricity yet, she canned what we didn't eat. But the best thing about the apple tree was yet to come.

Like I said once before, us boys slept upstairs. One cold morning I took my usual glance out the

THE END OF THE ROAD – A BETTER PLACE

back window to see what I could see. Lo and behold there under the tree was a huge buck!! "There's a buck—there's a buck!!" I yelled as I leaped down the stairs, but we'uns had no gun. I ran back up to see if he was still there, but he was gone. Soon after that Jimmy got a gun (he was a teenager then). I never got over the sight of that buck under that apple tree. The rest of the time we lived there I never went by that window without look'n out.

We didn't have much trouble leaving the yard here. And often got permission to go up to Maggie Boliver's with Brother Richard or James. The only boy of Maggie's who still went to school yet was Harold. He was about Jimmy's age. Back in those days everyone spent their spare time cut'n firewood, because the winters were long and cold. Out back of Boliver's barn was a stand of white birch. Most farmers didn't like it much 'cause it took over the pastures so fast. Well, it was a good source of firewood and only six-seven inches in diameter. It sawed good green with a cross cut saw or even a bow saw. One wood cut'n detail really sticks in my mind.

One fine fall day as a chilly wind blew across the frosted grass, James and Harold took me and Tom to help in the birch woods. Us young-uns would climb to the top and once they bent over, the older boys would chop 'em down: tree-ridin', a hair-raising descent—brought about by the force of gravity!! Great fun was had by all.

Our guardian angels were sure on hazard duty. What else could have kept us from being mangled?

JOURNEY TO THE BACKWOODS

Another escapade there at Boliver's took place at butchering time. Not want'n to miss out on any adventure, I ran up there just in time to hear old pig squeal'n and raising a big fuss out back. I saw Maggie try'n to get the hog out of his pen a few feet so Harold could drop 'em with a .22 shot to the brain. Old porky must-a figured this was a chance fer the great escape. See'n it was now or never, he came crashing out before Harold could get the drop on him. Down the driveway went Mr. Bacon at a high lope. Harold leaped through the back door and came out the front with the .30-.30, stuff'n shells in it as he ran. By then ol' side pork had hit the gravel road and was head'n west at full gallop. Harold led him a mite and touched 'er off.

It was a neck shot—I was impressed. I'd never heard of anyone shoot'n a hog with a .30-.30. All sorts of unusual things happened there at the end of the gravel road.

Things got perty serious a few times. Once Mom had to go visit the doctor. She wouldn't be back till late, so we had to stay at Maggie's after school. We stayed to supper, and Maggie gave us tea to drink. I never had tea before, and I got sicker than a dog, vomited all over. I still don't like tea and that was fifty years ago.

A few years back I went to New York fer a reunion. I took a drive up the Jerden Falls road to where Maggie once lived. Trees now cover everything. The old barn fell in many years ago and then the farmhouse burned after that. You'd never knew

THE END OF THE ROAD – A BETTER PLACE

anyone lived there. It was even hard to bring back the memories. At first, I felt almost like I'd never been there. But I shut the truck off, closed my eyes. I heard the voices, the laughter, and recalled the smells. A tear came and I smiled—and I thanked my God fer Maggie and her boys. They were fine nabors.

Associate yourself with men of good quality if you esteem your reputation: for it's better to be alone than in bad company.
—George Washington

CHAPTER EIGHT

WINTERS AT THE HOMESTEAD
Circa 1952

Three of my heroes, left to right, Uncles Vinny, Tony, and George in the early 1930s

JOURNEY TO THE BACKWOODS

The first winter there at the old homestead was one never to be forgotten. Number one priority was keep'n warm. Many times a cold wind moaned out of the north. Boy, it was frigid upstairs in that old house–Brrrrr! Me, Tom, Richie, and Jimmy would all huddle around the round oak stove and get as hot as we could. Then up the stairs we'd run, me and Tom in one bed, Richie and Jimmy in the other. The beds were the old iron-and-post type with piles of blankets on 'em. We dove into bed and thrashed around till the sheets got warm. Then we'd cover our heads and just leave a hole to breathe out of. 'Course at that age we had to claim half the bed. We got in some awful arguments if'n one got on the other's side: kids!!

I especially remember that winter 'cause I got a terrible fever. I was hallucinating and I sweat so bad the sheets kept get'n soaked. Ma put cool washcloths on my forehead and changed the sheets. We had no money to go to a doctor so you just toughed it out.

As the sled roads froze up, Uncle Vinny was go'n down the old Bush road to cut pulpwood near the Dead Swamp. Sometimes Jimmy stayed out of school and went to work there, times were hard. Besides, they brought out ash firewood, it was green but ash burns green. We needed lots of wood.

I spent all the time outdoors that I could. 'Course by the time we got home from school it was 'bout dark. But on weekends I could hear the pines out back sighing and call'n me to come and explore.

WINTERS AT THE HOMESTEAD

There I found rabbit trails and weasel tracks. If you look carefully and your senses are keen, the animals will teach you. "Boy-oh-boy," sez me, "if'n I had a gun and some traps, I could become a woodsman." Sometimes I'd chase them fresh rabbit tracks, and they came right back to where I started. Just like Uncle George said they would. I needed a dog too. But how to talk Mom into that. All she said was we couldn't hardly feed ourselves. But I remembered the promise to myself, someday I'd have a dog and a horse. Yes-sir-ree, someday.

In the evenings, when Old Man Winter became almost unbearable, and we had to stay in, Mom had a project to ward off cabin fever. Crochet rugs—big rugs. She showed us young'uns just how to loop the needle and don't get it too tight. But I recall the first one I made. Instead of flat it turned out like a huge soup bowl.

I longed fer a gun and a hound.

And so winter had its form of daily-ness: pack'n wood in and ashes out. Most exciting fer me was listening to hear the jingle of tug chains when Uncle Vinny came by with the big black team of Percherons, Doc and Dan. They were hitched to the big log'n bobsled that had belonged to Grandfather Roch. How I dreamed that I could drive them sometimes. But that was the last winter he had 'um. In the summer he bought a tractor.

The lilac tree out near the big pine looked all bleak. Winter had truly come to the barren trees. The waterfowl and songbirds had left fer warmer climates. Now we just saw chickadees and an occasional crow, and the noisy, obnoxious bluejay. Sometimes at night I could hear the great horned owl up near the Oak Hills. Rabbits and grouse had better watch out!! Old Long Talons was a silent killer. Yup, another great white winter had arrived.

The first part of winter Uncle George was again helping Uncle Vinny cut logs and pulp. Sometimes Jimmy went to help. One night Mother kept opening the door to listen 'cause they was quite late and it was get'n cold and no menfolks. I heard a knock on the window and someone rubbing the frost off. When I got over there to the glass, there appeared a bobcat—face to face!! I screamed and jumped just as Jimmy laughed. I ran outside to see this furry wonder. They had four of them that Uncle George had caught near the Dead Swamp. At that time the county had a fifteen dollar bounty on 'em. That was a lot of money in those days. I remember stroking the sleek fur and look'n at the sharp claws. Yes-sir-ree, all the stories were true. Uncle George was indeed a great trapper.

That same winter Uncle Tony was cut'n some timber up on Grandpa's lot. 'Course I started in on Ma. "I have to go!!" became my battle cry. It's a wonderful thing this soft heart mothers have. The next Saturday there I was, half a dog trot try'n to keep up with Tony as we headed fer camp. We followed the sled track, and I never missed anything. Every rabbit and squirrel track drew my attention. I saw grouse tracks that came out of a hole in the snowdrift. Where did this grouse come from I just had to ask Uncle. He showed me where a few feet

WINTERS AT THE HOMESTEAD

away the grouse dove in the night before, safe from owls and the sub freez'n cold. This was real learn'n, I reasoned. I couldn't never learn this at school.

As we hiked on, I became even more aware of tracks in the snow. I even forgot Uncle in front of me. He stopped, and I bumped right into him. He was pointing at some tracks that were two by two. "Fisher cat," he said. Of course I just had to know what it looked like. "Sorta like a cross between a weasel and a fox," he said, "black with a grayish brown head."

As we walked I kept try'n to visualize this unusual varmint. We got to camp and I was overjoyed to see it again. We spent the day there not far away cut'n a few logs. Tony faced the trees with the ax and I helped cut 'em down with the crosscut saw. Boy, did I ever get tired pull'n on that saw—Whew!! Uncle probably could have done better by himself.

You know, my woodsman logger uncles were some of the best foresters I ever knew. They only cut the mature trees and those that were go'n bad. Uncle Tony seemed to know every tree in the forest and what its condition was. Here I was be'n taught in the folklore of the Adirondack Mountains.

As evening fell it started to get really cold. The trees were snap'n and pop'n from the frost. But Old Tony never hung up the saw till it got good and dark. Then we headed out the mile and a half to home. My ear flappers were up aways, and my ears got cold and then didn't seem to hurt anymore. I never said anything to Uncle fer fear he'd think I was whin'n. After we got home and my ears warmed up they hurt something awful. Uncle had left with his old Model T truck, and we had no phone of course and it was thirty-five below out. So Mother just did what the old pioneers did. She cut a big potato in half and hollowed out a place fer my ears. I had to hold them on all night. I remembered roll'n around on the floor hang'n on to them spuds. I was moan'n and groan'n something fierce. How it hurt. A couple of days later the skin all fell off, but they healed all right. It was a severe case of frostbite.

I returned to the woods, the river, the camp-the game-with a feeling somewhat, that of a prisoner escaped from his chains.
—Jedeiah Smith.
Famous mountain man of the beaver trade.
One of the few, if not the only, man of the mountains to carry a Bible.

CHAPTER NINE

SPRING BRINGS NEW ADVENTURES
Circa 1952

Winter was slowly losing its grip. The sun became warm, the maple sap flowed, and we started to hear that age-old trueness of the season. The wild geese could be heard, if not always seen, lifting our spirits as they passed over with that musical honk'n. Songbirds returned, wild flowers graced the hills and backwoods. In the distance the Oak Hills turned green. The old apple tree out back grew its wonderful fragrant blossoms. Truly, the Creator was a God of the greatest imagination.

Us kids, of course, sprang right into spring. Hunt'n fer birds' nests and seeing the different colors of the eggs. We discovered that birds, like the meadowlark, who nested in the grass, had spotted eggs that camouflaged themselves. Out'n the woods we'd occasionally find a wren's nest woven on a limb,

SPRING BRINGS NEW ADVENTURES

A shy Uncle Tony with a nice trout

boy-oh-boy, this had town beat every which way. Except fer one thing that is—bugs! As soon as the weather warmed up, out they came, ready or not. But in spite of 'um, we'uns were hav'n a good time all the time.

It came to pass I began to long fer Uncle Vinny's farm. Tom and I would walk up to Boliver's Corners every chance we got and follow the old Tote Road through the woods right to Vinny's place. We helped

JOURNEY TO THE BACKWOODS

clean out the calf pens. Me and Tom and Mike was start'n to chew tobacco about then. Uncle Vinny bought Days Work plug fer Mike, and he'd give us a chew. One of the Kloster boys from the Belfort Road was helping that spring and we gave him a chew. He got perty green around the gills and vomited all over, looked like he'd been drawed through a knothole. It's too bad we all didn't get sick. I guess you could say we were climb'n Fool's Hill.

We loved it there at Vinny's old farm. Grandma lived there and was still in fair health. Us Three Musketeers usually got on her nerves. What one didn't think of the others would. We'd play tag running all over and jump her flowerbeds. She'd come storm'n out with the broom and threaten us, madder than a wet hen. 'Course, we always tried to look as innocent as a new-laid egg. I remember she had a flour sack cut in strips tacked onto a short handle. Be'n it was a farmhouse there was no shortage of flies hang'n around the door. She forbid us to open the door without shoo'n the flies away first with her homemade fly chaser. And if'n things got too hot around there fer us, we'd beat it down to the barn and the hay mow. I regret not be'n more respectful; she'd had a hard life.

That barn was a marvelous place. Its high hip roof and massive beams caused us to stand in awe. Grandfather and the family, with help from Mennonite nabors, had built it. Up in the haymow we dug tunnels and climbed to lofty heights to jump into the soft hay. It was the best trampoline in the whole world.

SPRING BRINGS NEW ADVENTURES

Once bored with that, we'd race back outdoors and into the pastures. We'd make believe we were hunters like Uncle George. We'd sneak along the rows of stone fences and stalk chipmunks, shoot'n at 'um with our slingshots. Or we just chased each other, run'n around like chickens with their heads cut off.

Having that out of our system and it be'n the start of summer, we'd pester Uncle Vinny till he took us to the hayfields. Uncle, smile'n with patience, loaded us all on the hay wagon and away we went, down the country road heading fer the flats to get hay. We passed Monnat's general store where he might stop on the way back. Sometimes Uncle would buy us a root beer barrel candy if we didn't get into too much trouble. Uncle Vinny had a gold tooth, and his heart was made from the same substance. On my first trip to the flats I'd not be able to get any candy.

Uncle George was down there wait'n on us, he had an old coupe car with a rumble seat in the back. Anyway, they unhooked the wagon 'cause first thing was to cut some more hay. Uncle Vinny hooked the little Farmall—a tractor—to the horse-drawn mower that had the tongue cut off. I jumped on the mower with Uncle George, Tom, and Mike on the tractor with Uncle Vinny. Round and around the meadow we went, once in a while Vinny stopped so's Uncle George could oil the machine. Fer a while I enjoyed the ride on the mower. Grasshoppers and garden snakes beat a hasty getaway at the sound of such clatter. Pretty redwing blackbirds fluttered here and there, nervous about their nests. Yes, this was the time of buttercups and butterflies.

It was a hot old July day and after several passes by the edge of the woods, I heard the forests call'n me again. Like a typical foolish kid, I just jumped off without warning Uncle George. I forgot the cut'n bar was six feet long. Before Vinny could stop the machine it had caught me and cut my leg to the bone. Load'n me into the old coupe, we sped to the country doctor. Dr. Dalton was a kind and gentle man of medicine, and he made every effort to sew up the gash between my howls of pain. Restraint was needed, so with Uncle Vinny at my shoulders and Uncle George at my feet, the good doctor completed the necessary treatment.

We hung around Uncle Vinny's like a bunch of strays, I guess that's what we were, with no Dad to do anything with us. Brother Mike's dad had left him and his mother when he was an infant. God the Father gave Uncle Vinny to us—three fatherless boys—born to trouble. Uncle Vinny was sorta a single parent 'cause he was a bachelor and a saint too. Fer it took someone with the patience of Job to put up with us three boys who just had to know everything right now, and usually did everything without any warning.

The old house at Uncle Vinny's had lots of rooms. It was built as a board'nhouse way back fer wayworn travelers. Then it was a church. And then Grandpa and Grandma lived there with a dozen children.

SPRING BRINGS NEW ADVENTURES

I loved that old house. It had few conveniences but lots of charm. Sometimes we stayed overnight, and at time fer bed we raced upstairs and leaped upon the feather-tick mattress. Boy, it was soft, you could hardly see over the sides. Forgetful young-uns that we were, Uncle was right behind us and would kneel with us and pray. Always a few short prayers, fer he well knew the patience of youth. "Hi—yi what lads," he'd say.

Us three whippersnappers usually had an appetite like an alligator. Seems we were grow'n like antlers in the velvet. When the hunger pains became unbearable, Grandma would fix us big bowls of bread and milk, and we ate it by the gallon. If she was in a good mood she'd take us into the parlor, order us to set still and crank up the old phonograph. How we loved to hear Old Uncle Josh. He made us laugh. He told about his experience go'n to the big city in one of them there department stores. And there was lots of neat stuff in that parlor like a stuffed great horned owl. He had impressive huge yellow eyes that looked awful real. There was a graceful cock pheasant with beautiful plumage, and old pictures of relatives. Look'n back, think'n about the old place gives a man memories that are throat catch'n.

Anyhow, summer was also a time fer country boys to be fish'n and we longed to fish bullheads up at Trout Pond. But that was above Belfort and we had no way to get there. So we cut a deal with Uncle Vinny. Every Sunday afternoon we helped him do the milking early, and then he'd take us boys bullhead'n.

JOURNEY TO THE BACKWOODS

Like I said before, Uncle Vinny had a heart of gold. And he was a happy-go-lucky feller.

You never saw three boys work so efficiently in your life. And no mischief either! We carried the milk up to the milkhouse, sometimes getting a big drink of warm milk from the strainer. We done everything Vinny told us. He'd smile and sing:

> In the big Rock Candy Mountains where the bums all go to stay,
> it's a land that's fair and bright, where the handouts grow on bushes, and you sleep out every night;
> where the box cars all are empty,
> where the sun shines every day, on the birds and bees and the cigarette trees,
> and the lemonade springs where the bluebird sings,
> the bull dogs all have rubber teeth and the hens lay soft boiled eggs,
> I'll see you all this coming fall in the big Rock Candy Mountains.

This was said to have been written in the 1920s, and was called "The Hobo Ballad" by a man named Harry McClintock. It's been said other versions were heard many years before that. The version that Uncle Vinny sang was a particular makeup of his own, having cleaned up the song for us boys, since some of the song was inappropriate, and us boys were wild enough as it was! It was obviously

SPRING BRINGS NEW ADVENTURES

wrote by someone who longed fer better times and had seen many hardships.

Uncle Vinny was no shade tree farmer. He had the cleanest barn and milkhouse. He really worked at it. His care of those cows made an impression on me fer a lifetime. No one took better care of their stock. They were never dirty or improperly fed. Winter time they always had clean straw night and day to lay on. When the lights went out at the end of a long winter day, the munching you heard was from contented cows.

Anyway, the chores all done we'd pile in Uncle's Chevy pickup with fish'n poles and worms and chatter'n like a bunch of squirrels. The truck wouldn't even get stopped and we hit the ground run'n. Casey Kloster was sometimes with us, and he knew the way to the big rock where we'd fish. We baited worms on and set bobbers and tossed out fer the big catch. We were a poor look'n bunch lined up there on that big rock. Sorta a Tom Sawyer and Huck Finn bunch. But we were the happiest kids in the world and the richest too. Back then life was beautifully simple.

The first thing Uncle Vinny done was build a big fire, 'cause it would be dark soon. And fer some reason the fish was attracted to the light. And you could see when yer bobber went under. When one disappeared everyone saw it and would whoop and holler. We tossed the fish into a pail. Uncle Vinny tended the fire mostly. He sat there the firelight leap'n off his thin face, his old cap sit'n a little

JOURNEY TO THE BACKWOODS

sideways and his expression lost in thought. Perhaps he was think'n how to keep these three high-voltage young-uns out of mischief. Like Father Flannigan's Boys' Home, Uncle Vinny was in the human salvage business. We usually stayed till midnight. Vinny had a hard time get'n us out of there.

As that first summer skipped by, Mother said she had to get up on the seven-acre lot near the Dead Swamp and cut that windfall. Half of it was flattened from that same hurricane-force wind that brought the wolves down. The bugs had changed with the weather, most of the mosquitoes and black flies were gone, now we had no-see-ums, deer flies, and horse flies. Mom had gotten down to old Ralph Merrilly's store in Croghan and picked up a bottle of Woodman's to help fight this new menace. They'd like to drive ya stark-raving mad. We put some fresh dope on our hat brim, course we could still smell it from a month ago.

Anyhow, up the old Bush Road we went every morning. Us kids stalked snowshoe rabbits, played Tarzan in the trees while Mother chopped and sawed that blowdown. As the days faded away, that little woman with big visions cut and piled forty cords of four-foot hemlock. She put it up on skids, so it wouldn't freeze down. I remember what hard work it was. Us young-uns sometimes helped her roll the blocks up those skids. The next winter, the pulp Mom cut was hauled out by Donald Moser and his father. They had a big black team of Percheron horses. They wanted to know how Mother got

SPRING BRINGS NEW ADVENTURES

those huge logs of pulp in such high piles. Ma told them she just made up her mind that it had to be done and rolled 'em up there with a peavey. A lot of folks today, I think, have lost that type of pioneer determination

Before we knew it Mom's threat about pick'n berries the year before came to pass. She handed us young-uns small pails and off to Bailey's Swamp we trudged. My goodness, what a jungle that swamp was. Spruce and balsam, snowbrush and blueberry brush, some places it was just impossible to get through. Once you made it to certain areas, the blueberry bushes were usually easy to pick from. They were high, not like the western huckleberry, which is mostly low to the ground.

And it was always hot, the sun blazing down upon us, and our feet always wet from the swamp water. I remember I hated picking berries. All I could think about was swim'n or fish'n or going up in the woods where someone was log'n. Mom always would warn us that the winters were long, and we'd better pick. Sure easy fer her to say that, I reasoned, she loved to pick berries. Us young-uns would put leaves in our pails and pick a few berries to cover them so it looked like we had a full pail, then we could leave and get on with funner things.

But alas!! Mom soon discovered our move and made us stay all day long anyway. I guess you could say our true character shows up when no one is look'n. We're all born with that trait. The only exciting times came when a bear was known to be prowling about pick'n berries himself. Then we'uns had to go about the swamp yell'n to scare old Bruin away.

We voiced our complaints to Mom that summer time was a time fer swim'n. So every chance we got we'd jump in Indian River or better yet pester Uncle Vinny to take us to Jerden Falls, so we could swim near the bridge. It was a good way to get the dirt and sweat off from the hay fields. Once in a while we bummed a ride over to Double Eddy on the Beaver River out of Belfort. Down below the power dam there was a series of boulders and fast water, and then a perfect pool, more like a pond. By now I could swim a little, so I paddled around not far from shore.

The older boys would swim all the way across and then tease us young boys. One day I took the challenge, and I swam and swam and got tired. About fifty feet from shore I couldn't go anymore so just dog paddled try'n to catch my breath. I was just about go down and remembered Black Creek and knew no one was go'n to pull me out. So with all the strength I could muster I finally made it to shore. I was a lot more careful after that.

One summer Mike came up with a baby raccoon. We were never bored with this masked bandit around. At first we'uns had to keep him locked up in the feed box. He soon tamed down though and became a great pet—and a great pest!! By and large he was a clever little bugger and would steal anything that wasn't nailed down. The older he got the

SPRING BRINGS NEW ADVENTURES

longer he would disappear till finally he never came back. Us boys really missed him. Rascal that he was, I guess he reminded us of ourselves.

Uncle Vinny always sang in the barn at milk'n time, but he loved to sing in the hayfield too. He was always in tune with the larks as he sang the old ballads, and haying season was learn'n and entertain'n. Uncle Vinny let Mike drive the tractor when it was time to load hay. Me and Tom were jealous and showed it. "It ain't fair," we howled. Uncle said we could soon take turns. So we teased each other and did a lot of roughhousing. If Vinny was work'n on the haying equipment, we'd run over to the big rock hill that stuck out in the flats. The stubble in the cut-over hayfield was hard on the bare feet. You could hear plenty of oohs and ouches as we hobbled along. Fer sure, the sounds and motions we went through would have made a great video today; at least it would be wholesome.

There is a time for everything, and a season for every activity under heaven.
—Ecc. 3:1

I shall lead you
      through
          the loneliness,
the solitude
you will not understand;
    but it is My shortcut
      to your soul.

In Loving Memory of
Lorraine (Young) M. Valentino

May 29, 1940

August 1, 2006

After Glow

I'd like the memory of me to be a happy one, I'd like to leave an afterglow of smiles when day is done. I'd like to leave an echo whispering softly down the ways, Of happy times and laughing times and bright and sunny days. I'd like the tears of those who grieve to dry before the sun, Of happy memories that I leave behind When day is done.

Krueger Funeral Home Inc.

CHAPTER TEN

MORE GROW'N UP

Us boys knew every creek within walk'n distance of Indian River. We also knew the trout situation in those waters. One hot summer day, with clouds menacing, we voted to fish the Spring Creek below the Bintz hill.

The one-lane blacktop wasn't too boring a walk 'cause of the huge maples that lined the road. Sailor Dog chased chipmunks into stone piles and us lads got into the usual horseplay. Starting down the Bintz hill, we noticed old Emmett out near his barn and waved. We then raced each other to the creek. The fish'n was good 'cause of the com'n storm. Up the creek we went through the thick tag alders. We all knew where the best fish'n holes were, so we kept warn'n each other "I get the next one." We got so wrapped up in our fish'n trip we didn't notice just

JOURNEY TO THE BACKWOODS

Happy summer days. Uncle Vinny on the load of hay. Snuffy driving, Tom on the left, and me hiding.

how black the sky had become. And then it started to thunder and lightning. We held a quick parlay and figured we'd better light fer home.

We made 'er to the road just as it commenced to pour. Just above the bridge to the north was a Monarch pine, and we made a break fer it, forgetting everything we'd been taught about stay'n away from big trees in a lightning storm. We were about forty feet away when—Bam!—lightning struck!!! We dove fer the ground! Splinters of wood flew in all directions. We were three scared boys. We laid there till all the wood and needles had settled and ran fer home like the devil was after us. I never got nowhere near a lone big tree again when a storm was near; we had barely escaped by the skin of our teeth.

MORE GROW'N UP

As summer turned into "dog days," Vinny, George, Jimmy, and a few other fellows went on a fish'n trip to the big woods, Massawepie! They came back with stories of wilderness, great trout fish'n on the alder bed flowground, Cage Lake, and Buck Pond. I drank it all in like a sponge. They told of see'n bear and big bucks. They had whiskers, and their clothes were torn and dirty. Yes-sir-ree sez me, sez I, these guys looked like real backwoodsmen. We zeroed in on Uncle Vinny till he promised, "Next summer you lads can go!" It was all we talked about fer days.

The Good Book sez; "To every thing there is a season, and a time to every purpose under the heaven" and it was now time to reap the oats. The old McCormick reaping machine was pressed into use. It cut the oats and tied 'em into bundles. Us boys followed along and "stooked" 'em six to a stack, heads of grain up. They were left out in the field till the thrash'n machine came around. It made its way from one farm to another; farmers would get together and help each other. Womenfolks would put on a meal that would shame any restaurant, even outdoin' a Baptist potluck. Secretly, I think the ladies were try'n to outcook each other, all kinds of meats, salads, and pies. There at those tables, usually outside in the shade, there was togetherness, and it made the bonds of nabors stronger. A piece of America was lost forever when the combine replaced the thrashing machine. Nabors would drift apart—who needed his nabor when you could do it all yourself? Sad, we've paid an awful price fer progress.

JOURNEY TO THE BACKWOODS

Usually when Sunday rolled around Ma marched us the two-and-a-half miles to the little white Catholic church in Indian River. We children didn't always follow willingly, but follow we did, down the gravel road where I'd gotten to know every stone and tree along the way. I knew just where every chipmunk's domain was in a certain rock pile. Or we might see the ruffled grouse. And even better, Wily Whitetail may have crossed in the night and left his footprint in the sand near the shoulder of the road. Nature was a wonderful thing to behold, and she made the walk less monotonous as we trudged down that old road.

Sometimes a kind nabor thought of us and came to pick us up. There at church the pastor was Fr. Paul J. Feeley, known to everyone as "Father Paul." He always had a radiant smile that showed a peace that could not be bought, begged, or stolen. It came from within, from the soul, knowing he was right with God and man. He was a handsome man, humble, energetic, and shiny of eye. He was never afraid to sweat in hard labor along with the flock of parishioners. He had become a servant in love for our Savior, loving us like Jesus would have, warts and all. God's people were his first concern, and he always had time fer those entrusted to him. Stopping by regularly to visit, fellowship, or just brighten someone's day with that peaceful caring smile. His earthly allotment amounted to twenty-five dollars a month and with this meager pay I saw him help many poor folks. Someone once said, "God surely loved the poor 'cause He made lots of 'em."

Fr. Paul J. Feeley (1913-1986)

Think'n back I can still see Fr. Paul set'n there on the bottom step of the church altar grinning from ear to ear watch'n us squirm fer positions on the front pew. One of us usually ended up set'n next to a girl—so we needed our space. I recall the first time we sat there. To get our attention he said there was a story told about St. Francis and the wolf who

JOURNEY TO THE BACKWOODS

lived in a cave. Everyone was afraid of this big bad wolf, but not St. Francis. Us young-uns, by then, were on the edge of our seats. He said the story was like Uncle George and the wolves—then he really got our attention 'cause about then Uncle was hunt'n wolves. From there he told us that we never had to be afraid because God loved us and would protect us if we keep Jesus in our hearts.

One late summer Sunday, when Fr. Paul cut the service short, look'n out over the congregation with a concerned expression on his face, he began, "Brothers and sisters in Christ, one of our own here came home some years back from that awful war. He needs help cut'n his winter's wood, an old wound has left one arm unusable to run a chainsaw or split wood. That brother is George Roch and next Saturday we'll have a wood cut'n bee near Frost Mills on his brother Vincent's land. Please come, and the women bring dinner."

It turned out to be a sunny wonderful day, and the country folk remembered Uncle George and the sacrifice he made at Guadalcanal. They came with saws and axes and trucks and food and kids. Here was the real church. I never forgot it, and Uncle George never did either. Many years later the church bishops moved Fr. Paul to a big city. Most every fall he'd come back to hunt and visit those he remembered so dearly, and Uncle always shot him a big fat buck to take back.

Like the rest of us, Fr. Paul knew he was a sinner saved by the grace of God through Jesus Christ.

MORE GROW'N UP

My memories of him give me direction and sanity in a world of "whose church is right and whose is wrong," because he never thought he was perfect, fer otherwise, I may have followed him or his denomination—rather than the Savior.

Ya know, some churches can claim tens of thousands of mental prisoners. They smile ya right in body, soul, and wallet, but Fr. Paul was fer real, and his life showed it. He's well remembered in this weary pilgrim's heart.

All too soon the season of confinement came to pass. SCHOOL!!!! One fall in particular us young-uns caught lice at school from someone. Ma had a real fit. We were itch'n and dig'n. She boiled our clothes and wet our heads down with kerosene, what a mess!! We smelled like stove oil fer days. But it killed the lice.

That fall Mom got a promise that if she cut the right of way, the power company would bring electricity up to the old homestead. I remember be'n out'n the rain pulling brush out of the way. It was a lot of hard work as we had only axes and bow saws. We would again do everything with almost nothing, in record time! Uncle Vinny came a few times and cut the big trees with his Homelight chainsaw. I remember he just bought it, a model 3-17, his first one. The Bolivers helped as we neared their place. That winter we would have electric lights, no more kerosene lamps. But we still heated water on the kerosene stove fer baths. We took one every

JOURNEY TO THE BACKWOODS

Saturday night in a big old wash tub—whether we needed it or not.

And this was another season to put by and make do. We never could afford a refrigerator while we lived there, but we got along fine. Everything was canned and put down cellar where it couldn't freeze.

When hunt'n season opened several fellas from the cities came to hunt with Uncle George. Uncle was noted far and wide as a great woodsman. One fellow I remember was named George Marco. I could never forget his car, a Hudson; he called it The Old War Horse. Us kids would peek in and admire the velvet seats and shiny dashboard. It was indeed an exciting Sunday afternoon when Mr. Marco decided to take us fer a drive. We kids thought this was just the cat's meow as the sedan floated down the road.

It was probably the second fall that Mom started cut'n Christmas trees to sell. They was a man named Francis Codish bought some land near where the Bush Road started. He was from a big city and was in the Christmas tree business. He'd come up with a big long truck and load 'em all up. I remember him as a very kind man always giving food and fruit to us and to Maggie Boliver's household also. Those were the days when an orange was a real treat, or a peach, even a pear. Kids get so much today that they wrinkle up their nose at such things.

Mother had a little ladder she'd made, and she packed it all over the swamp. When she saw a good tree that was fifteen to twenty feet tall, she just put the ladder against it, climbed it and cut the top out. It was always wet in the swamp and when it snowed it was a real mess. The huckleberry brush along the trails would get you soak'n wet. Us kids toiled along drag'n the trees out to high ground. John and George Boliver would come with the team to haul 'em out. That was the only part I enjoyed—when the horses came. Us kids could jump on the wagon or sleigh and just feel the power of those big draft animals. That tree money bought us new boots or maybe a coat if'n Mother couldn't find hand-me-downs. This went on fer several years, and there came another man to get trees. His name was Art Bettinger. He too was a man of immense generosity, bought us bags of flour, sugar, and to the delight of us kids, CANDY!!! Us kids saw Art as a great man with a big heart.

And fall was the time to observe the great Canada geese wing their way south. My senses were always tuned fer that wild call, "honk, honk, honk." Such a marvelous sight, see'n them in the perfect V formation, call'n to each other, lest one go astray. And when one started to fall behind, it would call frantically as it tried to catch up. It was such a lonely call. Geese mate fer life unless one dies. They seem to have more dignity than a lot of humans.

I like a bit of mongrel myself, whether it's a man or dog; they're the best for every day.
—George Bernard Shaw
(1856-1950)

CHAPTER ELEVEN

A BACKWOODS LOVE AFFAIR
Circa 1953

By the time I was nine I'd heard many stories about the famous Massawippi Camp. Actually, it wasn't just a camp up in the big woods, it covered a huge area with places like Brindle Pond Camp and Big Sand Lake, to name just a few.

I believe I was nine when I first got to go up into that big woods of bears and beaver, hungry trout and playful otter, big bucks and brush wolves—it was a howling wilderness.

Just after haying, Uncle George, Uncle Vinny, Leo, and Andy Kloster planned to go to Massawippi Camp to cut wood and do some fish'n. Leo and Andy took their old Ford tractor and a wagon to where the road ended, a place called Burganers', just above Long Pond. In them days it was a hunt'n and fish'n lodge with cabins.

JOURNEY TO THE BACKWOODS

Left to right, Uncle Tony, Gilbert, Dad, Mom, Pat Phillips

Me and Brother Tom and Cousin Snuffy were the rest of the party going in. Was we excited!! While the menfolks loaded provisions onto the wagon we asked a million questions—How big are the trout?... How big are the bucks?...Will we see any bears?? Golly, we must have been an awful nuisance.

After a short visit with old man Burganer we climbed on the wagon and were off!!! The road was full of huge boulders and mud holes; creeks had to be forded; it was a rough ride indeed. But us youngsters never paid it any mind, we was too busy taking in the country. Virgin forest lined the

A BACKWOODS LOVE AFFAIR

ancient trail. It was a beautiful, wild, and undefiled backwoods. Chipmunks and squirrels scampered from the "wheeled horse" that intruded and passed through their quiet domain. Sometimes we'd see deer, and a couple of times, when Uncle George was walk'n up ahead, he'd motion for us to halt. "Looky here, boys," he'd say and poke at what looked like dog dung—"Wolves," was his reply before anyone could even ask. I noticed it was full of deer hair, and my trapping instincts would get all riled up about then. Some folks might a thought I'd already been out'n the woods too long, seeing me there poking apart wolf dung with a stick.

We had a tough time climb'n Parky Hill. They was flat rocks with a creek run'n down over 'em. A couple of times the tractor got stuck, but the men always got it out. It was get'n late in the day, long shadows were telling us dusk was not far away. Us boys started to ask how far it was to Massawippi Camp, fer the sun was get'n dangerously low, and we thought about wolves and bears and such.

It was dark before we reached camp. Uncle George had walked on ahead cut'n blown down trees out of our path. He even had a lantern lit and a fire go'n in the cook stove when we pulled up. It had sure been an exciting trip for us kids, but we were tired. Uncle Vinny made sure they wasn't no snakes or mice in the bunks and took down the light mattresses off the rafter braces. They'd hung them there on wire last fall to keep varmints out. We helped unload the wagon and had a quick bite

JOURNEY TO THE BACKWOODS

to eat. Us Three Musketeers laid in the bunks and listened to the men talk about hunt'n and fish'n till eyelids forced us to sleepy dreams.

Morning found us out'n the woods exploring. The spring creek that trickled near camp caught our first attention. Then we slipped across the old road to spy into the old Massawippi Camp. The porcupines had long since took it over, and it was lean'n terribly bad towards the south. I peeked in through the half-open door and wondered about all the hunt'n parties that had enjoyed each other's company. This was the first camp built up in this wilderness. Many, many, many seasons past, the old timers had built it; my grandfather Johnny Roch, Lawrence Company, Leo and Andy's dad, and a few others. Somewhere I saw an old picture of many bucks and a bear hung on a pole near this camp. *Boy, what a place to come and hunt*, I dreamed as I leaned on the old doorsill. The hunts of those gun-tote'n old-timers passed before me—live scenes in Technicolor.

Uncle Vinny called me out of my daydream to breakfast. We had cornbread and bacon and lots of hot coffee. I liked coffee, but Mom wouldn't let me have any at home. We never had it 'cause Ma said it weren't good fer kids and would stunt our growth.

At breakfast I overheard the menfolks discuss just how they'd pull down the old camp and burn it. Leo said we had to get rid of the quill pigs. They were even chew'n the seats up in the outhouse. They was a-feared the varmints would get into the new camp next. So after our hearty meal we all gathered around

A BACKWOODS LOVE AFFAIR

the decrepit old cabin. They hooked a chain on each corner and pulled with the tractor. The weathered hide-a-way took quite a lot of pull'n to bring her down. Then Andy put some kindling under it and lit her. We stood ready with pails of water and shovels in case the fire might spread. Recent rains had left the forest damp so we had no trouble. The men all looked a little sad as the flames leaped high. Fer sure they had many pleasant memories of hunts in days gone by. This cabin in the big woods had sheltered 'em from many storms. Us young-uns thought this to be another great adventure.

The week passed so quickly. The men fixed the camp up and took us fish'n up in Massawippi Pond. It was mostly a big beaver dam. Mallard ducks quacked and took off spray'n water in all directions. Beautiful wood ducks flew off without a sound. I thought this to be the most beautiful place on earth. Little did I realize how many places like this was up in this neck of the woods.

The trip out was quiet 'cause us young-uns knew school would start soon. I wanted to stay up here forever. This was a real education; this was really liv'n. Yes, the trip out left long faces. Even the men were quiet. Fer they too realized that we all loved the wilderness, partly because it held the solitude which would revive the soul. Some things are loved because of their value—other things are loved because they are just plain loved.

Once we were in the pickup and headed towards Indian River, we commenced to pester Uncle Vinny.

JOURNEY TO THE BACKWOODS

We were planning a trip fer next year, and we'd not even got back home. Vinny finally agreed that we would go next August if'n we got the haying done in time. Us Three Musketeers all shouted we would help every day. Uncle Vinny smiled and rolled his window down—and spat a big stream of tobacco juice.

The next summer we'd heard International Paper Company had started a road into the big woods from Burganers'. Us boys were paranoid it might stop our fish'n trip. But Uncle Vinny never broke a promise, and we finished hay'n in good season. We would walk this time and carry our provisions. We put everything in pack baskets, loaded up, and away we went.

Sure enough, old D-8 Cats had pushed a truck road as far as Wolf Pond. They were really log'n. A tougher look'n bunch of men I never saw. I knew this was to be my lot someday. I remembered how I stood in Croghan look'n across to the big log decks at the Block Mill.

We asked the log'n boss where we might park our cars out of the way. Mosquitoes and black flies buzzed about his face. He looked like a serious fellow but nevertheless was very friendly. We shouldered our packs and made our way past the log'n crews who were deck'n logs along the road. We hiked on up to Massawippi Camp the first night. Boy, it brought about the same excitement that it did last year. The cabin still held a kind of mystery fer me. Us boys weren't very tired 'cause we'd only had to

A BACKWOODS LOVE AFFAIR

walk a few miles. So we sat around that night in a trance and listened to all the stories of the old days. Of great hunts and hardships, tough winters on the trapline, and friendships. Some lasted and some through jealousy—gone forever.

We pulled out early next morning follow'n the wagon road to a place called Kelly's Camp, we turned and left there. Us youngsters were get'n a little tired but said not a word to anyone. We were determined to show the men that we could handle it.

On this trip there was myself, Brother Tom, and Cousin Snuffy. That covered us whippersnappers. The men included Uncle George, strong of hand and great of heart, Uncle Vinny, with a heart of gold, strong, robust Brother James, also able-bodied Casey Kloster, and Herb Kampnich, easygoing, kindhearted, slow talking, slow to anger, just a joy to be with.

Somewhere between Kelly's old camp and the alder bed flow ground, things got a little lively. Jimmy was point man out through the brush and stepped on a large hornet's nest. Of course, Tom was behind him plodding along tired and didn't notice the commotion after James had passed. Tom came along just in time to be the recipient of a bunch of mad hornets. All of a sudden Tom went into this here wild dance and howling at the top of his lungs. He dropped everything he was carry'n and dove off into the brush, hands wav'n about his head like a wild man.

JOURNEY TO THE BACKWOODS

Yup, them there black hornets done get perty savage all right. Anyway, by then of course the rest of us cleared away and Uncle Vinny went to check on Tom. He had several large nasty stings all right, most on his hands and face. Of course, by then he was wail'n most pitifully. But they determined the stingers were a long way from his heart, so Vinny just put tobacco juice mixed with mud on 'em and it took the sting right out. Brother James hung a blanket over himself and retrieved the goods. We made the alder beds late in the afternoon. Was we tired!!!

We had to wade the river near the head of the flow ground on an old beaver dam and camped on the knoll near the spring on the right side of the river. Uncle George built a lean-to in no time and had a cheery fire go'n. After a quick supper, us boys rolled up in our blankets, listened to the lonely call of the loon, heard the little spring laugh'n and gurgling as we slept the sleep known only to those who have been so exhausted, yet so full of gratefulness. We were a bunch of happy boys, I'll tell ya.

Bright and early we were awakened to the sound of ducks hav'n a quack-along. The men were already down fish'n and us boys wasted no time get'n there either. Uncle George was out there with his split-bamboo fly rod catch'n the big ones on the White Miller Fly. Us young lads cut long, slender maple poles and wound black fishing line around the end, hooked an earthworm on, and there it was. The best made-in-America fish'n rod a boy ever had.

A BACKWOODS LOVE AFFAIR

And we all got nice trout too. Boy, we had a feast over hardwood coals. We stayed a few days and fished to our heart's content. After a downpour one evening, our lean-to got perty wet. No one carried plastic in those days. In fact, everyone was too poor to even have a tent.

But Uncle George and the other men always had a campfire. And every evening as we sat by the embers, memories always would glow, and those stories, what a way to impart to the youth the past, how to conduct oneself and live.

Beaver were get'n too plentiful there on the alder beds. Those ol' flattails were all business now. Uncle George said he'd better come trap'n soon, as the beaver would dam up the little spring and the brook trout wouldn't have no place to spawn. He caught the beaver the next winter. But little did we know a couple of decades later acid rain would ruin far more than the beaver.

The next day we dried out and went explor'n down below the old dam. It was built sometime around the turn of the century, I guess. It backed up a whole lot of water and logs. When the ice went out in the spring they blowed the planks and away she went!! Logs and water hurled down river towards Harrisville and the big steam-fired sawmills, what a sight it must have been. Now all that remained was rocks and logs that had formed the dam. Just a reminder of bygone days when men were men and logs meant beans on the table. Seems like my grandfather dumped logs on the ice here.

JOURNEY TO THE BACKWOODS

Mom told a story once about a lumberjack who cut his foot half off with an ax in the dead of winter. Up here so far from civilization and no medical help, they figured he was a goner. The foot got infected in a couple of days, and the boss said he'd see he got a ride out on the next supply sled, which was another couple of days. By then gangrene had set in and his foot and leg was turning green. The cook be'n a resourceful fellow and always felt sorry for the way the woodsman were treated, decided to help the man. He got the biggest old boot he could find, cut a thin liner out of salt pork and made the logger wear it all the way out on the sled. The trip took two days and when the doctor cut the boot off why the salt pork was green as green could be. And the ol' boy's foot was clean as a whistle. Saved his leg and probably his life.

Anyhow, where was I, oh ya, we were headed downstream from the old dam. We'd went about a mile and Uncle George suddenly whispered us to a halt. We all crept up to the log he hid behind to see what the hide and seek was all about. Down near the next bend was a family of otter. They'd run up the bank and slid down into the water. They sure looked like they were hav'n fun. I thought I'd like to try that with them. But they'd be afraid. It's the age-old fear of man put there so long ago. After fifteen to twenty minutes of that entertainment, we fished awhile then went back to camp. That night as I drifted off to sleep I was sure I heard logdrivers' voices from the river.

A BACKWOODS LOVE AFFAIR

Next day we headed fer Cage Lake, and us boys got even more excited, if'n it were possible. Uncles George and Vinny told us stories on the way. I heard them comment about all the wolf sign in the old burn we went through. Deer sign was scarce.

We knew we were close to Cage Lake 'cause the timber changed drastically. Big spruce became plentiful, and us kids would look up at 'em in wonder. Jimmy and Herb couldn't touch hands, Herb on one side of the tree and Jimmy on the other. At that time I believed Cage Lake to be like heaven. Be'n how we were all pretty tired, I crawled out on a knoll and watched the floating clouds that seemed in no hurry. I was glad I wasn't either. For here was a place that spoke of peace.

The next morning the men had a couple of rafts built from dead spruce logs and leav'n us boys to watch they pushed off out into the lake. The big brook trout lurked there beneath the lily pads and Uncle George had the medicine fer 'em. Out there on the rickety raft cast'n the White Miller fly again and fool'n the hungry trout. He made a graceful silhouette against the morning mist. Those two-pound native brook trout that Uncle brought to shore were of the most brilliant colors, and fat. My-oh-my, what memories I have of that lake. After a few days though, we had to leave. We'd try and head off cross-country and hit Big Sand Lake.

We got too late a start!!

About halfway there we hit a terrible patch of windfall and had to keep bearing right. What a jungle! It was hot and hard hik'n over that blowdown. Uncle George hadn't been through there since before the war when him and my Dad trapped here. We got all turned around and ended up back at the river below the high banks, and it got dark. Us young-uns just couldn't walk anymore and every time they stopped we'd fall asleep. The men would build a little fire and after half an hour make us go on. Uncle George said we'd make it to Brindle Pond Camp soon. I was so-o-o tired I could hardly put one foot ahead of the other. About midnight, up ahead I could hear Uncle George say, "Here's camp, boys." It was so dark I couldn't see my hand in front of my face. But us kids let out a yell of gratitude, and the woods behind us came apart.

Wolves, snarling and growling!!!!

"Hurry!!" Uncle said, as we raced for the cabin. The wolves were really carry'n on by now. They howled deep from empty bellies. It was a vicious-sounding chorus. Herb lit a lantern and Uncle George stood in the doorway with his .32-.20 pistol drawed. "One of you young lads howl," he sezs. So one of us got down by the door and howled. A wolf answered about one-hundred feet out'n the dark. Uncle shot, and the wolf yelped. Next morning we saw where the other wolves had ate the one that was hit. Later that night all the men took the lantern and went fer water. Us kids jumped in the top bunk and waited. We could hear the howling and growling and the shoot'n. Boy, were we scared.

A BACKWOODS LOVE AFFAIR

A considerable time was spent the next day rest'n and clean'n up the cabin. It was obvious that it had been built only with hand tools. Even the table and counter near the stove were half logs. Uncle George said that he and my Dad had built it fer some rich fellers who just used it to hunt in the fall. I believe they was from Rochester. They'd built it in the '30s. No wonder Uncle could find it in the dark. We sure was glad we could use it. After we cleaned it up, we cut some wood. Those were different moral times in America. The cabin wasn't locked, and it was open to all who might have need of it. But you always left it better than you found it. A few years later, once the road was in, everyone locked their camp doors. What a tragedy, I thought.

While we were there Uncle George said we'd walk over to Grassy Pond Camp not far away. On the way over Uncle said that before the war he and my Dad was trap'n hereabouts and had buried a bunch of traps late in the spring. They were in an old copper boiler near the old cabin. War came, and this was the first chance he'd had to come and look fer 'em.

We reached the old cabin and found it in bad shape. The porcupine had took it over and the walls were get'n rotten. It was a great place fer us boys to explore. We searched every inch of that old cabin, careful not to step in the porcupine dung.

Uncle couldn't remember after fourteen years just where they'd buried the traps. Sez he, "If'n you young lads find 'em you'll all get ice cream when we get out." And guess what? I found em!!! I just happened to kick one of the many piles of wolf dung near camp and kicked the handle of the boiler, can you beat that!! What a trip to remember. It's been half a century, but I still haven't forgot.

And here's yet another story of the Massawippi Country. Like I said, Dad and Uncle George built Brindle Pond Camp and used it fer trap'n. Back in those days just before the war and during the war, beaver were real scarce. In fact, you were only allowed four per person.

After Uncle George joined the Marines and went to war, Dad still trapped some out of that camp. He left Burganers' one morning early on snowshoes in early spring, figuring he'd make it to Brindle Pond 'fore dark. Dad hiked along at a good pace and only stopped once near Wolf Pond. It was about sixteen miles to camp. He happened to look back as he nibbled on his lunch and noticed someone follow'n him. He knew right off it was the game warden!! He then took off walk'n slower fer he wanted to get to camp right at dark. He was a corker, he was.

The warden stayed on Dad's trail all the way. Just before Dad got to the Oswegatchie River near the high banks, he picked up the pace. Get'n to the river the ice was already go'n out fer the weather was warming considerable. Dad stood there not know'n what to do next. Should he turn around and spend the night at Massawippi? But then he'd bump into the warden. The whole thing would be terribly embarrassing.

A BACKWOODS LOVE AFFAIR

Dad already had his four beaver, and the warden wanted to see the camp and make sure Dad didn't have no more. Just then a large cake of ice floated down and hit the bank near Dad, and he jumped on. Taking one snowshoe off, he paddled furiously for the other side. Just before his "ferry" hit, he put the snowshoe on and jumped off. He hurried up in the edge of the woods and hid. It wasn't long 'fore the warden came along. Dad recognized him then, standing there look'n where Dad's snowshoe tracks just stopped at the water's edge. Then he looked up and across and here the tracks just started again. He stood there and took off his hat scratching his head. He knew no man could walk on water lest it was God or by the power of God. And he knew enough about Jean Terrillion to know he'd never been spotted wear'n a halo—not by a long shot. Dad looked west and guessed the sun would set in about an hour. The warden would have a long walk back to his car. Dad turned and made his way to camp.

Them was the sort of games that wardens and potential violators played in those days. Perhaps the warden would get the next laugh.

Many, many years later I was in Watertown get'n some beaver and otter tagged at the head office of the Fish and Game Department. The old head warden came out to tag 'em for me. As soon as I presented my license his eyebrows raised and he said, "You any relation to Jean Terrillion?" "Yup," sez me, "he's my Dad." He sighs and sez, "I never did catch him."

I don't think he really knew the whole of it. You see, Dad became a carpenter and built the log building that was this headquarters fer game wardens. I reckon there wasn't any hard feelings on either side.

A lot of folks did what they had to do in them days to put beans on the table. Get'n so nowadays a feller can't hardly afford to gather fish and meat and trap fer profit. Seems like the well-to-do have turned it all into a sport.

And Fish and Game Departments have a biologist behind every tree. It looks like a lulu to a lot of us who view the thing from the sidelines. A game warden is the one who knows what's go'n on. And he should be given one assistant and lay off the rest of the entourage. All the money saved should be used fer winter range to increase game populations. One warden told me it made too much sense, so they'd never do it.

Anyway, as young lads, we took only a few more fish'n trips to Massawippi. Through much jealousy, some members of that hunt'n club didn't want Uncle George to belong. They said he killed all the big bucks and caught too many fish and beaver. So he left. He took it hard too. That place was never the same without him.

One summer Mom wanted to go to Big Sand Lake, and so we loaded up—Tom, myself, Snuffy, Mom, and Brother Johnny, a dyed-in-the-wool city boy.

Someone left us off at Gregg's outlet and we started out. It was hot. Clouds of deer flies did their best to bleed us dry. We'd been follow'n the state

A BACKWOODS LOVE AFFAIR

boundary line 'cause it crossed Big Sand outlet near the lake. But the blowdown was several trees deep, and lots of it. Mom was get'n concerned 'cause the afternoon shadows was show'n up. And Brother Johnny was repeat'n over and over, "This is for the birds. This is for the birds." I climbed up on the windfall and sorta found a trail if'n we stayed on 'em. We walked from one to the other fer about an hour but still hadn't gone far. Johnny gave up and crawled under a top to nap. Mom was tell'n him to get up 'cause we had to go on. About then one of us climbed a tree and could see Big Sand Lake about a mile away, and we all yelled, Ya-hoo.

Youth is a wonderful thing. How quickly we recover.

By the time we reached the lake, it was dark. Uncle George told us to camp on the end near the inlet. Having got there exhausted, we rolled out our blankets and went to sleep. When daylight arrived we discovered a wooden platform not far away. On it was piled a tent, stove, fold-up cots, and a canoe and paddles. Us boys thought someone had just abandoned the whole outfit. Mother said it belonged to some hunters who, no doubt, fly in come fall. She even found a name and address on a tree.

Anyhow, we put the canoe and paddles to good use. There is a beautiful sand beach there and we made the most of it. Mother spent most of her time cleaning up the cache of goods. The squirrels, mice, and porcupines had made an awful mess. In between swim'n and canoe'n we cut some wood fer a night fire. Mom thought it was a good idea 'cause they was wolves about. We caught very few fish as acid rain was already destroying those beautiful lakes.

As the evening shades fell, we built a campfire. Yes-sir-ree, it's the universal sign of friendship. We all had a cot to sleep on and again reasoned that this was really liv'n. Here we were again soak'n our souls in the wilderness. It was a quiet, peaceful serenity that exists only in the deep woods.

Just over the ridge from Big Sand was Rock Lake, probably more beautiful than Big Sand. It's water so clear you could see the bottom in fifty feet of water. Uncle George said it never had any fish 'cause the water needed lime or something. We planned a short excursion over there tomorrow.

The camp firelight danced off the big spruce trees nearby. We laid there look'n over the stars. It was a great way to spend the evening, learning what they were and where they were—the great starry hosts. Those stars assured us of another pleasant wilderness tomorrow as we drifted off.

"What was that?" Mom shouted. "What was what?" I responded as I bolted awake. "Hark, listen," she whispered. Mom was a light sleeper and missed nuthin', but I started to figure she'd had a dream or something, and I just laid back down. Almost to sleep, I then heard what she'd feared: ha-o-o-o-o-yi-o-o-o-o-o-o. I sat up and answered and they called right back. "Stop that," Mom scolded with fear in her voice. "You'll have the whole pack down on us." Poor Mom thought it was a pack of wolves, and be'n

A BACKWOODS LOVE AFFAIR

the rascal I was, I didn't tell her they was loons over on Rock Lake. They hollered again, and I squalled back. Mom had fear in her voice, so I quit.

By then everyone was awake.

Snuffy put some wood on the dying embers, and Brother Johnny pulled his cot real close like. We went back to sleep finally and along towards morning someone yelled, "I'm on fire." Sure enough, I don't remember whose blankets caught on fire. I remember we dragged it to the lake and doused it. What a night.

We didn't have any more nights like that. Mom finally somewhat believed me that the howling yell was indeed the wild, hysterical, laughing loon. We did break a paddle though and Mom said we'd have to pay fer it. After we got out, she wrote to the name on the tree, it was the man who owned the stuff. He was so impressed from her honesty and the way she cleaned the outfit up, he sent her a pack of fancy cheeses. In fact, he sent something fer many years at Christmas.

Yup, it's true what Mother always said, "Honesty pays."

Fer all practical purposes, the last pleasant fish'n trip to the big woods was when we were about fifteen years old—me, Tom, Snuffy, Davy Proulx, and his nephew.

By then there was a gate at Burganers'. Once the log road was in, non-camp members couldn't drive on up. International Paper, who owned all that clear

JOURNEY TO THE BACKWOODS

to the forever wild Adirondack Park, leased it to hunt'n clubs, of which Massawippi was one.

So anyway, some adult dropped us off at the old Kelly's Camp Road. This time I had my old town cedar rib canoe. It weighed about one hundred pounds and I determined to carry it to the alder beds to fish. It got awful heavy 'fore I got it there, but I made 'er. We had a great time as usual except fer one problem. We hadn't planned our food reserve and by the time we went to Cage Lake and back, we ran out of grub. We ate a lot of trout, and smoked some to eat as we headed out—a day early. Our pickup person was to get us on Saturday near the high banks.

I recall devouring food like a wolf once we made it out. I never forgot that lesson. And all the hunt'n and fish'n trips since, I've always had extra.

All things bright & beautiful,
All things great and small,
All things wise and wonderful,
The Lord God made them all.
—Cecil Frances Alexander
(1818-1895)

CHAPTER TWELVE

TRAP'N MASSAWEPIE - THE FIRST YEARS
Circa 1955

I shall never forget my first trap'n venture at Massawippi. I was eleven. Uncle George and Brother

Start of the great Adirondack Camp.
Uncle George is center holding the ruler.

TRAP'N MASSAWEPIE – THE FIRST YEARS

James had been up there trap'n through the ice in late winter. The road had been plowed 'cause some outfit was log'n there all winter. So along about the last of March, us young-uns got to go one weekend.

The road had broke up by then because of spring weather.

Brother James had to go to work fer some sugar'n outfit making syrup. It was just Uncle George and me, Tom, and Snuffy.

The near finish of Massawepie camp. Great shelter while on a backwoods journey. Herb Kampnick with the peavey.

Uncle had a few traps set on the way in and picked up a couple of beaver. He told me I could set a trap on Wolf Pond if'n I wanted to. The beaver was eat'n themselves out of house and home. Uncle George showed me how to set a "ladder" set through the ice. I had carried in a 1½ Newhouse trap, which

JOURNEY TO THE BACKWOODS

was very strong. I didn't have any big traps as yet. We spent a wonderful weekend at Massawippi. Them was shine'n times and still dear in my memories. Uncle caught some beaver and otter on Massawippi Pond and up at Lee's Creek. Once it was a big log'n camp. Nuthin' was left anymore except a clearing in the forest. He said his Dad, Grandpa Roch, had sleighed logs from there fer Mr. Lee, many, many seasons past.

The story was told how Johnny Roch had a beautiful team of blue roans which he was most proud of. And they could pull too!! Gramps pulled up there to the header (a rollway that held many logs) one day to load. Now each rollway had two men who was mighty handy with a peavey. Which, fer those who never saw one, was a long ash handle with a steel pike in the end and curved steel hook that let a logger roll a log that sometimes weighed over a ton. At any rate, they loaded Gramps's sled while he went in and had a bite to eat. He hurried back out 'cause another teamster just pulled in to load. Climb'n on the sled and keep'n his reins steady, he chuckled to his team.

The big roans dipped their heads and came into their harness, but they couldn't move the load. Gramps had seen the extra logs the boys had put on while he was eat'n. A crowd started to gather as the boys with the peaveys commenced to who-raw Gramps a little. "Johnny Roch, we thought them Percherons could pull?" Gramps never said a word, he just *Gee-ed* the team to the right and spoke to

TRAP'N MASSAWEPIE – THE FIRST YEARS

them in a serious voice. Most log'n horses know when it's time to get down and pull, and pull they did. They broke the sled loose from the snow with a side pull and were on their way. Gramps stood up on that huge load of logs and smiled and waved. Ah—victory is sweet.

Well it was out Sunday night and back to school. But my mind was not on read'n or rite'n or arithmetic. No-sir-ree, how could this boy, born to follow the ways of the wild creatures, pay any mind to school things? Here I had a trap set fer beaver in Wolf Pond and a big beaver would fetch me twenty dollars. Why, that was nigh onto a fortune!!!

All week cooped up in that classroom, my heart at Massawippi, I never thought Friday would come. Mercifully, Saturday morning found us hik'n on up the road again. Uncle George caught some otter in the inlet to Wolf Pond. So he told us boys to go and pull my trap on the pond—if'n I had a beaver or not. He went on up to the camp to skin and get a fire go'n.

We snowshoed on over to pick up my traps. But when we got to the pond fear struck our hearts!! The ice was go'n out and my set was forty feet from shore!! What to do now. Goodness, Uncle was halfway to camp, so we were on our own. There was still rotten ice out to the set, but it would never hold me. But leave it to a gather'n of young make do cobblers. We cut long poles with our axes and wired 'em end fer end till they reached the set. Then I cut a light dead pole five feet long fer a walk'n stick. I figured the ice would hold as long as I kept my weight distributed on the long poles.

I started off. FEARFULLY!!

Using the short pole to steady myself, I made it to the trap. I had to pull up the branches, which the trap was on under the water. I grabbed a holt and heaved. Up she came, and with a huge beaver drowned in the trap. I was so excited I stepped off the pole with one foot as I yelled ya-hoo!! Tom screamed, "Watch out."

Good thing he did. For if'n I'd got off that pole, I surely would have sunk. What a whopper beaver. I learned later it was near eighty inches. Uncle George said he heard me yell clean up to the camp. I'll tell ya that beaver was heavy. But we was so excited it didn't matter. We fetched it to camp, about a mile and a half.

Uncle George was all happy fer me. Laid it on a small log table and took out his Sharade pocket knife. He skinned that big beaver clean in twenty minutes. Uncle sure know'd about such things. What a hunt'n and trap'n education I got from Uncle George.

And still another time a few years later I had another close call on the inlet to Wolf Pond. I'd set a couple of beaver traps, big number four Blake and Lambs, on a beaver dam. It got real cold and when I came back to look at 'um, the ice had covered everything. I chopped a hole where I thought the first one was, removed the ice, and kept feel'n fer the wire on the trap. They was that there green algae-like stuff

TRAP'N MASSAWEPIE – THE FIRST YEARS

all over and before I knew it, I stuck my hand in the trap!!!! I panicked fer a minute then stopped and forced myself to think. It was below zero and I was alone, so no one was go'n to hear me yell for help. The wire was fastened to a stake driven out beyond my reach. I could see the stake stick'n out of the ice but couldn't reach it. I'd stuck my right hand in the trap so chop'n the ice with my left was very slow. I couldn't pull the trap out of the water far enough to pull down the spring to relieve my hand. And to top it off, my hand was starting to turn numb. It didn't hurt much, but I knew in this temperature I'd lose my hand in short order.

I commenced to pull and yank with all my strength. Yank and pull, yank and pull. Part of my problem was the drown'n lock slid down the wire, which in turn had made the wire even shorter. As at other times in my life, I soon believed I wasn't really alone. And soon I started to pull the trap further and further out of the frigid water. I soon had enough slack to put both feet on the springs and free my hand. I never pulled that trick again. After that when I couldn't locate a trap, I'd poke around with a stick. Like Ma always said, "You kids just don't know the danger."

Easter vacation and long weekends gave the only free time to escape to the backwoods to trap Massawippi. But when I reached fifteen, I received a "time out" to trap there all spring. It was a miracle and all documented in a later chapter.

CHAPTER THIRTEEN

ONE OF THE WORLD'S BEST NABORS
Circa 1952

We went up to the woods every chance we got on weekends.

I think this was the winter Jimmy went to work fer Harold Moser on the farm. He boarded there too.

He worked hard and was very responsible. He was well liked, and they treated him fairly. I remember they sold us a quarter of beef every year very cheap. They were good nabors even though they lived halfway to Croghan.

That Christmas our one present was a new sled each, at least fer me and Tom. So we spent our evenings walking up the road to the hill near Maggie Boliver's and slide'n all the way back down to the house. We didn't have to worry about cars come'n along 'cause ours was the last house on the road.

ONE OF THE WORLD'S BEST NABORS

A 21-year old Croghan R.D. 1 youth serving with the First Air Cavalry is Lewis County's seventh fatality of the fighting in Viet Nam.

Sp-4 Thomas H. Kloster, son of Mr. and Mrs. Reuben Kloster, was killed Nov. 13 at 5:45 p.m. while in battle 60 miles northeast of Saigon near the Cambodian border.

Word of his death was brought to his parents Friday morning, Nov. 15, by Sgt. Brown, of Camp Drum, and on Friday afternoon, Lt. Confer, of Camp Drum, also visited the Klosters verifying word of his death.

Circumstances surrounding his death are being awaited by his parents.

Sp-4 Kloster had been in Viet Nam since Feb. 19, and was stationed near the demilitarized zone until about three weeks ago, when (Continued on Page 5)

SP-4 THOMAS H. KLOSTER

Tommy Kloster, loved by everyone, missed by everyone.
He was a true reflection of his parents.

Over the next few winters we often went down to slide with Rueben and Norah Kloster's younger children. Out behind their house and barn in the moonlight, sometimes twenty to thirty below zero, we'd race down the hill and into the draw. We had such fun. "I went the fastest," someone would shout. Sometimes childlike arguments ensued over who indeed won the race.

The Kloster boys didn't lack ingenuity by any means. They tamed their young bulls and heifers so they could hitch them up like horses. While mostly child's play, sometimes they dragged wood and did other chores with them. Rueben, or "Boob" as everyone called him, always had several head

JOURNEY TO THE BACKWOODS

of cattle for their use. He milked 'em and Norah separated the cream. They then fed the whey to the pigs. Seems like they raised 2two every six months. They butchered spring and fall. They always had good look'n hogs.

With seven kids to feed (and plus sometimes half the naborhood), Rueben raised a big garden too. He and his wife worked very hard to provide fer their family, but you don't find a whole lot of people like that today who don't live out of a store. As to further save money, Norah knit wool socks fer the whole family.

Saturday night Uncle Vinny picked up us kids, and we'd all flock over to Norah and Rueben's place to be entertained by way of their newly-purchased Zenith TV. Uncle Vinny really got into the wrestling. This was long before it turned into such demonic foolishness. His favorites were Yukon Eric, Farmer Boy, and Vern Gaunya. He sat beside the old round oak stove and whenever he had to spit tobacco juice, he just leaned forward, opened the stove door—never tak'n his eyes off the TV—and let fly, and he never missed.

Somewhere between wrestling and a Charlie Chan movie, Norah served bologna sandwiches and the best start-from-scratch chocolate cake in the world. Washed down with fresh milk, what a treat. It was one of the few times me and Tom got store-bought bread. Norah always had some 'cause she had so many lunches to put up fer her family. Otherwise, she baked bread just like most of the other women in the area.

ONE OF THE WORLD'S BEST NABORS

Like I said once before, sometimes Norah had half the naborhood to feed. Me and Tom, and Snuffy and Dale Lyndaker spent almost as much time there as we did at home. Or some of their many relatives would show up or the VerSneider boys would come down. Sometimes the house was so full you couldn't find a place to sit down. The folks of modern medicine say that adult human hearts are the same size. I beg to differ with the good doctors. They didn't know Norah. If'n you ever experienced her hospitality you knew this was a special person. How poor life would have been without her.

I guess what lingers most when I remember this great lady is that I still hear her hearty laughter. When that dear woman laughed, she could force a smile on a drug store Indian.

One of her sons, Tommy, and I became the best of friends.

We went to log'n competition together. He was the only person I ever knew who no one could ever say anything bad about. What a wonderful personality and warm smile, always cheerful and helpful. He got sent to Viet Nam and died there. His memorial service was at their home and that night I went there with what seemed like the whole county. Cars were lined up and down the road. I had to walk fer half a mile to get to the house. I shall never forget old Rueben and Norah near the casket. I'll never forget their grief, never. Perhaps it is true, the good die young. It still hurts fer a lot of us when we remember him.

The only person worse than a cheap person is a religious person who is cheap.
—Dale Francis Terrillion

CHAPTER FOURTEEN

THE OTHER BEST NABORS, AND THEY HAD HORSES
Circa 1953

There's an old say'n that best describes the relationship between man and horse. "The outside of a horse is good for the inside of a man." Tis true, you know. And the horse Molly filled a great void in

Picture taken at Mike Zehr's sugar camp.
Andrew Lyndaker second from left in the back.

JOURNEY TO THE BACKWOODS

my youth. Up the main road just past the old country schoolhouse lived Andrew and Inez Lyndaker on their small farm. You remember, I told you a little about 'em awhile back.

Like so many homesteads in that neck of the woods, there wasn't no shortage of rocks. It was a sight to behold. The more you picked up, the more they multiplied.

Andrew, be'n a mite old-fashioned, and poor to boot, did all his farm'n with a team of horses. The first time I recollect see'n him driving 'em he was plowing right across from the schoolhouse. When recess came, all the other kids ran and played. Not me. No-sir-ree!! Forbidden to leave the schoolyard, I'd lean up against that maple tree near the road and watch those horses pull that old Oliver walk'n plow. Their muscles would bulge as they broke the sod and fought the rocks, Andrew hang'n onto that bouncing plow with the reins over his shoulder. Years later he would comment in his dry humor sort of way, "Whoever took this land from the Indians and thought they'd farm it didn't have much sense."

Andrew, be'n a respectful Mennonite Christian, didn't hold with foul language. Never would he consider uttering a naughty word. But follow'n that plow with Molly horse go'n straight out would try even Saint Peter's patience. When the plow crashed off a big rock, Andrew needed a purpose fer his frustration so he'd shout, "Molly, you old blockhead, ya slow down." Molly never missed a lick, her head tucked and a little to the side and muscles straining.

THE OTHER BEST NABORS, AND THEY HAD HORSES

That was the closest "Brother Andrew" ever came to naughty words all the years I knew him.

So I leaned up against that grand old maple and wished I was over there bust'n clods with my bare feet. Then the school bell would bring me out of my dream. Fer I had been ride'n Molly on down this here old road next to Roy Rogers and Trigger. And Roy was a-sing'n "Happy Trails!" Man, I hated that school bell.

Molly wasn't a big horse as drafts go, probably about 1,600 pounds. She was a solid red sorrel chestnut color and looked to be Percheron and a little Morgan and, of course, all go.

Dale Lyndaker on the great horse, Molly

JOURNEY TO THE BACKWOODS

My dream'n finally paid off at hay'n time. I got to drive them while Andrew placed the hay on the wagon. Those were the days of the old hay loader hooked behind the wagon. Loose hay. Then when the wagon was fully loaded, we headed up into the barn. Molly pulled so hard she practically took the load up the barn bridge by herself. Poor old Prince horse tried to keep up, he never could. The single tree on his side was almost worn through from rub'n on the iron wheel of the wagon. Boy, that old wagon was sure hard to ride over the rocks. And whenever we got out into the road, those wheels would grind on the gravel.

Try'n to get a load of hay once almost turned into a disaster. Occasionally hay would get all wound up in the gears of the hay loader and the wheels would just slide. This particular time Andrew couldn't cut it out with his knife. He then decided the only way was to burn it out. I drove the horses out of the windrow of hay and held the reins real good while Andrew set the tangled wad of hay on fire. We should have unhooked the hayloader from the wagon. Hindsight is always 20-20.

Soon the horses smelled the smoke and heard it burn'n, and they got real nervous fast. All of a sudden they took off run'n and I couldn't hold 'em. The stampede was on!! Andrew tried to get back up on the load of hay, but it was too high with the wagon bouncing along. "Turn 'em!!" he yelled. I pulled as hard as I could on one rein and they turned towards the cherry trees and stone fence along the hay field.

THE OTHER BEST NABORS, AND THEY HAD HORSES

When they got right to the trees I yelled, "Whoa," and pulled on both reins, and they stopped!! Andrew got the fire out and we went back to hay'n. I never forgot how to control a problem horse after that. To me there was no better feel'n in the world than drive'n those draft horses. The smell of leather and horse sweat, the jingle of tug chains, it all helped a boy grow up. No doubt about it, Andrew was a special nabor.

Like I said before, Andrew's homestead was a stump and rock farm. He milked about a dozen cows by hand and sold milk in the big station cans to the cheese plant in Croghan. Folks today use those cans fer flower pots and what not. He also sold us milk fer fifty cents a gallon, if we could pay fer it or not.

Say! This reminds me of a story I once heard. Seems like this Quaker farmer had a cantankerous old cow. Like they used to say, "The devil was in her." Anyhow, this here old bovine had it in her head to kick or slap the Puritan with her tail every chance she got. He tied up the weapons and then she'd rock back and forth. Finally the old boy felt like he might lose it one evening when it was hot and he was tired. Stand'n up, he pointed a callused hand at her head and said, "Thou knowest I can not strike thee, but does thou knowest I can sell thee to a Presbyterian?"

Well, get'n back to Brother Andrew, greed had no place in Andrew's life. Paper money was just something you had to use to purchase things. He cared less about money than any person I ever knew. Silver and gold don't build friendships that last.

When we started the new log house on the main road, Ma and Richie cut all the cedar (the walls were cedar logs) down in Andrew's woods. He even hauled them out fer Ma with the team. And you can bet the price was right.

I can recall when Uncle Vinny would go down to Andrew's in the fall and press cider. Andrew had a small apple press, and we'd set on his porch and make some squashings. Sure was good stuff. There was old orchards all over that country that the homesteaders planted. The bears climbed them in the fall to get the apples and broke down the limbs, but some lived on.

Andrew's nabor Alvin Zehr had a one-eyed old mare named Jill. She was a wonderful old horse with the quietest disposition you ever did see. Andrew borrowed her once, so I could rake hay down on the flats and get the hay up before a rain. That sweet mare never did anything wrong. What a joy to drive.

Ralph Shaw borrowed her once to skid logs and hired me to drive her. Well, I was beside myself to say the least. This horse was so smart, we didn't have to even drive her in the woods. Ralph was on the landing and unhooked her and sent her back up the skid trail. She'd come to me and I'd hook her to a log and send her to the landing. The horse flies were awful. What wasn't sweat on that poor old horse was blood. Right after lunch one day, I'd just

THE OTHER BEST NABORS, AND THEY HAD HORSES

hooked her up when she keeled over and couldn't get up. Like I said before, I was about twelve years old at the time, and was I ever scared.

I ran fer the landing yell'n, "Ralph, Jill's dying!! Jill's dying!!" Of course, Ralph came run'n to witness the death of a horse he'd borrowed. Probably think'n, *What will I tell Alvin?* We sped up to Jill who was still on her side, breathing heavy. Ralph sized up the situation and said, "Talk to her. Stand behind her neck and pet her." So with tears in my eyes, I saw Ralph get out his knife. He has to put her out of her misery, and we don't have a gun. I just knew she'd broke a leg. Ralph knelt down behind her back with the knife and reaching over, cut the bellyband on the harness, stood up, and poked her with his boot and said, "Get up, girl."

To my joy she stood up!!! Was I ever tickled, Jill had kicked a horsefly on her belly and got her foot caught in the bellyband. I didn't see that. When I'd turned around she was just fall'n over. There was a safety on the side of the band that breaks if a horse gets hung in it, but fer some reason it never broke.

This job was late in the summer and the honey bees were really active. One day at lunch Ralph said, "I'll show ya how to hunt bees." This sounded like another a great exciting adventure fer me. He took a jar lid from his water jug and sat it on a stump. Then he put in sugar and water and stirred it up. We just sat back and waited. Right quick-like a honey bee buzzed right down into that sweet mess and commenced to load up.

JOURNEY TO THE BACKWOODS

Ralph gently leaned over and sprinkled white flour on Mr. Bee. The honey maker was soon full and took off. Ralph whispered, "Watch which way he goes now." I had very good eyes in them days and pointed off into the beech forest. We went about fifty yards and sat down with the jar cover near us. Soon a bee came, then another!! They loaded up and took off. I watched carefully and pointed, but Ralph shook his head no. Golly, I figured that we'd get up and go after 'em.

He whispered, "We'll wait fer the one that has flour on his rear end." Sure enough the next bee was our trailblazer with the white rump. He filled his pouch and flew higher this time. Ralph said the tree was get'n closer now because the bee's line of flight had changed. We went through this charade a couple more times. Finally Mr. Bee's trips were real short and that meant the tree was real close. And so it was. The last time he loaded up and left, he went straight up into a big old growth white ash. This was great, sez I, jump'n up and down. "Let's cut 'er down and get the honey."

But Ralph said we'd have to wait till the bear den up in the fall, so they wouldn't find it and destroy the bees. He said you must leave one-third of the honey and replace what you took with sugar. Then be sure and cover the tree up real good so's the bees wouldn't freeze. That made sense, sez I. If'n one was to live from the forest, one must take care of those things out'n the woods.

My Drug Problem

I had a drug problem when I was young.
I was drugged to the church on Sunday morning.
I was drugged to church for weddings and funerals.
I was drugged to family reunions regardless of the weather.
I was drugged to the bus stop to go to school every weekday.
I was drugged by my ears when I was disrespectful to adults and teachers.
I was also drugged to the woodshed when I was disrespectful to my parents.
Those drugs are still in my veins: and they will affect my behavior in everything I do, say, and think. They are stronger than cocaine, crack, or heroin, and if today's children has this kind of "drug" problem, America would certainly be a better place.

—Author Unknown

CHAPTER FIFTEEN

THE NEW HOUSE
Circa 1955

After a few years in the old homestead, Ma bought three acres of land down on the main road from Alvin Zehr. We started the cellar and you never saw so many rocks in your life. Ma worked like a Chinaman with that pick and shovel, but what to do with all those rocks? Well, she used tons in the walls and septic system and still had huge piles left over. So she dug big holes and buried 'em under the driveway. Those that were too big to lift she rolled with a stone hook. It looked like a huge peavey.

Once the cellar walls were done, Uncle George came and started to put on floor joists and subfloor. It was always an interesting treat to have Uncle George around. If he wasn't nail'n or saw'n, he'd tell us boys stories. We really ate 'em up.

THE NEW HOUSE

Mom on a breadbakin' marathon.

For many years after Uncle came back from the war, he could only raise his left arm part way. He'd been hit with shrapnel in the shoulder. Uncle George was a Marine at Guadalcanal. So when we put the logs up for the walls (they were put upstanding), us boys held 'em and Uncle nailed 'em with two large spikes. There were no power tools, and we worked very hard, even the holes were all drilled with a brace and bit. I remember see'n Uncle peel big long shavings with his big wood-block plane.

It was so far to walk down from the old homestead every day to work on the new house. I got so tired and bored from walk'n that dirt road that I made another vow. When I got old enough to get a car I'd never hitchhike again, and I never did.

JOURNEY TO THE BACKWOODS

So Ma then decided to camp there near the new house that summer. We built a tin lean-to and became like the old-time woodsman. Eat'n over a campfire and pile'n green ferns on to smoke the bugs away. Sometimes it was hard to get to sleep at night between the buzz'n and blood let'n. But we made it till fall and then we had an old-fashioned work bee to put the roof on. All the nabors came.

It was great. Virg Lehman even brought a Cat and did all the back fill and landscaping. The entire roof got put on in one day. There was lots of good food fer everyone 'cause many woman folks came to help. After the hard days work they even had a small keg of beer as everyone relaxed and visited. "Many hands make light work," Mother always said. It's almost impossible to have bees today. No one wants to be bothered. No one wants to give a little of their precious time. Sometimes I think only through some disaster will people become real nabors again. And here's another thing, today there are so many people on government programs they may be better off financially than you. A body has to be real careful who he helps. Some folks figure the world owes them a liv'n.

Anyway, the new house with all the modern conveniences sure was nice. It was soooooo much warmer than the old homestead. And they was lots of good rabbit hunt'n close by. I even got to trap a few weasels. I tracked 'em in the deep snow. The varmints' tracks changed direction as often as young

THE NEW HOUSE

boys' thoughts. I tried everything to rid the critter of his silky coat, and sometimes I catched 'em.

And I soon began to trap muskrats over across the road in Indian River. Every one I caught was around seventy-five cents. There was no other jobs fer a young boy around there after school. It was sure a lot more enjoyable than go'n to the classroom. Out there follow'n that river I learned all sorts of things that only Mother Nature could teach me—and it was never boring. I didn't get no lectures or a slap when I stared out the window at the wonders of creation. Only soft subtle things like the songs of birds, the ripple of the water, the winds play'n in the trees. I not only learned but got food for my soul as well. "Be still and know that I am God," that's what it says in the Good Book.

Mom was always in need, try'n to finish the new place. Dad didn't send the thirty-five dollars a month like he was supposed to. So her tree cut'n in the fall was mighty important. Them was the days a quarter looked as big as a dinner plate. And a greenback, why they was tough to come by. Fer us, dollars were scarce as gold bars. Now we had a light bill, (about six dollars a month) and furnace oil to buy (sixteen cents a gallon).

Somehow or another, she got in contact with the owner of the Fenton House in Number Four. It was there she'd worked as a chambermaid when she was fourteen.

Number Four, at one time, was a summer playground fer lots of wealthy folks. They came near

JOURNEY TO THE BACKWOODS

there on the train and then by horse-drawn coach. There was several hotels and lodges there to satisfy their every whim.

Mom could cut Christmas trees there, but it was a long way from home. If'n we couldn't get anyone to drop us off, we had to go by way of shank's mare. I remember those long walks to Belfort, across to Kirchnerville, and up the Number Four Road. Sometimes it was one or two in the morning 'fore we got home. I'd be so tired I would try and lay down beside the road and go to sleep. Mom would prod us on and sing while we walked. "Sing'n seems to help a troubled soul." That's what Johnny Cash said. Sometimes she sang "How Great Thou Art."

Walk'n along at night we heard great horned owls hoot'n, foxes bark, and sometimes wolves howl. They really tuned up. That always got my attention and would interrupt the boredom.

Near the Fenton House was another old hotel that was closed up. It was boom'n when Mom was a girl. She told of a great tragedy there one summer night.

Like most of those places, a small bar most always done a brisk business. A local woman, sort of a Calamity Jane type, usually could be found there. This old gal was known fer her vulgarity. On one stormy night the place had plenty of folks exercising their elbows and were feel'n no pain. Lightning struck real close, and most everyone got a little quiet. Not Ms. Bar Patron, she stated she was not afraid of no blanky-blank lightning. Moments later, a bolt of

THE NEW HOUSE

lightning struck her D.E.A.D.!! Only her!! Mock'n God is not recommended. The owners of the Titanic learned that also.

The come'n winter looked like another poor folks Christmas. Mom made enough from the trees to pay the taxes, fill the stoveoil tank, and buy flour and sugar. I had so desperately wanted a Daisy BB gun. Someway I got hold of a Sears Roebuck catalog and saw it displayed there in all its glory. Every day I looked and hoped and yearned. In my boyish way I prayed, surely God would help.

The day before Christmas I was look'n out the window through the icicles when through the fresh snow drove a car. *Who was this?* I wondered as two men got out. Mother met them at the door. "Mrs. Terrillion, we're from the Salvation Army and the VFW, and we'd like to leave some things for Christmas." "My yes," Mother replied. From the car they brought a few boxes and Mother gave them each a nice fruitcake. It was glad tidings fer all. Us young-uns danced around the gifts, whooping and laugh'n with glee.

But there was no Daisy BB gun.

There was some toys, a doll fer Bonnie, and some warm clothes. Those acts of kindness have always been with me. I can never pass by a Salvation Army kettle at Christmas. The ring'n little bell warms my heart, and my eyes sometimes get misty. Down memories trail I still remember that Christmas so long ago. And every now and then I send them good

JOURNEY TO THE BACKWOODS

saints money from my tithe. Few churches have a track record to match the Salvation Army.

There at the little white Catholic church in Indian River every summer, they had a church picnic with good food and games. What do you suppose was right in the center of the table of prizes? Yup, a Daisy BB gun.

But it cost ten cents to play a card. I combed the roadside ditches like Sherlock Holmes look'n fer pop and beer bottles. If'n I found ten I could play, and I did find ten. Up to the table I went, determined as a homesick salmon.

The bingo numbers rolled away.

I placed my kernel of corn, with precision, on the card whenever Ed Proulx called the numbers out. But alas, I lacked cover'n one number. I was the saddest boy alive. Uncle George saw me as I stumbled about from one game to the other. Suddenly his hand was on my shoulder, "Daley boy, why so gloomy on this fun day?" I quietly informed Uncle of my financial plight and wondered aloud why I couldn't win the BB gun. "Ten cents you need," stated Uncle reaching in his pocket. Boy, that dime looked bigger and better than any I ever had. My attitude changed in the blink of an eye.

Thank'n Uncle, I tore off fer the table of treasure. Put down my big dime with renewed hope. The numbers rolled again, and they came fer me. I won the prize!! I leaped up off that bench like a fox after a field mouse. They handed me my gun, box and all. "Uncle George," I yelped as I raced about. "I won it,

THE NEW HOUSE

I won it!!!" A happy boy ran up the road. Who sez God don't hear the simple prayers of children?

The church picnics are no more than a memory now. They gave them up a few years later. They sold beer there in huge washtubs on ice. Mother always voiced her anger. She said how could the church justify make'n money right beside God's house sell'n booze? She was right but she got overruled anyhow. She should have washed out their mouths with soap like she done with us if'n we said bad words.

I wonder if Christ had a little black dog?
All curley and wooley like mine;
With two long silken ears and a nose, round and wet,
And two eyes, brown and tender, that shine.
I'm sure, if He had, that little black dog
Knew, right from the first, He was God;
That he needed no proof that Christ was Divine,
And just worshiped the ground where He trod.
I'm afraid that He hadn't, because I have read
How He prayed in the garden, alone;
For all of His friends and disciples had fled-Even Peter,
the one called a stone.
And, oh, I am sure that little black dog,
With a heart so tender and warm,
Would never have left Him to suffer alone,
But creeping right under His arm,
Would have licked the dear fingers,
in agony clasped, And, counting all favors but loss,
When they took Him away, would have trotted behind
And followed Him quite to the Cross.
—Anonymous

CHAPTER SIXTEEN

THE DOGS
Circa 1955

Most of the folks around that neck of the woods had rabbit hounds, coonhounds, and foxhounds. When we were still up at the old homestead I happened by Maggie's place one cool evening and discovered a boy's gold mine. The Boliver's bitch had a batch of pups, mostly of beagle descent. With a joyful heart, I stumbled in to look over "boy's best friend." There in a box near the old cook stove, on a bed of old rags, was a black-and-white wiggling mass of whining and howling pups that needed to be cuddled. And I picked out the runt of the litter. She whined and squirmed. Puppies smell wonderful, and who could refuse one?

The cold, dark, early spring night couldn't dampen my spirits. With "Bullet" tucked safely in my coat, I raced fer home. "Mom, Mom, look what

JOURNEY TO THE BACKWOODS

Left to right, Davey Proulx, Dale, Snuffy.
Sailor dog front and center.

Harold gave me. My very own pup!" Mother had a major fit!! "We can't hardly feed ourselves, and this dog will have pups when she grows up." Mom really carried on. "You'll have to take her back."

"No-no I can't do that," I cried. I retreated to the porch, clutching my precious friend in my arms. I ran and hid in the pines. Lean'n up against a tree, I sat and held Bullet and told her what a great rabbit dog she'd be. We'd roam the woods and hunt together. I'd get a gun and....

We sat and shivered together, just a couple of misplaced pups. A young moon rose, and I could see

THE DOGS

Mom stand'n on the porch call'n me to please come back to the house. I shuffled back and begged and pleaded fer my pup. She came up with a box to put her in and made me go in and eat supper. I wolfed down my food (after we said grace) and with Ma shake'n her head, I got permission to check on my pup. "Put your coat on," she scolded.

The clear chilly night seemed colder than it was 'cause a breeze was a-blow'n. A fox barked... a great horned owl hooted, and the stars all sparkled friendly-like. It was too early fer crickets and frogs. If'n I was just old enough to stay out in the forest, maybe up at Gramps's camp, no one would bother me there. I could hunt and fish and trap all the time. Or maybe I could go west to the great mountains. Uncle Leslie had been all the way to California, and the few times I saw him he had a big smile and would say, "Go West, young man, go West." But how far could a penniless nine-year-old get? Still, it was a dream. Bullet whined. I held her close. There we sat on the porch enjoying each other's company—one lonesome pup—one lonely boy. Bullet had to stay in the woodshed fer the night.

Next morning bright and early 'fore school, I ran out to check on my hound. She whined and came to me, and I knew she was hungry. I gave her part of my cornmeal mush. She gulped it down like only a hound could. That day at school was the longest I ever had. All I could think about was my pup. I never thought Uggy's old Ford would ever get me home. I leaped out, leave'n my books, and ran fer the woodshed, yell'n fer my dog. She wasn't to be found. I asked Ma where she was, and she just said, "I told you we couldn't afford to feed a dog," was all she said. My heart was broken. I sat on the steps and sobbed and cried, call'n for Bullet hope'n she'd come run'n out of the night. I refused supper and stayed there call'n fer my hound. My soul was truly downcast. But the Good Book sez that God is a Father to the fatherless. Sit'n there, the emptiness I felt overflowed down my cheeks. How I missed that pup. I renewed my vow again. Someday I'd have me a dog and even a horse, and no one would take them away.

A boy's best friend. Dale at new house, 1955.

THE DOGS

It wasn't long after we'd moved into the new house that Jimmy got a female hound from the Dekin boy about his age. We all had great hopes that this would be a great rabbit dog. Indeed, the first winter as just a pup she took to those rabbit tracks like a duck to water.

Before we knew it, Mom's fears came to pass. She had a batch of pups. And they looked like a Heinz 57 variety. Yup, they were mongrels all right. But what did it matter to me and Tom and Bonnie? We played fer hours on end with 'em, only a couple of months old when tragedy struck. The mother went off one day and found a dead cow behind a certain person's barn and was feeding on it.

This feller, being of low moral character, shot the dog, but she made it home barely alive. We heard her that afternoon whining over behind a lumber pile near the house. Her chest all blowed open, she looked so pitiful. Us kids all cried and cried. Jimmy came home and put her out of her misery. In those days, every time someone saw a dog, they automatically figured it was chasing deer and killed it. Some of those people around there were the sorriest lot that ever was. The same people who did this were usually the ones who would shoot a doe in July.

Well, we had four pups to raise, and we raised 'em. Ma would only let us keep two, so we kept Brownie and Prince. That Brownie grew up to be the hunt'nest dog you ever did see. He once kilt a porcupine while out'n the woods with Uncle Tony. You ought to have seen the quills, covered from nose

JOURNEY TO THE BACKWOODS

to ears and even some in his body. We put a pitchfork down over his neck and pushed his head to the ground. Then spent all night pull'n quills. He was so gritty a dog you had to really watch him when you were hunt'n, or he'd still take another porky.

That dog got to know the sound of Tony's old car and ran over to the corner and jump in. Once while up near the Jerden Falls, Tony got between a cub bear and its mother before he realized it. Well sir, the cub bawled, and mother charged. Old Brownie raced in there and put up such a fight that the sow forgot all about Uncle Tony. When the dust cleared, the old sow was back against a tree and Brownie dare'n her to fight. He was so fast she never could get a hold of him. Tony got up the Tote Road a ways and called the dog.

A few years later, Prince and Brownie was run'n up the same road ahead of Tony, and a couple of nuts shot them both. They told Tony they were "wild dogs," and they attacked them. It was a dirty deed, indeed. We saw all kinds of wierdos come up there in the summer from the cities. Tony never quite got over that, and he got even more reclusive in the years ahead.

About a season later, I got a dog that was mostly husky from a nabor because he killed his chickens. "Husky," I called him. The only problem with Husky dog, he liked to chase everything, as long as he could see it. That meant deer too. So I had to keep him tied unless I went hunt'n or out'n the woods. When I went to Uncle Vinny's farm once, I took Husky.

THE DOGS

Uncle had some of his prize calves in a one-acre fenced area. Of course Husky got out of my sight and attacked these fine young bovines. Uncle heard the commotion and put a stop to that and demanded I tie up the dog fer the rest of the day.

Awhile after that I was head'n up to the woods and had to pass a farmhouse that had a big, ugly police dog. This here dog used to come out and chase me. I'd run over in the woods and hide or climb a tree. He scared me half to death. I didn't know how Husky dog would take this intrusion by this beast. But I knew Husky was such a scrapper and that he might just give that cur a little grief. Next trip, I just marched right up the road like I owned it, Husky dog trot'n alongside of me. Sure enough, out charged the brute, and Husky lit into 'em. Boy, did the fur ever fly. Husky was so fast that big dog never had a chance. And there I was just a-howl'n and yell'n, giving my dog all the support I could.

Husky turned that there menace inside out. Well sir, big dog soon beat a hasty retreat fer the barn, and me and my hero went on up the road, my head held high, like a British soldier walk'n up the King's highway. That dog-gone dog never did bother me again, even after Husky was gone. He'd see me come'n and tuck his tail between his legs and hide. He never forgot who was top dog. That Husky dog was my great companion up at Gramps's camp the year I quit school and spent the summer there. But hey, that's a later chapter.

JOURNEY TO THE BACKWOODS

"Old Bloop," Uncle Vinny called him. Mike named him Sailor. He was sorta another Heinz 57 variety. But you could at least see some sled dog ancestry come'n through.

He was a great all-around dog. Quite large, with ears that went halfway up then flopped over. He was fearless too. He'd tackle a bear or bull, didn't make no difference. He could hunt about anything, and was smart enough to figure it out.

Snuffy discovered Old Bloop liked to pull a sled, and could he ever pull. Equipped with only a collar and a long rope, Sailor dog would just about yank the sled out from under you. Down the old road we sped, laugh'n and arguing about who should set up front. What a grand time. Course the Western Flyer sled didn't have no brakes, so if'n we were headed down hill we had to drag our feet. And if a car was come'n you had to ditch 'er. We just steered fer the snow bank and crashed. Poor Old Bloop would come to a sudden halt. The car driver would stop and look at our wreck, shake his head, and smile. Probably took him back down memory trail. A bunch of boys never had more fun than us. We was poor in gold but rich in ingenuity and country life.

Old Bloop disappeared in his prime. Just like so many other dogs. Some trigger-happy lowlife run'n around with a gun play'n judge, jury, and executioner.

I have heard it said many times that a good index to character is a man's ability to make friends with children and with dogs. I believe it to be true. The man who can interest a boy and make friends with a boy and who can win the confidence of a dog must be all right. Children and dogs, usually, are good judges of character and of human nature.

—From the sermon,
"The Saint of the Rank & File"
by Peter Marshall
Mr. Jones: Meet The Master,
by Catherine Marshall

CHAPTER SEVENTEEN

OLD TIMERS
Circa 1955

Up the main road beyond Uncle Vinny's place lived an old bachelor named Emmett. He was a wise man, having lived many years as a millwright for sawmills and other jobs.

Like Uncle Vinny and other bachelors around that neck of the woods, he was lonely fer companionship. He and Vinny were the best of friends, so

Left to right, Uncle George, Aunt Mary,
Mom, Grandma Roch, and Uncle Vinny.

OLD TIMERS

every couple of weeks, usually on Sunday night, he'd drop in to visit. Of course, us young lads were always around to sit and listen to old log'n tales, hunt'n stories, and things that happened in unusual fashion. They all just fit right into my dreams.

Emmett usually brought a bottle of white wine, which him and Uncle Vinny would sip on as they talked. They were sociable and never drank much. Just like Mother always said, "Moderation in all things."

I was always awed by Emmett's knowledge of so many things. In Harrisville there was a sawmill that sawed veneer fer spy gliders during World War II. Like a lot of businesses at that time, certain things were hard to come by, especially engines. They couldn't get a big enough diesel to run the saw, so what was they go'n to do? They got Emmett there to figure this out and Emmett knew that farm engines were the most plentiful, so he ordered two of the biggest two-cylinder that John Deere made at that time. He hooked them both to the same shaft, and tuned them up real good, and really sawed veneer. They used a thin-bladed saw with a big arbor to keep it saw'n straight. I only wished I'd have been older, so I could have absorbed more of this great knowledge. Hardly any young people today will ever get this opportunity because they're brought up to sit around and play with computers or watch TV or become obsessed with sports. Young people today haven't been taught to respect their elders and learn from them. Parents look to the public school system to teach them everything, but as everyone knows, it ain't work'n so great.

As any good educator knows, schooling is more than textbooks. Anyone who has tried to keep kids' minds riveted to books has learned that the subject must be kept interesting. Books are certainly a part of the learning process. In fact, reading is probably the greatest source of education there is. A good reader has access to thousands of people who were the best at what they did. But kids need hands-on experience, watching good professional people with trade skills work at what they're good at. Children need to be taught to work hard, to create, and to take pride and fulfillment in their job. We don't need no gifted and talented classes either. Every human has gifts and talents. Someone just has to help develop them. Society and education have put so much importance on get'n an office-type desk job that has lots of advancement, they completely overlooked the trades. This is where the majority of people are employed.

America has lost so many of these jobs because we've failed to transfer the skills of a craftsman on to the next generation. I don't know where this happened. It probably started in the sixties. Like Benjamin Franklin, I'm a great believer in apprenticeship. For a man who wants to work with his hands, there is no better school. Christian schools are the answer, they could have retired folks come in and pass on their skills. Man—how did I get off on this? Anyway, let me get back to some old timers.

OLD TIMERS

A few times a year, some old Mennonite men who knew Uncle Vinny real good stopped by to chew the fat. As I remember, it was Menno Zehr, Mike Zehr, and another fellow who I've forgot. They were a joyful bunch and I suppose wanted to talk to someone out of their church group. Not to mention they sneaked out with a small bottle of blackberry brandy. They didn't figure it would go over too well if'n the minister or their wives knew they took a little nip on special occasions. They knew Uncle Vinny wouldn't tell. Besides, didn't the Savior turn water into the finest of wine at a special occasion?

However, fer many men and women, it's best not to touch ol' John Barley Corn at all. The stuff has ruined more lives than all the wars combined. Well sir, these old boys would have a right good visit, and hearty laughter was common. Vinny would sit in his favorite spot on the wood box next to the cook stove and enjoy his guests. Uncle Vinny was like that. Never too busy to be a good nabor, he wasn't concerned about next month's payments because he didn't have any. She was always cash on the old barrelhead.

There was another feller who stopped by a lot. He was Mr. Snyder, the calf and cow buyer. Once a week he would stop to buy calves for the sale, and Uncle Vinny would sell him the calves that he didn't want to raise. Uncle had a special cow called Susie Bell. He raised every heifer calf she had. Boy, this cow would give the milk. She'd fill that milking machine and push milk clear up into the air lines. She was a great look'n cow too. Mr. Snyder would tell Vinny he had the best look'n cows in the country, and he should have known. He'd try and buy that cow every time he came, often offering Uncle unheard of prices at that time fer a cow. We liked to see him come by 'cause he'd always kid around with us young whippersnappers. He'd come after us with both hands out like a bogeyman and tell us if'n we didn't behave he'd take us to the auction sale. We'd all run fer it and hide. There's just no way around it, Uncle Vinny's farm was the best place to grow up.

A couple of summers I stayed at Uncle Leslie's farm to help put up hay. It was near the south end of the Texas road.

Like all those old farmers of the country, Leslie was a creature of habit. You could set yer watch by whatever he was do'n every morning. He went to the barn at 5:30, let the cows in at 5:37, washed off their bags at 5:43, got the milk strainer set in a cream can at 5:58, and put the first milking machine on at 6:00 sharp!

About then I stumbled out to help.

He had mostly Guernsey crossed with Holstein. They gave lots of rich milk. He always took a pint of pure cream off the top of a cold can in the cooler. This cream was fer his oatmeal after milk'n at 8:45. The granola crowd of today would surely gasp to see him pour that on his cereal. And to add his insult to their injury, he used nuthin' but pure "dairyman's" butter on his bread. And if'n that don't give 'em hardening of the arteries, he smoked a pipe and chew'd

OLD TIMERS

besides. And I'm sure they want to know how long he lived eat'n all that there animal fat. Well sir, he lived to be a hundred!!

I suppose his stress-free life down on the farm helped a whole lot. And like I was say'n, his habits didn't hurt him either. Saturday night milk'n was always early. We had a quick supper and off to the settlement fer his Saturday night pool games. His wife usually went to a movie, as I did. Every Sunday summer afternoon (after church) he went trout fish'n usually up at Indian River.

He had a real down-to-earth character who hauled his milk to town. The ol' boy had a rickety two-ton truck with high racks that flapped like duck wings and half a load of quack'n boys. Uncle once asked the milk hauler what his boys' names were. Sez he, "I just named 'em Avery, Tom, Dick, and Harry. Then the wife didn't trust me to name any more, so she took over." And yes, funny it was, but he really was fer real.

The old boy couldn't always keep the milk truck run'n so Uncle sometimes had to make a run himself. His only rig was a faded old Caddy four door. He'd take out the backseat and load the cream cans right in there. I think he farmed fer fifty years there and never owned a truck.

He did have a tractor and a team of very old horses. I didn't get to drive 'em much. When he started on that there farm, he owned a nice pair of black mules. Put'n in the hay one afternoon a big storm came on sudden-like. He unhooked the hay

JOURNEY TO THE BACKWOODS

loader and took 'er fer the barn. Wouldn't ya know it, there came a cloudburst just as he started up the barn bridge to the hay loft. Part of his barn bridge was cemented rock and with the rain splattered on it, the mules figured this thing was not safe. They stopped and stood look'n this over as only mules can. Uncle said he whispered, he yelled, he threatened, and he even took a torch and held it under their bellies. Them mules just stood their ground and finally the water just ran right out through the load of hay. Uncle kept good his threat, he sold 'em the next week and bought a team of horses.

Uncle always raised his own bulls from calves. When they was a yearling and in the barn tied fer the winter, he put the fear of man into 'em...least most of 'um. I saw him take a short piece of shovel handle and every day when he fed he'd give 'em a light whack on the back. After a few months of that, they feared him like the butcher shop.

It was my job to herd the cows to the different pastures morning and night. The day pasture was up the road, and I always kept a few cows between the old bull and me. He feared Uncle, but he sure bellered at me. Sometimes he tried to linger back and get close to me. But I always had a fist full of rocks and would nail him a few times. He'd look at me with those bloodshot eyes and rumble low in the throat.

A few years later Uncle hired a footloose hobo type of fella to help with hay'n and such. One of those big bulls caught the old man out in the

OLD TIMERS

barnyard and killed him. Mother always said, "Don't never trust a bull." Most of 'em scared the liv'n daylights out of me.

Anyhow, the hay was unloaded with one of those big hayforks. You stuck it into the load and pulled it with a huge rope on pulleys, then tripped it to land in the loft. My job usually was torture. Up there a few feet from the metal roof, I had to replace the hay with a pitchfork or the hay stems would roll and compact, make'n it almost impossible to pull out come winter. I bet you could have fried an egg on my head. When I got behind—which was often—Uncle hired Tom Rivers to help. He was a big easy go'n lad near twenty. I saw him as a knight in pitchfork armor. I've forgotten a lot of names over the past half century, but I'll always remember Tommy Rivers.

I got a dollar a day plus room and board, which always went to Mother to buy school clothes. Perhaps that's why I had such a dislike fer the classroom early on.

I guess I didn't tell ya about Surly Coyouier. He was a liv'n legend when I was a pup. He was mostly French and a handsome rascal, and double tough. He was a proven woodsman who became famous partly because of his feet. Ya see, he wore those sixteen-inch leather logger's shoes year around without socks. Forty above or forty below made no difference to ol' Surly. He was a great red-blooded sawdust savage.

Then came the big war.

He figured if anything was tougher than log'n, it would be war. And be'n a patriot and all and his

JOURNEY TO THE BACKWOODS

relatives from France be'n butchered, he had to take action. He and several other loggers enlisted as a tank crew. First thing the Army told him, "You will wear your socks." "Yes, Sir," Surly would reply out loud. And under his breath would say, "Till you leave—Sir."

Anyhow, outgunned by the bigger tanks, Surly and his crew developed the old hit, run, and hide style of fight'n. Surly be'n the driver, he showed the enemy what kind of stuff an American backwoodsman was made of. He made 'em pay dearly fer their butchery. Make no mistake about it, war is a terrible thing. I heard an old soldier once say on Memorial Day: "Anyone who finds glory in war belongs in an insane asylum." And I'm reminded again from the Good Book, "A time for peace and a time for war." Where was I? Yup, Surly's crew told that only his driving saved them many times over and, of course, the Judge of all look'n down to care for them.

Be'n just a young-un, I only saw Surly in town on the street as we passed in Vinny's pickup. He'd wave, and ol' Surly would wave. Then one hot summer day I was traveling by way of shank's mare again head'n fer Uncle Vinny's when a car pulled up. A new '56 Ford two-door hardtop with all the windows down. "Hey, young fella, how about a lift?"

Surly Coyouier!! Was he kidd'n or what? I mean I opened the door in a trance and just floated into the car. There he sat in person, the world's greatest logger. His rolled crusher hat sat on a full head of hair. A light beard didn't hide his weathered face or

OLD TIMERS

his genuine friendly smile. "Sheriff got aholt of me said a man's lost up north, and they can't find him. Wondered if I'd help." On the backseat was his pack basket with his camp'n gear and blanket stuffed inside. When I got out of the car and he drove off, I knew I'd been in the presence of greatness.

He got old like most of us do and retired to the Bateman Hotel in Lowville. He had no family, leastwise wife or children. The last time I saw him was on the street kind'a gimp'n along, and he still didn't have any socks on. I don't know if'n he ever made his peace with God or not. Sure hope so. It would be great to see him there when the roll is called up yonder. I have a belt buckle that belonged to his family from France, given to me by a distant relative. It's one of my treasures.

When the weather went foul and we couldn't make hay fer a few days, Uncle Vinny had a cure fer that too. Every summer he had a small log'n operation up near Frost Mills on his big wood lot. Those days were so precious to me, headed fer the backwoods. Vinny never had to wait on us once we caught on to the routine. In the back of the old Chevy pickup, we were loaded way ahead of time and horse'n around. If'n Uncle caught us raisin' Cain, he would threaten to leave us off at Ernie's place. You never saw three rascals turn into choirboys so fast in all your life.

Old Ernie was a little scary-look'n to us younguns with his sparse beard, and he looked as serious as an old owl. At least he looked like a owly old coot.

JOURNEY TO THE BACKWOODS

He lived in a ramshackle cabin surrounded with every conceivable piece of junk you could imagine. His yard consisted of a well-beaten path weave'n in and out through his savings account to the door. Brother Tom, Snuffy, and me would gaze in awe as we rode by on the way to the woods.

Ernie lived on an Army pension, or so the story was told anyway. Seems like he was a World War 1 vet or charged up San Juan Hill. Anyhow, it was one of them there dumb arguments that killed a lot of good men. They should put the ones that start 'um on the front lines.

Well, finally one day there sat Old Ernie on the Belfort Hotel porch sip'n on a beer. It was a hot sultry day threaten'n more rain. We'uns were surprised when Uncle swung in right up to where Ernie was sit'n. Said he was go'n to have a beer with Ernie. That sort of shocked us, 'cause Vinny never did it before. We were sorta shell-shocked in the back not want'n to get out. Ernie looked fearsome as ever. Uncle sensed the problem and offered to buy us a Mission orange soda. That did it. We bailed out—on the off side. Keep'n a wide berth around Ernie lean'n back in his chair, we entered the hotel to claim our prize.

Back out through the door, we slid around the corner and watched Vinny sit down next to Ernie. "And how's your day, Ernie?" sezs Uncle.

"Why, couldn't be better," sez Ernie. "Just this morning I went to Croghan to do some trade'n and met a stranger in a new sedan on the bridge go'n into town. We both got to the bridge at the same time and each waited to see who backed up to let the other come across. The feller in the new sedan finally shook his fist at me and yelled, "I never back up fer a fool!" Well, I shoved her into reverse and yelled back—I always do!" Old Ernie was a witty character.

Secretly I think Uncle stopped there that day 'cause he wanted us to not fear Ernie anymore. From then on we learned he was a kind and gentle man who had seen enough bloodshed and human ignorance and anger to last two lifetimes. Once the cat was out of the bag, Uncle stopped at Ernie's once and a while to visit. His house was like his yard, but clean. There was everything from soup to nuts piled here and there. His younger years were lived in great poverty, and he couldn't force himself to toss anything. He should have run fer public office 'cause neither money or power could have ever corrupted him.

His sweet wife's name was Mae. She was quiet as a mouse whenever we was there. She just let Ernie be Ernie and loved him. Her hair was white as could be. I thought her to be most ancient. They had no children, but I think they loved the children of all their friends. She always gave us cookies or something while we waited fer the adults to come out after buying some parts or just visiting with 'em.

Do not squander time, for that is the stuff life is made of.
—Benjamin Franklin

CHAPTER EIGHTEEN

MISFIRED GUNS AND UNUSUAL HUNTS

Circa 1956

A week's catch of 35 beaver, 5 otter, 40 muskrats by Uncle George, 1957. George's boys, Reggie, George Peter, and Roger.

JOURNEY TO THE BACKWOODS

Somewhere about the age of eleven or twelve, I had my first gun. It was an ancient single barrel Stevens that had certainly seen better days. I traded an otter skin fer it. I called it the ol' Smokepole. It was a hammer gun, of course, and what was really unique about the thing, you couldn't put a shell in it unless you drove the pin out that connected the barrel to the breech. The lever that was suppose to open it was broke down inside, and I didn't have no money to get it fixed.

Well, this old 12-gauge held a perty fair pattern, and I commenced to shoot some grouse whenever I could get a couple of shells from Uncle Tony, 'cause he didn't hunt no more. Of course Mom found out I never took the shell out of the old weapon unless I shot it. It was just too much work to drive that pin out, so I hid the gun in the woods and left it loaded. Mom would carry on about me shoot'n myself in spite of my best to persuade her that I was careful. I had to keep it hid don't you see 'cause I overheard her telling Brother James to get this gun and destroy it. Mercy, a hunter needs a gun!! I used that gun fer years and don't know whatever became of it. It's likely lay'n somewhere out'n the woods.

But the gun to take the cake belonged to my Cousin Snuffy. It was an old double 12-gauge that he bought from an antique dealer in Croghan. It too was a hammer gun, a nostalgic look'n sort of a weapon.

The purchase was made one morning when us Three Musketeers went to the milk station with Uncle Vinny. I think Snuffy paid $10 fer it. As soon

MISFIRED GUNS AND UNUSUAL HUNTS

as we arrived back up on the farm, we beat it down to the pasture to shoot this wonderful piece. Snuffy loaded both barrels, cocked the right hammer and ca-bang—boom; and Snuffy fell back on his behind. "Boy-oh-boy, does that thing kick," he quirped as he rubbed his shoulder. He opened it and there like we surmised both barrels had discharged. So we held a short conference and decided to try the left barrel with 'em both loaded. The only problem was no one would volunteer to test it again. Not to fear though, our Yankee ingenuity soon kicked in. One of us ran and got some trap'n wire, and we wired the old blunder bust to a tree. Then we hooked a string to the trigger and got behind a bigger tree and gave it a tug—bang was all we heard. We knew we had it figured out.

So Snuffy used that gun fer years. We even took it to the big woods on our trap'n ventures. On one of those trips the deer were hav'n another tough winter, so we cut an occasional balsam fir or birch to feed 'em. One area where a few deer hung out had only tall balsam and no birch. All we had was a hatchet and didn't want to spend an hour peck'n away on those big trees. Uncle Vinny told Snuffy to shoot the top out of a couple trees with the old double barrel. Snuffy took aim where the tree was about four inches through and ca-blam—boom. Snuffy went fly'n back in the snow but he cut that tree off slicker than snot. We all had a good laugh.

Then my favorite was a 86-model Winchester in the .40-.65 caliber. It belonged to Grandpa, though I

JOURNEY TO THE BACKWOODS

never knew him, only in stories Mom and my Uncles told me. But I got to know him through this fine old piece. As Gramps got old, that old long octagon barrel was heavy. Gramps got a little careless and struck the barrel in the snow, plugged it up, and when he shot it the end of the barrel bulged out. So he cut it off with a hacksaw or some crude tool.

Naturally, this old rifle was a black powder. Gramps loaded the brass himself with his own hand loader. I still got it.

So anyhow, when I was twelve a bunch of us went up and hunted near the power line this side of camp. Uncle George left me off to have the first watch. I could hear Tom and Richie and Snuffy barking as they drove the brush corner. All of a sudden out bounded a big fat dry doe. My heart was hav'n a runaway!! She ran by me, and I blasted away. Every time I'd shoot, why that black powder would leave such a smoke screen I'd have to move to see my target. 'Course, I was so excited I fergot to look at the sights, and I never cut a hair. Perty quick here comes Uncle George, rustling through the woods like a breeze on autumn leaves. I took a good ribbin' over that and don't you think I didn't.

Since then I've had the barrel replaced like the original. Only I had a .45-.70 barrel put on it. It shoots like a dream and is so accurate.

The old folks said when times were tough Grampa killed fourteen deer one fall and winter. One for each member of the family. Sometimes, as

MISFIRED GUNS AND UNUSUAL HUNTS

I look at that old gun against the wall, I wished it could tell me stories.

Like I said once before, from time to time Uncle George's fame as a hunter reached the ears of city folks. Some were men of importance and had more money than they knew what to do with. They'd get to know Uncle and want him to take them hunt'n. Most were pleasant and loved the taste of venison but didn't savvy the ways of the whitetail.

I remember one such feller. His name was Harry. An old man perhaps seventy-five, he'd owned part of a brewing company once in Buffalo or Rochester. One pleasant late October day while the ground was still bare, old Harry showed up fer a hunt. Well sir, Uncle gathered up a bunch of us young-uns to put on a drive and took old Harry to a stand. It was down in the swamp below the old homestead. While us youngsters headed around to make a drive, we took in the splendor of the autumn. My, what color, the oak and sugar maple, beech, birch, white ash, and red maple. What a life fer a boy born to follow the ways of the wild creatures. Pine squirrels scurried here and there and scolded each other, giving fair warning that they didn't want their cone caches tampered with. A bluejay squawked out to the forest creatures that man was here. What a racket!! They were indeed the forest crier. Golly, one of these days I would get me a gun, and I'd hunt bluejays.

Us boys finally got around the end of the swamp and commenced to yell and bark. The grand idea was to scare the deer of course and chase them out to old Harry and Uncle. Boy, that swamp was thick. Some places we had to get down on our hands and knees to get through. About halfway we heard some shots where old Harry was at. Did we ever get excited then. Our voices picked up tempo, ah yes, the exuberance of youth. When we got to Harry we discovered two other men there, and they were dragging a buck out. Uncle George was calling 'em every kind of lowlife you could think of. Seems like old Harry wounded this buck and those other guys were behind him, and they ran down and finished it off and claimed it. According to law in New York, whoever fired the last shot and killed it owned it. Good grief, no wonder Uncle was so upset. These people call themselves sportsmen. You bet. More like a bunch of horse thieves.

When I was about eleven years old, I fell into a real meat hunt one night. Uncle George found an apple tree up near the old Martin place on the Belfort Road. And see'n me tortured in my spirit, not be'n out'n the woods enough, he took pity on me and asked me to tag along. I don't remember who dropped us off out on the road so's no one would see any car, for folks would know what we were up to then. Uncle George had left his car down near Indian River village and we'd have to hoof it there when we were done.

We got to the tree about half an hour 'fore dark. About thirty feet from the apple tree was a huge monarch of a beech tree. It was about four foot on the stump, and the trunk only went up six or seven

MISFIRED GUNS AND UNUSUAL HUNTS

feet then turned into a hundred limbs. It was a perfect place to sit and wait fer Wily Whitetail.

Uncle swung up and then pulled me up. He whispered instructions to me in a very serious tone. Uncle was always very serious when he was hunt'n. He motioned fer me to get comfortable, and we settled in to wait.

Now it's been said that patience is a virtue that man never possesses and women seldom do. But they never hunted with Uncle George. We sat there in that tree fer hours, my rear end was sore on that hard limb. It was darker than a grave-digger's night. You couldn't see yer hand in front of your face. Uncle was chew'n tobacco, and I never heard him spit. He always had a way of lean'n forward and let'n the juice dribble on a limb. You didn't expect Uncle George to make a sound—and he never did. It was no doubt this endless patience, old Indian tricks, but mostly God, that helped him survive as a Marine in Guadalcanal.

Once in a while I thought I heard a leaf rattle on the ground, but it must have been a mouse. About the time I feared I'd have to shift around, Uncle touched my arm, and I knew something was up.

I don't know of anything that moves slower than a whitetail move'n to feed. It is the slowest of slow motion. My heart started to hammer up into my throat!! I hadn't heard anything, but Uncle sure had. There!! I finally heard a deer munching on an apple. *What's Uncle waiting fer,* I thought? I was get'n so excited I feared I might start to shake, surely the deer would soon hear my heart pound. Suddenly Uncle's flashlight cut through the eternal darkness. I saw two large eyes glowed and then the .22 rifle Uncle had borrowed from Brother James shattered the quiet peacefulness. The eyes vanished. We sat still as Uncle turned off the light.

Now what? I thought. Someone might have heard the shot. No. Uncle knew what he was do'n, that's why he'd borrowed James's .22 rifle. The only thing I heard—other than my heart was some rustling where the eyes had been. It was the deer's dying movements I reckoned. After what seemed like an eternity when it was only minutes, Uncle turned the light back on, and we climbed down. We went to where the deer had been and sure enough there was a young buck with medium antlers shot right between the eyes. I held the legs and Uncle gutted it out, and propped the cavity open so's it would cool out.

We then hiked out and down to the settlement. We saw a couple of cars come'n once we hit the road, but we jumped off into the ditch and hid. Uncle took me home and then got the deer. I was so excited I couldn't sleep even as tired as I was. I laid in bed with my hands behind my head think'n how great life was in the backwoods, especially around Uncle George the great hunter. Remember me tell'n you all about the wolves up at Gramps's camp that tried to make dinner out of old Uncle Tony? Well sir, they was everywhere around Indian River at that time,

MISFIRED GUNS AND UNUSUAL HUNTS

harassing wildlife of all sorts and even dining on beef when nothing else was available.

South of Indian River a couple of miles was the Moser farm. Like everyone else that had a stump farm around that neck of the woods, they kept their replacement heifers in a certain pasture. One morning as they looked upon the hill, they saw a very dead heifer laying there. And eating on it was a very live large wolf!! They did what any sensible homesteader would have done: they shot it.

Now in those days you had your skeptics just like now. "Those are western coyotes moved east," sez the government officials. However, this one that killed the heifer weighed eighty pounds. Eighty pounds!!! Ain't no coyote ever weighed eighty pounds, not to my recollection anyway. And I've been everywhere coyotes lived.

The area was get'n overrun with them critters and the county finally put on a $25 bounty. Us backwoods folks just thought that was the greatest thing since the internal combustion engine. And Uncle George picked right up on it too.

Course Uncle still had the bad shoulder and had to shoot with one arm. But no matter, he'd just rest the old 32 special across whatever was handy and when the carbine barked you never had to wonder. Whatever he shot at was dead.

Uncle trapped some of the varmints but would rather waylay 'em in ambush. Down behind his place was a large marshy area known as Putman's Swamp. Uncle had scouted the wolves enough to know that

JOURNEY TO THE BACKWOODS

they holed up there every day. And they had to cross a big hay meadow to get there. Which they did every morning about daylight. They was a cattle gate just in the brush on an old hay road that Uncle chose fer his place of ambush. He'd watch the weather and when it looked just right, he'd sneak down there in the predawn and wait. The wolves would burst from the timber and head fer the swamp. Uncle George would lay the faithful carbine over the gate, lead 'em the proper distance and collect himself $25. He'd smile a little and say, "Amazing what a feller with one arm can do."

He'd shoot a few and hang them in the tree near his house. Lots of people would stop and check out these "coyotes." Some said they might have a little feral dog in 'em. Perhaps. But I've been to Alaska and trapped wolves, and these critters had some of that also.

I shall be telling this with a sigh somewhere ages and ages hence: Two roads diverged in a wood, and I–I took the one less traveled by, and that has made all the difference.
—From "The Road Not Taken"
by Robert Frost

CHAPTER NINETEEN

HIDEOUTS AND SECRET PLACES
Circa 1957

Us boys were get'n about the age fer hideouts and secret meetin's and such. Besides me, Tom, and Snuffy, we'd met Davey Proulx who lived near Jerden Falls. The Proulx's lived in the last house in that whole area. Jerden Falls was once a thriving town there on the Oswegotchie River. There was a big tannery there. Remember, I said my Grandpa Roch hauled hemlock bark there, which was the main ingredient back then fer tanning hides.

Anyway, every once in a while Davey would invite me and Tom up to spend the weekend. We'd explore the forests and if'n it was summer, we'd fish the river. Boy-oh-boy, we spent some great afternoons fishing over at the falls. That river was a gracious, beautiful flowing body of water back then. We sure caught lots of brook trout, even an

HIDEOUTS AND SECRET PLACES

Trout Pond and the very rock where we spent many happy nights around the bonfire catching bullheads.

occasional brown. And we sure took advantage of the swimming hole down near the bridge. It was just a wonderful place to grow up around that neck of the woods.

I remember that old house was just as cold as the old homestead we'd lived in. Once in a while we'd go up in late fall. Davey's folks had some apple trees out back by the garden about a hundred feet from the house. One morning us boys had just woke up and looked out the window. There was deer under the apple trees!! Dave's parents had spent the night in town, so it was just us boys there. We bounded down the stairs. Davey grabbed a gun and we eased up to the back door. We opened it a crack without a sound and peeked out—no deer!! We ran outside in our underwear and looked everywhere, but they'd vanished. We talked about that fer months after that.

Dave's dad worked in one of the mills in Beaver Falls. And get'n out of Jerden in the winter proved a bit much, so they bought a house in Indian River. And us boys spent a lot of time hunt'n and fish'n together.

Then we figured we should have a hideout, a camp where we could spend a night once in a while. You know, a secret place fer boys of adventure. Back behind our new log house at Indian River was lots of woods and pasture belonging to a nabor. Us boys discovered a perfect spot in a grove of cedars. We knew Mr. Nabor wouldn't mind our harmless camp. After much planning and laying out our measurements, we designed an elaborate camp complete with bunk beds, stove, and table. We decided to build it from thick latex paper Davey's dad brought home from the mill. It was quite waterproof and went on easy. The more we worked on it, the more we changed our elaborate design 'cause we suddenly realized this hideout was suppose to be fun.

By and by we planned great hunts and fish'n trips from our hideaways, and we even got so foolish to plan deviltry. Someone would come up with a case of beer that older friends would buy, and us boys learned how to get drunk. Then we'd spend the night there at camp so's the grown ups wouldn't find out. Once we got drunk and left the camp fer Indian River settlement. We got to the bridge over the river and stopped to discuss our next move.

HIDEOUTS AND SECRET PLACES

I was so intoxicated by then that I couldn't even stand and fell off the bridge down onto the rocks. It's a miracle I didn't get killed. I laid there and moaned and groaned awhile, and the other boys got me to soft ground. They all gathered around me like a bunch of chickens overlooking a June bug. Man-oh-man, was I sick. Fer years the very smell of beer started my innards to convulse. Yes-sir-ree, the devil was in us all right. This alcohol could well have been an invention of Lucifer to start us on the road to hell. It was about this time I lost the close feelings I had with God. I had become the prodigal son and ran off to root with the hogs. It would be many years before I'd realize that my wild oats had grown into dreaded weeds. Those times would bring nuthin' but shame.

Probably one of the dumbest things us Three Musketeers ever did happened near Uncle Vinny's barn. We were coming back through the pasture one day from a big hunt and started toss'n hard cow chips at each other. Well, it wasn't long before someone tossed some a little softer. One thing led to another and before you knew it we had a full blown manure fight go'n. We'd hide behind black cherry trees and fling it at each other—"a-ha-gotch-ya!" Before long we were a sight fer sore eyes, I'll tell you. And we decided enough was enough.

When we got to Vinny's he took one look at us and shook his head. "Hi-yi what lads!!" he sez. Then made us get near the hose and proceeded to wash us down. Afterwards I heard him tell Grandma that

JOURNEY TO THE BACKWOODS

'Boys will be boys." It was about then Uncle Vinny said a Western movie was come'n to Lowville. Said it was called *Shane*. "If you boys stay out of trouble fer the next couple of weeks, I'll take you." Yippie!! Yahoo!! Stay out of trouble? Why, we became downright upright and forthright. If'n they was such a thing as halos we'd have grown 'em. You bet!! I had never been to the big theater before. It was something I always remembered. And the first time I ever saw Wyoming. Yes-sir-ree. What a treat that was. 'Course Roy Rogers and Trigger still were my main heroes. And always have been–down the trail of memories. "Happy trails to you."

You will never amount to very much.
> —A Munich Schoolmaster
> to Albert Einstein, age ten

CHAPTER TWENTY

FURTHER'N MY EDUCATION
Circa 1959

School was get'n to be a real problem in my fifteenth year. I had picked up some useful information there, but more and more my wandering mind was entertain'n some nonsense. So I spent more and more time trap'n and hunt'n than ever. About the first of March, Brother James stopped by and said he was go'n to Massiweppi camp and trap beaver. That did it!!

My gifted and talented mind went into action.

I had to figure just how I might hornswoggle them nuns into throw'n me out of school fer a few weeks. So I just quit the homework. Every day I left school I sorta dropped my books into the wastebasket near the door. 'Course the janitor figured it out right off and left 'em sit'n there. And I just picked

FURTHER'N MY EDUCATION

I'm a happy trapper.

'em up every morning. Well sir, all that didn't sit well with the good Sisters. The one in charge sez one afternoon, "Mr. Terrillion, it's obvious you don't care anything about academics. You are just wasting our time at the present. Until you can apply yourself, you'd better take your books and stay home." Them was sweet words to hear!!

Sweet Mom had another fit, say'n she didn't know what she was go'n to do with me. Well, sez

JOURNEY TO THE BACKWOODS

me, sezs I, "Mother, while you're try'n to work out something with the school, I'll go up with Jimmy and he won't be alone. You never know what might happen." To Mother, it seemed like the logical solution to her backwoods boy.

We loaded up our traps and wire in Jimmy's old Ford, drove to Bergeners, and left the car there 'cause the road would turn into a muddy quagmire in a few weeks. Fer now, it was still froze and log'n trucks were come'n out. Uncle Vinny picked us up and drove us to the camp. That old camp looked like a long-lost friend. When I walked in, the old smells drifted off the logs, the bunks, and the stove. Fer a moment I stood in a haze, overcome by emotions remembering the times spent here with Uncle George and the others. Jimmy barked, "Well, get a fire go'n or you'll be cold tonight." I hopped right to it and in no time the old barrel stove was crackling out a warm tune. Uncle Vinny helped us get settled and bid us a fond farewell.

Jimmy made a big johnny cake that night in an old tin oven he sat on the stove. Johnny cake was our major food served with maple syrup. We had a little bacon too but not much. Brother said we'd have beaver meat in a few days.

Four o'clock seemed like the middle of the night. Course I didn't know what time it was but I heard Jimmy start'n the fire. Br-r-r-r it was cold. I yelled out through a breathing hole in my blankets, "How cold is it?" "Only twenty-six below," Brother said. "Only!" I coughed. "Old woodsmen don't pay any attention

FURTHER'N MY EDUCATION

to cold weather," sez Brother. He knew that would get me out fer sure. We ate our humble breakfast, strapped on the snowshoes, and hit the trail.

The traps were heavy, but I wasn't go'n to whine. No-sir-ree. This beat the boring hum-drum classroom any day. 'Fore long Brother had quite a lead on me. We was head'n fer Big Sand outlet and Emerald Lake outlet.

The leather on the ol' webs creaked against the harness, music to this child's ears.

We snowshoed past all the old familiar places—the road to Lee's Camp, and Kelly's Camp. We crossed the river, which now had a log'n bridge over it. That meant we could cross once the ice started to go out. There at Brindle Pond Camp we turned down to the river again. Go'n past that old camp sure brought back the memories from that night years before when the wolves followed us. Down at the end of the pond, near the river, was a huge beaver house. We put in a couple of sets. On up the river we came to some bank beaver. They'd been come'n out even in the cold to cut some maple, so we made a set there also. We turned up Big Sand outlet and found a large beaver colony there. Using maple fer bait, we made more sets. Chop'n holes through the ice was quite a challenge. About the time you was get'n through, the water came up in the hole and every time you swung the ax, you got a minor bath. We needed an ice spud but didn't have one.

It was a long hike back to camp that night. We walked in after dark and lit the lantern. I built a fire while Jimmy made another johnny cake. We gulped down our supper. Man, I was hungry as a wolf. The wilds made a boy feel like one. We picked up and hit the sack. And I was soon dream'n of big beaver in our traps.

The next morning it was just as cold. We pulled out on the snowshoe trail in the moonlight. It took a few miles to get the kinks out, but in no time we were at Brindle Pond. The set there had a beaver. We hung it in the tree and went on. Next one had a toenail. Brother figured out what happened and reset it. Up at Big Sand we had two more, and we skinned those. We figured to get to Emerald outlet and put in some sets, which we did. Then we started the long walk back again, and picked up the beaver at Brindle. We didn't have time to skin it so we packed it in our pack baskets. That night I fell asleep on the bench with the skin'n knife in my hand. Brother just rolled me into bed.

And so the spring went. We caught some beaver alive, so we bled 'em and had beaver meat. Mighty good too if'n they was eat'n maple or birch. But once and a while they'd get into some hemlock and taste just awful. Yuk!!

The weather got nice, and we could go without snowshoes, but pack'n them beaver was tough work. Near the end of season a couple of fellers came by with an old pickup. They belonged to the hunt'n club also there at Massiweppi. We had a nice bunch of beaver hang'n there on them rafter poles. You could see the jealousy in their faces. Times were

FURTHER'N MY EDUCATION

hard, and you'd have thought they'd be glad fer us. Mother always said jealousy is big in the world. She was right.

I sure didn't look forward to come'n out to the settlement. It seemed unnatural to leave all that quiet and peace and return to school.

There was scars left on my soul those years in school. It was like a constant open wound. The other kids picked on me fer my naive backwoods personality. I had to wear the same clothes every day 'cause we could only afford one good pair of pants a year. Once a bully threw me down at a ball game and tore my pants. One more year and I'd be sixteen. I had big dreams.

THE WOODCUTTERS
A Finnish Folk Song
(English Version)
by Lousie Kessler

'Neath the pine trees woodmen are singing
As they send their sharp axes swinging.
In the clear cold air sounds are ringing;
Bravely work the woodmen bold.

Now a mighty pine tree is falling,
Words of warning woodmen are calling.
O'er the snow the logs they are hauling;
Bravely work the woodmen bold.

CHAPTER TWENTY-ONE

WHEN MEN WERE MEN
Circa 1959

The more I hung around my Uncles and their log'n, the more the timber gripped me, even consumed me. I started down that long log'n road into life's occupation known around that neck of the woods as a lumberjack. Just the mention of that word put a spring in my step. The spirit of the old loggers, whose days harkened back to the Swedish misery whip, haunted my dreams. And see'n is how Uncles had let me run a power saw, why I was almost kin to ol' Paul Bunyan himself.

I'd saved about thirty dollars from sell'n my fur and bought a used McCulloch chainsaw, a 3-25 model gear drive. Strut'n around the woods with that thing really caused my head to swell and my muscles too. Yup, I really thought I was do'n a big stroke of business. I squealed with ecstasy every time

JOURNEY TO THE BACKWOODS

Dale and Snuffy with their first bucks. 1959.

a tree hit the ground. "Yee-ha!" I'd yell, or if'n I felt really great I'd yell "Timber!"

I took to cut'n firewood fer five dollars a cord. Ridiculous wages by today's standards, but I thought it was really great. Seemed like it didn't matter in them days what you did, if'n it involved hard labor it just didn't pay much. To me, the main thing was I got to be out'n the woods—the best place on planet earth. Yes-sir-ree, them was the days of hames and hand pumps and handlog'n. And this woods work was ticklish business.

Make'n it pay was always a question of high finance. Or come to think of it; low finance. The days of the woodsman work'n fer a few shekels were mostly gone. However, big paper mills and sawmills

WHEN MEN WERE MEN

still controlled the scale rule. Ya know, a few people will rob you with a six-gun, but there's a whole passel of desk-hounds who will rob you with pen and paper and rulers.

That summer at age fifteen, I more or less weaned myself of farm'n. Husky dog and me spent many happy hours fish'n when I wasn't cut'n timber, or exploring and scout'n fer places to trap come fall. And long hot days were passed at the old swimm'n holes. Every once in a while I still helped Uncle Vinny or Andrew put up hay. I owed it to 'em.

But mostly my love affair with that ol' McCulloch kept me cut'n pulp or logs or firewood. My clothes would get perty ragged, cut and torn on the brush. And long about dark many nights as I arrived home, you might say I looked to rip, ravel, and run down at the heel. Mom sometimes put patch upon patch. Log'n was sure hard on pants.

Shoes were always a need. So soon as I got some jingle in my jeans I went over to Widrick's Shoe Repair in Lowville. Old Mr. Widrick had once built log'n boots fer river drivers back when men were men and loggers were real men. No doubt about it, those were the days when boys became men in their teens. I asked if'n he could make me a pair of caulked shoes with sixteen-inch tops. His face just kinda lit up and said he'd be mighty pleased to build me a pair. Well sir, it was a couple of weeks fore I could pick 'em up. There in the big storefront window by the door was my shoes. He had 'em feet first so's all the town folks could tell what a pair of log'n boots looked like.

I sure was proud of them there new boots. They changed my whole personality, made me feel good that I could work with my physical strength, so I might have something to share with others. There's a lot of people in this old world who live off the backs of hard work'n folks. And I didn't want to

Uncle Tony with pet fox. About 1930.

be one of 'em. And I guess I sometimes stood them old loggers on too tall a pedestal. It ain't good to be proud as one would become arrogant. The Good Book talks against it. I used to sit and listen to ol' timers brag on long-gone loggers and hunters who had passed on. I guess I was guilty of immortalizing the old woodsmen more in death than anything they ever were in life.

By and by, the season of the hunter brought about the spirit of Indian autumn. The dreaded classroom tried to occupy my feelings. But I would not be robbed of my passion fer the woods and all the varmints and critters.

That school year (which I knew would be my last) I'd been put in Sister Mary Charles's class. She was very old, and looked to be stern as a dictator. Sit'n up there at the head of the classroom, she looked almost ancient. I feared her like a dread. I wondered if'n all the stories I'd heard were true.

One snowy fall day as I sat and listened to her explain the fine points of history, I fell into a deep and pleasant sleep. My gifted and talented mind just reasoned that if'n I couldn't be out'n the woods I might as well shut down, which it did. The quiet disturbed my great dream. There I was stalk'n this big buck only to wake up and be look'n in the face of Sister Chuck. (No disrespect meant.) I could see she wanted to smile but knew she'd lose control over the whole outfit.

"Mr. Terrillion," she quirped, "if you're going to sleep, must you snore?" I snapped up in my seat. "No

JOURNEY TO THE BACKWOODS

Sister, I mean I'm sorry, Sister." My throat was pretty dry as I stammered out the words. She continued, "I don't understand it. Your oldest brother Gilbert was bright, and Wilson was bright, Richard was smart, Thomas also is bright. Let's see, did I leave out any?" They claimed she was ninety-two and had taught all my brothers. "Yes, Sister, Brother James." She gave me an even sterner look and replied, "Oh yes, James. He was sort of a dreamer like you. And you'll be a ditch digger because you don't apply yourself to your studies." I thought I'd seen a lot of honest men dig ditches, does that mean I should be ashamed of 'em?

Anyway, she was a great school teacher, but she was just another one who didn't understand there was other important things in life besides classroom learn'n. Besides, I figured a scholar was a person who learns more and more about less and less until he knows almost everything about nuthin'.

Near the last of hunt'n season my fifteenth year, Snuff, Tom, Davey Proulx, and myself hiked up to Gramps's camp. Not having a deer rifle of my own yet, I was tote'n Uncle Tony's ol' Model 12 shotgun. I was sit'n up against a tree near the falls by the river. An ancient runway passed ten feet away. Off near the camp a saucy bluejay squawked at a pine squirrel. The forest crier, I thought, as I huddled against the shotgun. He hadn't better come over here and announce my position or I'll be tempted to blow 'em into tomorrow.

WHEN MEN WERE MEN

Tom and Snuffy were com'n on down the ridge look'n fer tracks. Davey was over on the next runway. I was just sorta dream'n about big bucks when a twig snapped!! Coming down the trail was a buck, not a big buck but a buck nonetheless. I could see the gray ring around his eyes and when his head passed behind a tree I quick pulled up the gun (old Uncle George trick) and at about fifteen feet I fired, hitting him in the neck. I had my first deer!! I leaped up and commenced to holler and yell. He was a beautiful animal. Was I excited and we would have meat fer the winter. Darkness had sifted over the woods by the time we got out. I was tired but thankful. It was the end of a perfect day fer the backwoods boy.

That fall and winter I did a bit of trap'n. I had traded fer an old Town canoe and floated the rivers. My catch that season included otter, mink, and fisher. Done a considerable amount of rabbit hunt'n too. I always had to borrow a dog 'cause my hounds kept get'n run over or shot. T'was still a terrible place to raise a dog.

School was yet hamper'n my life out'n the woods. Spring muskrat trap'n had to be done after school and weekends. I caught a few beaver too. I was get'n awful independent, don't ya know. Ride'n that school bus the five miles from Croghan took forever. It made all the stops to let other kids off. And they just s-o-r-t-a walked off like time was nuthin'. When the metal box jalopy got close to our cabin, I was at the door. The driver, old Ike, was an easygo'n fella and sensed how bad I needed to get at my muskrat traps.

JOURNEY TO THE BACKWOODS

He'd throw the door open quick when he stopped. My first leap out took me ten feet. I changed clothes in record time, grabbed my gun and hatchet, and raced off fer the river.

My sets were parsnips on old logs partly submerged. When a trap was gone my heart would commence to hammer!! Sometimes the high water made it very difficult to get to the drowned muskrat. I'd fish around fer the wire and pull up my prize. And it was worth between a dollar and a buck and six bits, real money when there wasn't any to be made nowhere else. Mother sometimes got upset 'cause I came home all wet. Trap'n season ended about April 15th and my sixteenth birthday was only a month away. Funny ain't it how a kid can't wait to be sixteen, then twenty-one, then thirty? And by the time yer forty you're wish'n you were sixteen again? Life is short, is it not? But when we're young, life seems like forever. However, it is written," For what is your life? It is even a vapour, that appeareth for a little time, and then vanisheth away."

It was about this time Uncle Tony just gave up on life and passed away at our place. Mom took care of him, and I remember him lay'n in bed and refuse'n to eat. A part of me died with him. The boy who seemed to learn something from every step in the forest, and Uncle Tony was a great part of it. He was no ivy-towered naturalist. He came from the old school. He learned it from those who had roamed the forest like him.

WHEN MEN WERE MEN

Take'n me along in that old Pontiac sedan, we hunted the wild ginseng. It was so hard to spot and hav'n the impatience of youth I would sometimes step on it without see'n it. "Back here," he'd whisper. And there it was with its tiny red berries, usually on the north side of an old rotten log. He was another great uncle God had given me along down that stretch of lonely years. I have always remembered his kind, quiet spirit. The fires of his life had smoldered and gone out. A lonely man he was, but great company, and now he was gone like thistle-down on a late summer west wind.

Found dead and alone!

Nobody heard his last faint groan,

Or knew when his sad heart ceased to beat; No mourner lingered with tears or sighs, But the stars looked down with pitying eyes,

And the chill winds passed with a wailing sound

O'er the lonely spot where his form was found.

>—This epithet was from the grave marker
> of the hermit Jimmy O'Kane
> at Stillwater in 1858.
> Courtesy of Adirondack Museum at
> Blue Mountain Lake, New York

CHAPTER TWENTY-TWO

MORE EDUCATION
Circa 1960

Education is a necessary part of youth. Fact is, a person should never stop learn'n, no matter how old ya get. That clever, wise, uneducated Ben Franklin once said, "The doors of wisdom are never shut." Like I said before though, education can mean different things to different folks. In this sophisticated world a man needs a considerable amount of classroom indoctrination if'n he's go'n on to be one of them there Rhode Scholars or look'n fer a high-pay'n government job. I wouldn't want to discourage any person from get'n a good education, in whatever field they desire.

Out West the story is told about a great cowboy who could rope and tie anything with hair. He was rope'n wild horses once, spent most of a day on two. After play'n them all out and hog tie'n 'em, he made

JOURNEY TO THE BACKWOODS

a comment. Sez Walt, "These here wild Cayuses are sorta like our kids. We send 'em to school and then to more schools and bigger schools. And you figure once they're out they've learned about all they need. But they never really learn what they should till you put 'em to work."

Some ol' timers on Cage Lake about 1930. Check out the raft. One of them might be Mike Zehr.

The trades today are looked down upon as some lower form of life. Yet the greatest person who ever walked this earth was a carpenter. What would this old earth be like if there weren't no one to pick up the garbage in the city, or no mason to lay the brick? No carpenter to build your home? No plumber or electrician? The list is almost endless. Let us not forget the farmer, miner, and logger. Without these three groups we would have no raw materials whatsoever. Have ya ever seen anyone who had no skill try and farm or mine or log? I have. It's hilarious and sometimes tragic. Society has this hang-up where the harder the physical labor, the less you should get paid.

MORE EDUCATION

America has indoctrinated its children into this philosophy, and we are now paying fer it. Try and hire some youth off the sidewalk of some settlement and get a day's work from him or her. Young people in high school and college are not taught you must pay your dues. They want to graduate and have everything in life right now—big wages, big car, every toy known to man. America has put herself in a dangerous situation. We've shipped our manufacturing jobs to other countries. There's millions of people who need these kinds of jobs as that may be their only opportunity in life. And the tax base lost? Small towns and cities with boarded-up windows. People living with little or no hope of employment. Well, anyway how did I get off on this again?

Like I was say'n, eight grades was enough fer me 'cause the rest of my education would come from older men who was good at what they did. So on the 15th day of May 1960 I walked out of the school and walked the five and a half miles home. I paused on the bridge over the Beaver River long enough to toss my work books in the current. Like a cedar log on spring runoff, they floated along nice as you please, head'n fer the Great Lakes and beyond. The feel'n was beyond liberation. Most teachers may have thought me a hopeless derelict. Little did they know I was a backwoods genius in the rough; I was well on my way to a Masters in woodsology.

It was a long walk home, but I was cheerful all the way. Each house I passed brought to mind who got on the bus there every day. The thoughts of some brought joy, some pain. Passing Don Moser's farm I remembered his father Jake. He had a generous heart. He brought his big team up to the old homestead that winter long ago to haul out the forty cord of pulpwood Mom cut. He didn't live to be very old, seems like he died of cancer. But while he did live, he lived by the Good Book knowing that everyone was his nabor.

Not far up the road was the old shack, which was part of his farm. The Mosers let some poor folks live there 'cause they had no other place to go. There was several children. I don't recollect how many. But I do remember the oldest was named Anna. Poor Anna, she had the self-esteem equal that of an earthworm. She didn't have the proper clothes fer a teenage girl. And the other girls picked on her. Even got in a fist-a-cuffs with her. I felt so sorry fer her—all of her family. Her dad was sickly and couldn't work much.

I remember Mom used to ask different ones fer clothes to take to them. I often wonder what great struggles in life they had to endure because of their poverty. Perhaps their Heavenly Father looked down on their misery and had mercy on them. And then approaching our house I could hear Mom mixing cement in the wheelbarrow. I prepared my mind fer the confrontation. Mother sighed, she reasoned that of the many perils of parenthood, her son Dale was a real gem.

But I had a plan. Old Davy Crockett once said, "Be always sure you're right, then go ahead." And I was sure enough go'n ahead up to Gramps's camp

MORE EDUCATION

and spend the summer. Me and Husky, my fish'n pole and ol' McCullough. Uncle Vinny said I could cut and peel some spruce pulp near the dead swamp. Yes-sir-ree, everything was just hunky-dory. By now Mom had told all the relatives of my great plan. Along comes my cousin from the big city. He was starting college 'cause he wanted to teach in the public schools and have a good retirement.

He shows up one night about bedtime, and I was try'n to get to sleep. And he commenced to yell'n, "Quit school and head for the backwoods!!? Are you crazy? Make a living working in the woods? You need to get an education and a degree so you don't have to work like a slave!!" Golly, he just kept it up and wouldn't let me sleep. So I told him hard work is what built this country, and I needed to get some sleep, so I could start early in the morning. That seemed to put a lid on everything. And I drifted off dream'n of a place so remote my guardian angel would have to look hard to find me.

Next morning I loaded up my grub in my pack basket, some clothes, and fish'n gear. The power saw was heavy but I figured I'd pack it till I got tired and set it down. Uncle Vinny dropped me off at the end of the Jerden Road by the old homestead. Mom had sold it awhile back, it sure didn't look the same. I stood there fer awhile look'n over at the big pine that once seemed like a challenge. I guess it was all right. So life has many challenges, and I was beginning another. And I would not be hobbled by society's restraints.

If a man does not keep pace with his companions perhaps it is because he hears a different drummer. Let him step to the music which he hears, however measured or far away.

—Henry David Thoreau

CHAPTER TWENTY-THREE

LOG'N, A LIFE'S DESTINY
Circa 1960

I went to the woods because I wished...to front only the essential facts of life and see if I could not learn what it had to teach, and not when I came to die, discover that I had not lived. So wrote Mr. Thoreau at Walden Pond. Me and Husky started out with our grub stake. Once I hit the big timber in the Oak Hills, I stopped often, more fer the soul than the body. Surely I was not the first to fall in love with the forest. But whose love was greater than mine? The old growth maple would spread their limbs and shelter me. Their trunks were strong and didn't pull away when I needed to lean on somethin'.

I was there in the safe embrace of the forest, the carefree day of a backwoods Adirondack country boy. Those woods were an unexplored textbook of nature's wonderment. I can still smell the rot'n leaves on rich earth, skunk cabbage and sarsaparilla, dogwood and sumac. Stalk'n dim Indian trails long since grown over with maple and beech, ash, and cherry. Here the mighty woodsman of yesteryear subdued the raw from the wild. It wasn't just a haven fer the critters. It was a place of endearment to me.

Finally at camp I threw open the door and drank in that fragrance—a cabin full of memories. Even Husky smiled and barked. "Trout fer supper, Husky," I assured him. Grab'n my line and hooks, I ran out and cut me a pole. Dug some worms out near the old barn and took off on a trot fer the river. Such freedom I felt as I bounded along down to the spring, where it emptied and splashed into the river. I shook with excitement try'n to rig up my backwoods pole. A trout jumped!! Finally, I baited my hook and tossed it in. Almost instantly the hungry brook trout grabbed it and made a run. I evicted it from its hiding place with a strong sweep of the pole. His beautiful bright spots glistened as he wiggled and flopped. Husky pounced on my catch as if to claim it. An hour later, I had me a fine mess of fish.

First thing I did once I got back to camp was build a fire. The cabin filled with smoke!! I jumped out and took a look, not a whiff was come'n out the pipe. Then I remembered Uncle Tony always checked the elbow fore he built a fire. I yanked it apart, sure enough, a huge mice nest had blocked it tighter than a drum. Cough'n and gag'n, I dumped it and stuck it back together. The old kitchen comfort took right off a-hum'n just like I remembered.

LOG'N, A LIFE'S DESTINY

There's something about the sound of trout fry'n and songbirds sing'n all ta-once. Me and my dog had a real feast. Along towards dark it clouded up and I had to shut the door; the bugs were anticipating rain. "Husky," sez me, sez I, "That's why them trouts was bite'n so good. There's a storm a-com'n."

Twilight comes early in the backwoods.

I had the old kerosene lamp lit in the middle of the table just in time. Boy, there came a downpour. I had me a pile of *American Hunter* magazines to read. Seemed like they was all about hunt'n in some far off place like Alaska, or Idaho, or the Yukon. I'd ponder over 'um till my eyes got heavy, and I turned down the lamp and jumped in bed.

From my bunk I heard Husky dog sigh with contentment, so did I. Often I thought how a dog is the only animal that will leave its own fer mankind. The cruel world seemed far away, and the ball game bullies even farther. I had resolved to rid my conscience of those schoolyard tantrum tyrants and academic wizards who had sat upon me and left permanent scars on my tender self-confidence. Fer now my spirit rejoiced 'cause through the pale darkness I could see the outline of the cabin built by the grandfather I had never known. I drifted off to sleep with the wind's soft-symphony in the trees. Here I was just a speck of humanity in the solitude of God's creation. The patter on the tarpaper roof was like a heavenly tom-tom, my song in the night.

My senses heard the soft drizzle before I was fully awake. I stuck my head out enough to see out the window and thought about sleep'n in. But Husky had other ideas. So I leaped out of the bunk and let him out. He made the rounds and marked his territory real good.

I put the makings of a fire together and the kindling caught and the little stove puffed and crackled.

Men that were made legends

I figured coffee would sure go good with my hot cakes this morning. I lifted the lid to fill the coffee pot and out jumped a mouse, the varmint made a clean getaway too. Well, I boiled out the old pot and made flapjacks. Boy-oh-boy, a breakfast fit fer a king, maple syrup and eight o'clock coffee. I can almost smell it now.

It about quit rain'n by the time I'd cleaned up the leftovers. I done decided I'd hike down and pick up my saw 'cause I'd left it near the Dead Swamp. Might as well get to log'n.

The sun began to peek out and the songbirds were hav'n a big time. Husky took off after a deer that bounded across in front of us. It took a lot of call'n to get him back. I cuffed him real good.

Wasn't long till I had ol' McCullough go'n and fell my first tree. I limbed it with my ax and then tackled it with a spud. Ya see, this spruce had to be peeled while the sap was up, the bark was slippery and wet. I was hav'n fun now.

The higher the sun got, the more humid it became and of course the bugs commenced to multiply and attack both me and Husky. I went and built a good punky smudge. They was smoke drift'n mostly over Husky. I had to tie him up 'cause he'd go hunt'n.

I was so excited to be cut'n trees and make'n stumps I hardly noticed the deer flies that drank my blood. This log'n was something a man could sink his teeth into. Our lunch consisted of rolled up pancakes with peanut butter and jam and water out of the creek. Sometimes I took a can of pork and beans fer lunch. I'd remember an old song I heard once..."I heard the whistle blow and I had to take a break—I'm eat'n beans from an old tin can 'cause that's the life of a lumberjack man." Every chance I got I'd read them old woodsman stories. The first loggers on this continent were called Shanty Boys in the state of Maine.

A tougher look'n bunch you never saw. I seen some old paintings, showed 'em sit'n about a crude cabin and even cruder stove, their longjohns hang'n from the rafter poles dry'n. These guys were an independent bunch. You could see it in their faces.

JOURNEY TO THE BACKWOODS

I always remember an old logger from Oregon who was too independent to work fer the company crew. Sez he, "Ya didn't have to know anything to work there. They blowed a whistle fer ya to get up. They blowed a whistle fer ya to go to work, and they blowed a whistle fer ya to quit."

Good loggers were independent.

Yup, log'n weren't fer the faint of heart. Be'n as how I was alone there fall'n trees, I made it a point to be extra careful. Limbing with an ax, especially.

The days just flew by, ya know. I was hav'n so much fun cut'n pulp and fish'n, why I didn't even miss human company fer a long spell. Then one Sunday morning I suddenly got lonely as an old loon. So I traveled out by way of shank's mare to the Boliver place fer a visit. After a few hours of another's voice, I headed back to camp. That night in camp the wind came up. Lay'n in my bunk, I figured it might storm. Yup, I had me a good visit with the Herbert Bolivers, even took supper with 'em. I wondered where Harold was work'n in the woods. He'd become a good logger. I smiled remembering how Harold was full of the dickens.

It seemed like a good night to reminisce, there in the eventide. Ya wouldn't think a sixteen-year-old boy could get melancholy about his past. I mean, how much liv'n can a sixteen-year-old already have? I was reminded of something an old timer said once. Sez he, "Some men live to be eighty and never live, while others live a whole life in a few decades."

LOG'N, A LIFE'S DESTINY

As my eyes grew heavy, I could hear old dead limbs rubbing against one another. They moaned in the wind like the ghost of Paul Bunyan. The wind brought the rain again. It swished against the pane. The spruce quit peel'n sometime in July. It was hot and humid. So I took to spend'n more time at the river splashing around to cool off. Husky would plop down and drink while lay'n in the water.

The only sounds were the chatter of a worrisome squirrel or perhaps a bluejay make'n enough racket fer a flock of most other birds. I took notice of the mink tracks under the over hang'n banks. I'd set a trap there come fall. Out on the island there was otter sign too. Lay'n there in the shade with my feet in the water, I took note of the wispy high clouds float'n by.

I was plan'n a trapline fer the fall and winter. Yes-sir-ree, this was the way a young man ought to spend his sixteenth summer, follow'n deer trails and explor'n otter slides. By and by I woke up from my nap. The song of the river had sung me to sleep. "What's fer supper?" sez me. Husky looked at me, head cocked sideways as if to say, "You talk'n to me?" "Yup, old friend, I'm talk'n to you. We still got time to catch a few trout." I ran up to the cabin, grabbed my pole and pulled my worm can out of the hole near the spring. Them worms don't live long in the heat, ya gotta keep 'em cool.

I decided to head up to Grandma's Falls as I hadn't fished there in a couple of weeks, such a beautiful spot. The river dumped itself about six feet

JOURNEY TO THE BACKWOODS

down into a big pool that always had foam over to the side; and always had a big trout hide'n there.

The sound of the falls came to my ears long before I could see it. Husky on up ahead suddenly stopped and the hair on his back all stood up. There were some big rocks that had caves in 'em just before the falls. Perhaps a bear had sought out the coolness of the caves. If it was a sow with cubs, she'd take me on, Husky, and anything else. I'd left my old shotgun in the cabin, now what to do? I held onto Husky and dropped my pole. Pick'n up a stick I tossed it up ahead. Lo and behold, out waddles a quill pig. My laughter had a tinge of relieved fear. We let old porky get up a hemlock tree before we made our way to the river.

After choosing a fat worm, I sneaked up to that pool covered with foam like ol' Hiawatha. Not a sound but the laugh'n of the river against the rocks. Husky sat nearby on a flat boulder. My worm hadn't even time to sink when wham!! The line headed upstream into the pounding waterfall. I hauled him out flop'n around, over a foot long, sunlight glistening off his sides of many colors. Be'n out away from the shore on a big rock, I feared I could lose him, so I beat it to shore to put him on a fork stick. Then I could put 'em back in the water to keep it fresh. Husky watching my every move to see if I would toss it down, so's he could take over. I pointed my finger at him. He laid his ears down and that showed he understood. After a while we had supper. We fought the deer flies back to camp.

It would be a week or so before the hot weather tapered off, and I could cut up the trees into lengths to skid them out to a landing. I figured I'd scout out some good fur grounds fer my trapline. We took some long hikes over near Frost Mills, Indian River, Oak Hills. We built cubbys (small lean-tos) fer fisher and bobcat. It sure was exciting to look fer critter tracks in the old tote roads. Every once in a while a deer would burst from cover, and Husky would give chase. Boy, he made me mad when he did that.

Dog days of August came, and the humidity was bad. But the nights started to cool off. It was time to be cut'n up the tree lengths. I loved to cut trees. I went after my work like I was kill'n snakes. The only thing that slowed me down was an occasional hornet that took offense at my project or the snarl of my ol' McCullough. A mud poultice usually took out most of the sting.

By the end of September we had the pulpwood cut up and hauled to the mill. Casey Kloster skidded it out fer me. I was look'n forward to my fall trapline, mink and muskrats.

TREES
by Joyce Kilmer

I think that I shall never see
A poem lovely as a tree

A tree whose hungry mouth is prest
Against the earth's sweet flowing breast;

A tree that looks at God all day
And lifts her leafy arms to pray;

A tree that may in summer wear

A nest of robins in her hair;

Upon whose bosom snow has lain'
Who intimately lives with rain

Poems are made by fools like me,
But only God can make a tree

CHAPTER TWENTY-FOUR

AN AMERICAN HERITAGE

Circa 1960

Trapping beaver

JOURNEY TO THE BACKWOODS

Early fall started out sad. Husky got loose and never came home. I feared someone shot him 'cause, like I said, just about everyone around that neck of the woods would shoot a dog if'n it was alone. I sure missed him, but life goes on. And I traded some wood cut'n fer a nice beagle pup. And before I could get him grown up, he got ran over that same fall. I didn't get any more dogs fer a long time.

Me and Snuffy had quit school the same year, so we planned to trap together that fall. We'd float Indian River one day and the Oswagatchie below Jerden Falls bridge the next. Different people would drop us off and then pick us up just before dark.

Manhood had found us when we weren't even look'n fer it. The uncontrollable number of mischievous things we did had long since been lost to society. In a few short years we'd went from "little rascals" to keepers of an American heritage, trapping. Sides, we were too young to hire out to a log'n crew and too sensible to ever work in one of them pulp mills. Mother, always worried about my future, would say, "Son, get a job at the pulp mill, and you will have a steady paycheck." It was a rut I'd never get into.

Push'n that canoe off every morning as the sun creeped over the rise gave a man a feel'n of real adventure. Like the voyageurs of old, trappers and trailblazers, men of renown. I always took the rear seat 'cause I guess I liked be'n in control. The long paddle seemed to fit my hand. Snuffy liked the front anyway. He could see what was around the next bend quicker. And be'n part Mohawk from his dad, he sure fit in there as point man.

Fall came in its magnificent way. Nature had painted the leaves with the best our Creator had to offer. The golden sugar maple leaves came twirling to earth to lie there like gold pieces. The smell of all the red maple already there was musty.

The Oswegatchie fled north, and had a good current to float down and was plenty wide and deep in most places. Fur sign was abundant and a trapper's dream. Otter had their toilets (usually a point of land where there'd been an old beaver house) and scat was everywhere at these places. Usually it showed they'd dined on crayfish and freshwater clams, which were plentiful, and stunk to match the menu. That reminds me of an outdoor gathering of a bunch of old timers where only one outhouse was usable. As one was come'n out the fella wait'n asked, "How is it in there?" Wave'n his hands the other replied, "Even the flies are dead in thar."

Our day trips were most always laced with encounters with wildlife. Ducks of every description took off quack'n their surprise 'cause we floated up on 'em so quiet. Muskrats we caught off guard busy with winter come'n on. Often we'd get within a few feet of 'em 'fore they'd dive, their long black tail wav'n a so-long salute. Many times we saw 'em swim'n under the canoe. Yes-sir-ree, this beat the classroom sez me, sez I. Right about then I thought about the poor souls sentenced there. But like I said

JOURNEY TO THE BACKWOODS

before, life has many choices. Perhaps mine would prove wrong; time would tell.

Mink are efficient little killers. We saw where they'd made meals of duck, muskrat, and even fish. Their IQ was ninety-nine times what a muskrat's was and if'n you were sloppy at your traps, you didn't get many. Every time I caught one, I'd snap it to clear the water off and fluff the fur. What beautiful little creatures. Made me think how out'n the woods something survived by kill'n something else, and I was part of the great plan of things.

Otter was always a joy to observe. They didn't usually give you much of a chance if they saw you. I recall one though that had some young hid in an old beaver house. She came towards the canoe, head and tail out of the water, and barked like a dog with bronchitis. She had a real fit till we was a long way below her territory. She'd dive under the canoe and come up behind and charge. Then dive and come up in front and bark. It was great entertainment fer a couple of backwoods young men.

Occasionally humorous things happened on the trapline. Brother Richard dropped us off once and wanted to float a short ways with us. He had along old Prince dog from Mom's and the cur loved to ride in anything. Well sir, all three of us piled into the Old Town Canoe, Richie in the middle, Old Prince just in front of him. Tippy canoe wouldn't take any stand'n on the sides, which Prince did as soon as we shoved off. You guessed it, over went the sleek craft and Richie leaned out and grabbed some willow.

AN AMERICAN HERITAGE

What followed should have been caught on movie film. Old Prince, use'n Richie fer a bridge, leaped up on his back and just walked to shore and didn't even get his feet wet. We sure did though. Our line down Indian River was much more of a challenge. The water was usually swifter and had a large amount of beaver dams across it. Be'n fall, ol' chisel tooth was fix'n up everything that looked like a dam. "Busy as a beaver" was an understatement.

We'd gotten really good at handle'n the Old Town. We sped down river like ol' Hiawatha himself. The beaver dams always had a spillway near the middle and we'd aim for it and shoot the rapids so to speak. It was a great challenge, and we figured we were somethin' all right. Our chests puffed up our Woolrich jackets. One late November day, with the wind gun'n icy pellets out of the north, we was glid'n downriver make'n record time. We was jump'n dams left and right. The blow'n snow caused us to keep our heads down, and we didn't notice how high Mr. Beaver had built up this here one dam. About halfway over it was plain to see we was in fer it!!

OVER WE WENT!!!!!

We come up gasp'n fer air. That water was colder than a banker's handshake. Make'n our way to shore, the only sound was our teeth click'n away. We needed a fire and fast. I always kept a few matches in a waterproof little case. They was worth their weight in gold. Stripping some birch curls off a tree, I quickly had a toasty fire go'n: a real white man's fire. If we weren't a sight fer sore eyes. Stand'n there naked as a jay bird and our clothes hang'n there from limb to limb. We'd salvaged all our stuff 'cause it was in the pack basket tied to the canoe. I burned up a pair of socks and I guess the worst thing hurt was our pride, which had gotten out of hand anyway. The Good Book sezs, "Pride comes before...a fall."

He who never made a mistake never made a discovery.

—Samuel Smiles

CHAPTER TWENTY-FIVE

BIG BUCK AND A SNOWSHOE WINTER
Circa 1960

Fall trapping season ended on a sour note. I'd left the Old Town hid in the willows till I could pick it up and someone stole it. To a woodsman, the worst thief that ever walked was a trap thief.

Uncle George growing old but could still get the big bucks. 1976

BIG BUCK AND A SNOWSHOE WINTER

Every cloud has a silver lining. That's what Mother always said, and I guess it's true. Hunt'n season sure ended like a dream.

Fer several years a huge buck had been hang'n around near Billy's clearing not far from Bailey's Swamp. Several hunters had shot at him, even wounded him. He was a smart ol' bugger. It was said he was at least a ten pointer. Uncle George decided to claim him.

On a cold December first day, Uncle lined up four or five of us to drive the south end of Bailey's Swamp. We got lost. George Peter, Uncle's son, had seen the monster while we was trashing around in that jungle. Uncle's rifle shots brought us out and he scolded us fer get'n all turned around. The brush was full of fresh snow, and you couldn't tell east from west.

Old Mossy Horns had come out and slipped through between the watchers. Uncle George calculated he was holed up in Uncle Vinny's sugar woods. He stood on the track think'n the ol' buck would double back and sent Richie and Tom on the trail. Uncle George told everyone where the best places to make a stand were. He sent me over on the Jerden Road just below Brouty's farm. There was a neck of woods there.

At that time I owned an old .30 Remington pump with a bore enlarged enough to shoot a .45 caliber. Its accuracy was questionable. I crawled up on a big rock about the size of a car, rested the rifle on the direction ol' Mossy Horns might come from.

JOURNEY TO THE BACKWOODS

It would be a long wait. By and by, I heard Richie come my way and then head back. His barking told me perhaps Uncle George out-guessed this old buck. No shot came.

About half an hour later, Richie and Tom was come'n my way again. Then I saw the most beautiful buck in all the world. He came out of the woods just up the road from me stand'n beside a big red maple and was as still as a Buddhist statue for what seemed like an eternity. As his head turned to look fer danger, all I could see was that magnificent rack. He jumped the fence, then the road, then the fence in front of me, he was so graceful and fluid he landed like a leaf. I had to keep my teeth clinched so's my heart wouldn't leap out. I hunkered down on that rock fer fear he'd see me. He passed twenty feet right in front of my gun barrel. I never had to move it. Just pulled the trigger!!

DOWN HE WENT!!!

And me, my goodness, I whooped and hollered like a Commanche and danced like a Sioux. Uncle George said he could hear me clean over on Vinny's sugar bush road. I was one happy sixteen-year-old, let me tell ya. I relived that moment fer months and told the hunt'n story till everyone around me knew it by heart. Old Mossy Horns was indeed a ten pointer. Years later someone who knew about such things measured it to score 160 more or less. It was a perfect rack and meat fer the winter.

December came in like December usually does, cold and plenty of snow. I dug out Uncle Tony's

BIG BUCK AND A SNOWSHOE WINTER

snowshoes. Fur was prime and the age-old craving to follow the ways of the wild creatures took control of me—again. It was another winter wonderland. Whiteness covered every rock and tree, front road and back road. It was a perfect snowshoe winter.

The stillness of the backwoods was the quiet of the soul. No distant rumble of a jet airplane or some pass'n car, only the rhythm of the heart. Your mind review'n good things and just where that fox would cross. Or a hollow log where you could catch a twenty-five dollar fisher. I'd caught a mink in the spring just below Gramps's camp. The next time around I figured it would be froze in, so I'd have to pull it up. To my surprise the trap was gone!! Some thief maybe had come down the river and found it. I stomped around look'n the whole area over. It was plain something was there and made a fuss. Perhaps a late coon had run off with my trap. I sure hated to lose an animal that might die a slow death in one of my traps. I concluded no human had been there.

The island out in front of the spring where I'd dreamed away many happy hours the summer before was worth a look. But to get wet feet in these temperatures might mean frozen feet. I hiked down the river, hope'n fer a place to cross over. A blowdown hemlock up ahead may let me onto the island. Taking off my snowshoes, I'd just started across when I spotted it. An otter under the limbs in my mink trap!! He had drowned there, a twenty-dollar otter. I could never express my exuberance; my excitement almost caused me to fall in. The way things

JOURNEY TO THE BACKWOODS

were turn'n out, I often had the feel'n I wasn't alone after all.

Part of my trap line was down behind our house near Putman's Swamp on Indian River. The long snowshoe trail I'd made to that area was packed down and a pleasure to walk. January's cold had made for lots of thick ice. A beaver colony had flooded the hay flats the fall before and was about as welcome as Robin Hood in Sherwood Forest. Haying was impossible with these eager beavers flood'n everything.

It was hard work cut'n holes through the ice to set traps but I loved every minute of it. The cold water came into the hole when you was almost cut through. And would splash up and freeze on your face. Old Jim Bridger would have been proud.

The weather had been very cold, and I'd caught nuthin' in several trips. Often it was after dark and I marveled at the flaming of the stars. Or when the new moon came and turned to full, I hiked my snowshoe trail, washed in the moonlight. Sometimes my imagination was my only friend. Look'n up, my breath seemed to freeze in mid-air. It was a joy to just be alive and be a part of the Creator's plan.

It's strange, ain't it? How critters know the weather will change days before it does? A January thaw was a-com'n and my next trip down to the flats saw a change too. Upon cut'n a peek hole to check my traps in the beaver channel, lo and behold there in one trap was a blanket beaver and in the other was a large otter!! I sure wasn't see'n things. There

BIG BUCK AND A SNOWSHOE WINTER

they was. I never chopped a hole out any quicker in my life. What a load to carry. My peck basket runneth over.

Home with my catch, Brother Richard was there home from college fer a few days. He took my picture there in front of the fireplace. Seems like in those days you got your picture taken near a team of horses, and automobile, in front of a house or near a fireplace, summer or winter. Anyway, I rounded out the late winter and spring trap'n beaver and muskrats.

Then came the fur buyers, usually in some old sedan, most always old men, shrewd as a serpent. I never knew if any were Jewish or not, but they sure knew how to haggle. They'd run their hands over the soft fur and shuffle beaver hides like a gambler deal'n a poker hand. They had a sort fer this and a sort fer that. You always had the feel'n they was try'n to hornswoggle you. And they had a roll of bills that would choke a bull. Fur buyers were very rich as I saw it.

The most honest buyer I ever knew was a very old retired farmer and trapper, Mr. Recha. He lived between Boonville and Utica. T'was a shame I didn't get to know him till the last few years I trapped. You sold him your fur knowing he gave you every penny he could.

A trip down there to his home was like be'n invited to a party. His faithful wife let you in after you left your furs on the porch. Then she reminded everyone to clean off your shoes. No doubt she remembered her husband was a farmer once. Mr. Racha would be sit'n at the table, hair gray as a wisp of smoke, his pad and pencil before him. "Come boys," he'd say, "sit and tell me what you've caught." His face beamed with sincerity and kindness. Not like a thin-veneer either. It was solid timber deep. Almost like on cue his wife brought mugs and filled them with coffee. Then he'd ask if we could stand a piece of pie. My, oh my, the first time I went there I thought, he's fat'n us up fer the kill. I went away that night ashamed of myself. His wife obviously did not share his pleasure in meeting trappers and buy'n fur. But she was a wife of noble character and did her best to make the best of it and make you welcome.

Yes, the old man did remember Old Spike the Indian and his wife who made those beautiful jackets. He'd reminisce as he asked about how so and so was get'n along as the lengthening shadow of life came upon him. He'd nod his head and say that feller used to be a great logger and a good man.

The pie, the coffee, the company was enough to make you forget why you came. What a gracious couple, and not a word of cussing or a bad report about anyone. This was a Godly home.

There in the corner of the kitchen was cardboard on the floor. Coffee and pie gone, he motioned to bring in our furs on the paper. The house was very, very clean. He usually had two sorts fer beaver and muskrats alike. He wanted us to know he made two dollars on beaver and ten cents on muskrats. His

BIG BUCK AND A SNOWSHOE WINTER

son-in-law hauled 'em to New York City and sold them at the big sales.

The last time I saw him he'd gone to Alaska to see a daughter who lived there. His eyes sparkled and his voice spoke with gratitude and excitement as he shared his trip. I have always remembered him warmly. You don't meet many like him these days.

To a friend's house the road is never long.
—Anonymous

CHAPTER TWENTY-SIX

THE YEAR OF SEVENTEEN
Circa 1961

Yours truly with a big bobcat and the infamous ten point buck.

JOURNEY TO THE BACKWOODS

There's a whole lot of younger Americans who never heard of the CCC Corps (Civilian Conservation Corps). It was the brainchild of the Franklin D. Roosevelt administration about 1933 or '34. It employed several hundred thousand men to plant trees, fight forest fires, and do conservation work in streams and national parks. Many of these men were from the cities and unemployed and didn't have a trade or even know how to work. Be'n the Great Depression, there was a lot of men who needed a job and the CCC came through in a big way. It was a wonderful outfit. Once I saw a documentary on the old boys. Several gave great testimonies on how the Corps made men out of them and gave them a hope fer the future. A lot of them ended up in World War II as soldiers. Those boys became great men.

There around our neck of the woods they planted tens of thousands of pine and spruce on that homestead ground the state bought back from the starved-out farmers. They did well in that rocky, sandy soil. Probably not as good as native hardwoods, but most were well on their way to be'n tall and straight.

A lot of small log'n outfits had begun to log these stands. You could bid on 'em at the state conservation office. Well, sir, I got me a sale up at Jerden Falls and bought me a new saw called a Lombard. Direct drive it was and weighed about half what my ol' McCullough did.

Mom never did learn how to drive a car, so about then she bought a Fordson tractor. She drove the thing all over to get gravel and up to Gramps's camp and to fish. I built a heavy duty trailer to hook behind and went to cut'n pulpwood 'cuz it was plentiful and dollars few.

That summer at seventeen was almost as happy as the year before!! Did I tell ya Uncle Vinny got married and was all lovey-dovey at fifty? Us boys didn't spend much time at the old farm anymore, and he was very lonely. He had completed his God-given mission—be'n there for three fatherless boys in our great hour of need. All of us should complete on this earth what our Heavenly Father has gifted us to do. And do it as pleasant as Uncle Vinny, and as well.

Didn't see much of Uncle George anymore either except in the fall to hunt a little. He couldn't see good and made a joke about need'n glasses. He killed a buck in Billy's clearing that fall, and it took him five shots. He ordered some specs.

His boys were grow'n into big boys. I mean b-i-g boys. He was teaching 'em the stonemason trade. Under Uncle George's guidance they built the most beautiful fireplaces in the Northeast. Reggie, the biggest, broke the rock with a twelve-pound hammer. I once saw him carrying a portable cement mixer to their barn. (We're talk'n a heavy object here.) As I drove by I honked my horn. He sat it down, waved, and pick'n it up again and carried it away. Those boys had the sweetest personalities and the greatest manners. George and Helen raised 'em right, all four of their children.

JOURNEY TO THE BACKWOODS

But like every family, times come that bring much sadness. The day before his oldest boy, George Peter, was to go into the Army, he was killed in a car accident. Uncle seemed to have lost a lot of life's meaning after that. He was never the same. You could see it in his face. And who could blame him? What one of us could face such a dark hour and totally recover from it? Not to mention the horrors of war he'd been through that still haunted him. I wished I'd have been able to share his burden. But I must confess I'm greatly lacking at those times of personal tragedy. And I owed him so much, much more than I could ever repay.

As I toiled away that summer out'n the woods, I noticed the bugs weren't any better than the year before. Mother said all these bugs seemed to do was torment a body, and take the enjoyment out of our summers in the woods. About the time I conceived they might drive me mad, I'd remember the old fish'n holes. So I went to see if I could encourage the fish to bite as good as the mosquitoes did.

The river there at Jerden Falls wasn't far from my job. I could swim or fish, whatever way my fancy leaned on any particular day. Sometimes I forgot my pole and just headed up to the falls to check it out, tossing a rock into the pool of sleepy trout. They'd scatter in all directions. "Yup, you could take the boy from the country, but you can't take the country from the boy."

I remembered that as early fall came, fur prices weren't very good and a man from near Boonville offered me a job on his farm, a big farm. He did a little log'n too on the side. It was look'n like a busy winter down on the farm.

Now I didn't really care fer dairy farm work 'cause it got a little monotonous at times. I mean, you milked 'em in the morning, and you milked 'em in the evening. Seven days and then you started on another seven. And clean the barn. I couldn't figure where all that manure came from. I just figured we was feed'n too much. But it was a job and fer the time be'n I needed a job.

By the time spring rolled around I was ready fer a change. It wasn't spring fever either. It was the mountain fever.

Clarence Kelly was do'n a lot of tree planting that spring. He'd bought some planters that was hooked behind his Fordson tractors. One man drove and the other sat on the planter. The trees came fifty to a bunch from the state nursery. A small metal wheel was attached to the side of the planter that made a click every six feet, and you stuck a tree in the ground. The planter opened up a furrow in the soil just under the seat. So there you sat listening to the purr of the tractor and the "click" of the wheel. But it beat milk'n cows and ol' Clarence was a great man to work for. And he demanded of us that our work be first rate.

'Course, you plant trees as soon as the snow starts to expose the good earth. Although it was spring, it wasn't warm by any stretch of the imagination. The pussy willows gleamed softly, nature's

JOURNEY TO THE BACKWOODS

pearls come to life down by the marshes. Still the wind was raw, and it rained most every day April into May. We worked like a bunch of galley slaves, twelve hours a day—daylight till dark. I remember my hands were so cold. We took turns. The guy on the tractor drove while the other planted a thousand trees then they swapped. If memory serves me right, we tried to get ten thousand trees a day!!

We were plant'n most of these here seedlings in beautiful big meadows, farmland that had once been cleared by toil and sweat and horses. We worked mostly in St. Lawrence County. I'll bet some of them old farmers rolled over in their graves as we put trees back on that rich sod.

The state forester had to guess the number of acres and then how many thousand of trees were needed. They delivered 'em five hundred to a bundle and kept 'em under cover till we planted. A lot of the soil was waterlogged of course and we fought daily to keep from get'n stuck in the quagmire. Clarence made big steel cleats instead of chains that sucked the soil instead of cut'n through it. But every now and then down you'd go. Mud up to your knees. We earned our $1.50 per hour.

Like I mentioned a little bit ago, the forester sent the trees out. Sometimes we came out just right, sometimes we ran out and sometimes we had several thousand that we didn't know what to do with. We gave them away to anybody that would plant 'em knowing that virtue is, most of the time, its own reward.

THE YEAR OF SEVENTEEN

Then before the trees leafed out, Clarence had us dig'n white birch clumps to sell to the nurseries. We took a spade shovel and cut the sod around the tree. Trying to leave a big ball of dirt attached, we wrapped it in burlap to hold the dirt and moisture. We had to jump on the spade to cut through the roots and sod. I think it's where they got the term "fallen arches."

One fellow I heard about sold birch clumps that wasn't. Well, let's just say wasn't totally grounded. He cut 'em off ground level, stuck 'em in a small bucket of cement, then took 'em and sat it in a bigger bucket and covered it with clay dirt. He sold 'em cheap and sold lots of 'em. And then skipped town. Funny how you remember people who hornswoggle someone. And like Mother always said, "Dishonesty never pays in the long run." And Mother was seldom wrong.

The month of May had a day of the heavy heart. Memorial Day around that neck of the woods meant most everyone visited the graves. It was a great reminder not only of loved ones laid to rest but also of the frailty of men. The Good Book sez; "We are like the shadows, that appear and lengthen and fade away."

If every man would keep his own dooryard clean,
soon the whole world would be clean.
—Johann Wolfgang Vaughn Goethe

CHAPTER TWENTY-SEVEN

MR. SLAYKO AND MURPHY'S LAW

Circa 1962

Grandpa Roch's logging team

JOURNEY TO THE BACKWOODS

When the warm winds of summer brought the sound of songbirds to my ears and the woodpecker called me again to the backwoods, a lot of small outfits were log'n pine fer pulpwood. It wasn't big enough for sawtimber. Being about six to seven inches on the stump, it had about twelve to sixteen feet of merchantable wood. You really had to sweat to cut and pile two cord a day, at seven dollars a cord. No matter how good you were at math, it comes up fourteen dollars a day. You furnished your own saw, gas and oil, ax, hardhat, and ride to work. But youth is resilient.

My old friend Davey Proulx came by to show me his new used car. We put our heads together (could have been dangerous) and hired on fer Mr. Slayko.

The small scattered wood we cut every day would have been enough to send less dedicated men back to the settlement, and beg fer a mill job. I shuddered every time my mind brought it up.

Chainsaws in those days were about as dependable as a modern-day politician. You just never knew when it would let you down. Spark plugs fouled daily; rewinds came apart hourly, and the chain must have been tempered in Taiwan. Be'n too poor to have a spare, we lost considerable time.

Then I cut my big toe half off!!

It was on one of those days when Murphy's Law was in force. I was make'n the most of a cool morning. Rain was threatening, and I sawed into my prize caulk boots. Blood burst forth immediately. It

MR. SLAYKO AND MURPHY'S LAW

commenced to throb as I hobbled over to Davy. We was pull'n the boot off when wouldn't you know it, along comes Mr. Slayko. He takes one look and sezs, "What in the Sam-Hill are you do'n? I ain't pay'n you to saw boots." Once you knew Mr. Slayko and had worked with him, you'd expect a comment like that. He was tougher than wang-leather, and built like a marathon runner. He worked on the run. Picked on the help in a somewhat good-natured way and expected ya to earn your pay. If anyone ever out-worked him I never heard about it. He'd cover-up any two ordinary men. Only George Moser could come anywhere near to keeping up with Mr. Slayko. They loaded every one of those four-foot pieces on to the huge trailer in the woods. Then hauled it to the landing and reloaded it into his trucks. Every day, rain'n cats and dogs or forty below zero, they got the wood out. He added new meaning to the phrase, "Where there is a will there is a way."

We got paid on Friday afternoon every week. Sometimes if he couldn't make it back due to a breakdown on one of the trucks, we had to stop at his house fer our wages. One evening when I pulled in to get paid, there he was sit'n under the hood of one of his old Fords with both heads off. And it was cold. Just a thin wool shirt on and grease up to his elbows. Peer'n out from under the hood he grinned, "Great night fer a cookout." (He loved to barbecue venison.) His wife seeing me there came out with my check, looked at his project sighed, "Don't you ever give up?" I surmised she was try'n

JOURNEY TO THE BACKWOODS

to wean him off log'n. He, still with that confident grin, sezs, "Nope."

Old King Cole may have been a merry old soul but no merrier than me and Davy out there in the woods. We went to work every morning fore daylight—we were log'n!! And our spirits were rejoicing. One of those pine stands we were cut'n was just across from the old CCC camp on the Harrisville Road. It was hot, and the bugs were drill'n us fer blood, but we were make'n the chips fly 'cause like I said, chainsaws weren't too dependable. At that time I was wearing a hardhat, and the sweat was leaking into my eyeballs. Anyway, my ax glanced off a limb and really cut my leg, Murphy's Law again, and the blood burst forth. Well sir, I yelled over to Davy, and we headed fer his car. We raced off with blood running into his floorboards. He looked down and drove off the road and crippled the front end of his nice Plymouth car. Good grief!! This log'n could be hazardous. Well, I got sewed up and went back to work. I was likened to the old saying, "He that never broke nuthin' never did nuthin'."

We finished that job and moved up near Beaches Bridge. I got rid of the hard hat and found an old beaver felt slouch hat that would absorb the sweat. We were on our way to hav'n fun again.

'Course, bull of the woods Frank happened to notice my new old hat. "Looks good on ya," he grinned. One sultry August day he came by from estimating timber. I was leaning back enjoying my lunch. I always carried it in a one-gallon old honey

MR. SLAYKO AND MURPHY'S LAW

pail. He carried a small cruising ax with a long handle. He sat down to visit and was tapping on the pail with the handle and said I carried enough homemade bread in there to feed the whole crew. He seemed to be studying some sort of mischief. I took off my hat and sat it on a stump next to me. As he got up he walked over to it and started pecking it full of holes!! Sez he, "This hat is too hot, it needs ventilation!!" My prize hat too. The thing might have expired to an early grave, but I sewed it up with rawhide and used it fer years. I don't know whatever became of it.

Somewhere on the number four road the next winter we were cut'n fer Frank and it snowed and snowed and snowed. The snow got so deep where Frank went with the Cat it looked like tunnels. Coarse cut'n that pulp you couldn't wear snowshoes and so the snow was so deep in the drifts, that it just left ya floundering.

Part of the crew was two men who were bachelors, uncle and nephew, ol' woodsmen, good loggers. They lived near the job so finally one morning as we could see they hadn't been out their driveway, yet we stopped. We decided that see'n how misery usually liked company we'd comfort each other. They welcomed us into the house. It was warm and cheery. We settled in fer a serious visit. They had cases of beer. They offered as one. We declined, as it was seven o'clock in the morning!!! You know, in a few years they was both dead from liver failure. What a waste, good honest hardwork'n men.

JOURNEY TO THE BACKWOODS

We just had to regroup as we were spin'n our wheels in that snow and go'n in the hole. Another cutter named Toughie had a whole car trunk fall of old McCulloch chainsaws and the gas tanks leaked on 'em all. He carried a bar of some kind of soap and when he'd gas up, out came the bar of soap to plug the hole. What a character. Sez he one morning, "I think this child will go home fer the rest of the winter and sleep it off." He did too. Hung around the house and ran out of wood. Then took one of his ol' McCulloughs and cut the porch off!! And cut it into firewood. All the while his poor wife screeching like an owl. She was on the warpath. Toughie just sez, "I never did like the porch no-how."

Like I mentioned, we had to regroup as we was get'n about as poor as skimmed milk. Davy went to work fer an outfit skid'n big logs, and I went to trap'n. I figured if I was go'n to have a poor winter, I might as well do something I enjoyed. I concluded I'd never cut pulp again in that deep snow, not fer love nor money.

How sharp the point of this remembrance is.
—Shakespeare

CHAPTER TWENTY-EIGHT

OLD HANK
Circa 1962

The next summer I figured maybe it was time I went in debt and bought a Cat from old Hank.

Left is Louie Kampnich and
Uncle Vinny loading black cherry.

OLD HANK

Now Hank was another one of those real characters. A voice like a lion, lived to close to a bar-room, green as June grass when it came to machines but knew timber probably better than any man I ever worked with.

Be'n more than twice my age, he'd already worked with the best loggers they was, when the big camps were really boom'n. Every once in a while I'd cut someone's trail that had worked with Hank, and they had a humorous story to tell.

Seems like old Hank and another grizzled logger about as tough, decided to spend the summer cut'n and cold deck'n timber several miles from the nearest truck road. They hauled all their fuel in barrels and had a big grub run and booze. Joe was one of those guys who'd rather work than eat or drink. 'Fore the summer was over, old Hank was to know what was meant by "Rode hard and put away wet."

Old Joe proved to be tougher than Hank. Out'n the woods by daylight and stayed there till the shadows were long and fading.

Day after day, rain or shine, deer flies, black flies, no-see-ums, Joe was building a big cold deck. Along towards the end of summer they were lean and mean. Old Hank lost about thirty pounds and his belt hung down like an unused piece of saddle girth. They was sit'n on a log one day discussing how much money they'd have come fall. Ol' Joe reached over, grabbed Hank's loose belt end, laid it cross the log and chopped it off. Sez Joe standing there with the ax in his hand, "You ain't gonna need that any more."

JOURNEY TO THE BACKWOODS

A great hunt! Back row left, Uncle George, Louie Kampnich, Bob Boliver. Front row, Leo Kloster, Bernard Boliver, Herb Kampnich, Lawrence Kampnich.

Another story made the rounds back when they was just starting to use trucks to haul logs in a big way. First thing Hank did was drink and drive. He got in a wreck and John Law told him he couldn't drive fer three months. So Hank went out in the brush to hook chokers fer a spell. And he became bored almost to perfection.

The Cat Hank was hook'n fer broke down out near the landing, so it didn't make it back right off. Old Hank got tired of wait'n and decided to take a toasty nap. Crawling into a brush hole, he was soon into dreamland. He never heard the fallers cut'n a big tree near him and of course they didn't know he was having a siesta. Down went the tree on Hank!! The limbs gave him a severe beating. Out of there he jumps, yell'n, "I'm all right!!" as if to convince himself more than anyone else he hadn't perished.

OLD HANK

Probably the wildest thing he ever got wrapped up in was a pig barbecue. Old Hank was on one of his notorious four-day drink'n sprees, and someone at the bar planned a cookout. This one was to bring the wood and someone else to bring the beer. Of course, not to be left out Hank bellows out, "I'll fetch the pigs."

Now old Hank had a sweet wife who tolerated his bar runs but had long ago took over the responsibility of the home. She had a job but made sure Hank had enough wood delivered to last the winter. And out back of their little barn she was raising, of all things, two butcher'n hogs.

Old Hank, of course, had neglected to tell his dear wife about his commitment to the greater area pig out.

The whole neighborhood laughed in silence.

One dark night, after Hank had drunk some courage over at the local hangout, he headed out to finish the dastardly deed. The pigpen was as quiet as a long forgotten graveyard. That is till old Hank arrived. Hank's plan was to get the hogs into the pickup and make good his escape. That way his wife would simply think they got out and ran away. After all, they only weighed about seventy pounds apiece. Well sir, anyone who has ever grabbed a pig can testify that they do not take it quietly. The tone of the squeal'n reached a heightened pitch and the ears of the startled wife. She called the local cop. He arrived in a matter of minutes and caught the hognapper red-handed. There stood old Hank looking

JOURNEY TO THE BACKWOODS

innocent as a new-laid egg. It took her a while to forgive him fer that fiasco.

However much of a failure Hank was at hog napping, he more than made up fer it on his knowledge of timber. There was once an export log buyer named Mr. Love who made the rounds buying veneer quality logs. Hank had a big deck of good cherry and Mr. Love came to buy. He was scaling 'em of course to get the total footage as to make payment. Every time Mr. Love put the ruler on a log to get footage, Hank would tell him exactly what was in it: 110 feet, 320, 240, etc. Pretty soon Mr. Love stepped back and sez, "I'll bet you a dollar a log you can't do that six logs in a row." The buyer would point to a log and Hank would call it. He called it thirteen times in a row. Mr. Love congratulated Hank on his knowledge.

But Hank couldn't file a saw for beans.

Our method of madness was: Hank done the fall'n, I did the skid'n, and while I was load'n Hank bucked on the landing.

Wheeled skidders had just become popular and were a great improvement over crawler tractors, much faster and cheaper to operate. We rented and then I bought one. Get'n back on the trail to hook a drag of logs, there would stand Hank. "Terrillion," he'd roar, "file mine saw!!" I'd made the mistake of filing his saw once, and he was hooked fer life.

We loaded with the crane for several years. It had single line and tongs. Old Hank hooked the tongs, and the log most always balanced. He was good at it.

OLD HANK

One old crane we rented had a wore-out pulley at the end of the boom. If I was load'n big logs, sometimes the tongs pulled out and caused the cable to whip slack, and it would fly out of the pulley. 'Course I'd have to shimmy up the boom and pull the pin for the cable was stuck alongside. In order to do that Hank had to hold up on the tongs to take the weight off the pulley. It was a sight to behold.

If we didn't look like a couple of shade-tree mechanics, there I was out on the end of the boom because once we got the thing in the air, it took half a day to get it back down and up. So we operated on it up in the air. The whole thing is about as believable as a bald-headed barber selling hair tonic. But there we was. Anyway, on one such coming-apart ordeal, Hank stood there under the boom while I shimmed up to unassemble and reassemble. Out on the end I was do'n an acrobatical maneuver trying to hold onto the big pin and get the cable back into the pulley, when lo and behold I dropped the pin and hit poor old Hank on the head. He sank to his knees and groaned.

Back down I came faster than a monkey after peanuts. By then blood was flow'n freely down his face. I led him to the pickup and raced fer town. Between racing along that old gravel road and trying to keep him from sticking his dirty hands in the injury, I had my hands full. We made it to a small town hospital in about forty-five minutes, never once within any speed limits. I was thankful we wasn't way back on some camp job.

JOURNEY TO THE BACKWOODS

I wheeled right up in front and led Hank to the front desk. By now the blood had dried all over his head and face. Lean'n over the desk, I sez, "Nurse, we need a doctor." She was fumbling with the normal paperwork and looked up just as Hank looks over. "Oh, my, gosh," she yelled and fainted. I have to admit old Hank was a sight fer sore eyes. He already had some teeth miss'n from a collision with a set of fly'n tongs years previous, also a broken cheekbone from a chain binder. I guess the poor nurse wasn't used to see'n men who lived life in the raw.

About then I spotted a doctor down the hall. "Doctor," I yelled, "we have a couple of patients here." He hustled right up, and I pointed to the nurse. He pushed a button and another nurse showed up. While the two nurses worked on their problem, the doctor led Hank to a room. I went in and sat down.

In a matter of minutes I heard Hank roar, "I'm not spending the night, I'm just telling ya that." Now I realize most doctors are well paid and that one was earning his. So the ol' saw bones finally got Hank stitched up and patched up, so we could leave the place, and it could get back to normal.

Press on; nothing in the world can take the place of persistence. Talent will not; nothing is more common than unsuccessful individuals with talent. Genius will not, unrewarded genius is almost a proverb. Education will not; the world is full of educated derelicts. Persistence and determination alone are omnipotent.

—President Calvin Coolidge

CHAPTER TWENTY-NINE

MARRIED FER LIFE
Circa 1967

I was work'n with Hank fer about five or six years when me and Geraldine started dating. I was haul'n veneer logs from No. 4 into Poland, New York. There was a mill there, I think owned by Jamestown Veneer. Of course I was skid'n most of the day and load'n, then I headed fer the mill. It was open all night and all you had to do was trip your load and put your name on the logs. Sleep was a real problem.

A logger is capable of figuring out anything. I picked up Geraldine on the way and down the road we went. At that time of night traffic was sparse and usually I'd need to nod off. Geraldine, of course, was sit'n in real close so I drafted her into service. She would steer while I caught a catnap. The road be'n perty straight and level, I just locked my foot on the gas pedal and away we went. Geraldine was just a chip off the old block. Her mother drove a log truck fer many years. In fact, she was carrying Geraldine's oldest brother and chang'n a tire when the iron slipped and hit her in the stomach. A few

Getting pelted with rice at Indian River, April 29, 1967

JOURNEY TO THE BACKWOODS

days later her son was born with a black eye. We sure done some crazy stuff back then. Do you know poor people have poor ways? And besides, it beat punch'n a time card. But many a night I went to roost without supper.

I sure hauled a pile of logs with that F-600 Ford truck. Me and that thing fit together like old Roy and Trigger. The trick was to make enough money to keep it in gas, tires, and engine and drive-line repairs and pay the road fees.

And the state police didn't make life any easier. The way they harassed log'n trucks you'd have thought the mob had hired us. Sincere they might have been, but they were set in their ignorance. And hadn't a clue (or probably didn't care) what hardships we went through to make a living. They surely loved to write them tickets fer a bad tire, a lightbulb blowed out, the muffler wasn't right, overweight—good grief. You see, to keep a logging truck totally up to snuff, you would have had to stop to a garage every trip.

Log roads back in upstate were nothing but old wagon roads. You couldn't afford to build good roads. No one reimbursed you fer it. So John Law nickeled and dimed you into poverty. Years later when I left New York, my driver's license looked like a scribble pad on the desk of a Philadelphia lawyer. They stapled on an extra length to mark fines onto my awful record—guilty of trying too hard to make an honest living in a corrupt world. (The county and state needed money.) But the law is the law. I

MARRIED FER LIFE

guess it's all water over the dam. Fer sure though, I'd have given up on it long before I did if'n I wasn't having so much fun!!

In 1965 or '66 I went for two physicals to be drafted into Vietnam. But because of a boyhood injury on Uncle Leslie's farm (broken cartilage in my knee) they sent me home. At first I felt like I'd let down my country. However, time would reveal how little that cause had to do with defending our homeland. It was more like a case of insanity.

Geraldine and I had gotten serious about each other and married April 29, 1967. Being the died-in-the-wool logger I was, I figured we'd only take a couple of days' honeymoon. The World's Fair was on in Montreal, Canada. We were married in the little white Catholic church in Indian River, a marriage made in heaven.

We settled into a small upstairs apartment in Croghan. Rent was $35 a month and being poor as anything, I figured we could put up with town for that price.

I'd gotten me another hound pup and kept her in a small barn out back. Being a pup and all alone, I figured her to howl once and a while, which she did. The barn stifled her lonely cries—or at least so I thought.

Next door lived two old maids. They never missed a trick. Somehow or other they figured out my hideaway pup and complained to the town mayor. He came to inform me of the town's dog ordinance, so I had to give my pup away. I decided that soon as I could afford it, we'd get out of town.

JOURNEY TO THE BACKWOODS

Woods work was hit and miss. All the big jobs seemed to be done, and winter found me driving log truck for hire. I was haul'n out of Redfield to Bernards Bay, for an outfit called Webb Lumber Company. It kept snow'n and snow'n. They was plow'n the road with a D6 Cat and even that came to a halt. We measured seven feet on the level and still coming down. Wolves had moved in because the deer were feed'n on the tops and limbs of our log'n. Tricky devils them Lobos was. A couple would lay down in the road while the rest chased the deer around on our landing yards. Sooner or later down the road the whitetails would come and be ambushed by the large pair. Driving up at daylight, there was the evidence in the road—blood and hair.

Hav'n snowed three feet overnight, on top of the seven we already had, they shut her down. It was such a blizzard the men decided to spend a couple of days at the Redfield hotel. Not me. I filled up my old four-wheel-drive pickup and headed fer home. They said I had some screws loose. But I already knew that or I wouldn't have been there in the first place. She was a bad one all right. It blowed so hard I couldn't see the road. And to make matters worse, every place there was a break in the timber there was two-foot drifts. The plow had gave it up sometime during the night, and there was no one else foolish enough to brave this disaster. Good thing as I may have hit 'em head-on.

I left the truck in third gear and the pedal to the metal. The momentum carried me through the

MARRIED FER LIFE

drifts. But as twilight neared, I could no longer see the snowbanks. Stop'n between drifts to clean out the grill, I feared that this was where I'd spend the night. I calculated I must be within two or three miles from the town of Lorraine. No, I told myself, self, walk'n wasn't go'n to get it. And then all of a sudden I could see the tops of electric light poles on one side and telephone poles on the other side of the road. I reasoned if I stayed right in the middle I could stay in the road. So using the poles as guides I forced my way along get'n into town about dark.

The place looked abandoned except for house lights, and I knew I couldn't get home. A quick check of my wallet told me I didn't have the price of a hotel room. Just maybe the township garage, where they kept the plows, might be the answer. Sure enough, the boys there were headed home, because they couldn't see to plow, but I could sit by the furnace all night. At least it was warm, and I wasn't out there look'n white death in the face.

Next day the roads were drifted in four or five feet deep. They headed out with the big blower mounted to an Oshkosh truck. Just out of town they chewed up part of a car buried right in the road. But they did get through, and I made it home.

Spring break up came regular as taxes, and see'n how the IRS would not take excuses in payment, I'd better come up with a plan. Jobs being a scarce as hen's teeth and not knowing which way to turn, I decided to follow the path of least resistance. I'd trap beaver through mud season.

JOURNEY TO THE BACKWOODS

Every morning I loaded up the temperamental snowcat and headed for Sand Pond Road. There I'd unload and take off to Muskrat Pond, Big Bear Lake, Loon Pond, and all waterways in between. I had to go up the back way 'cause club members at Massiweppi had a jealous fit about me go'n up the road. The message was conveyed to me by Jim Yousey, who at the time was woods-boss for International Paper Company.

Anyhow, like they say, ya do the best with what ya got. So I built a snowshoe trail way up in that backcountry till I could use the snowcat on it. I built snow bridges across rocky draws where the creeks had left high snowbanks. I left home early and got back late. My sweat, many times, froze to me before I could get back to the truck. More than once I considered giv'n it up, but there was no other work that time of the year. We had a new baby, Tina Marie, and a good blanket beaver would fetch $20 to $30 maybe. I finally got my trail near Bear Pond and remembered something John Quincy Adams once said, "Patience and perseverance have a magical effect before which difficulties disappear and obstacles vanish." As I viewed the beaver flow ahead of me, it was no longer the winter of discontent.

Of course, the days didn't get any easier but at least they were rewarding. Beaver began to appear on the boards. The hungry wolf would not appear at my door. I couldn't say the same about the mangy alpha tax wolf, however.

MARRIED FER LIFE

The weather started to lean in spring's direction. I hoped my snow bridges didn't soften too quick. I'd be in a world of hurt. The softer snow was hard on the drive belt on the vintage snowcat. Finally, one day at Muskrat Pond, the chain jumped the sprocket. There I was with a bunch of beaver and evening shadows sneak'n up on me. And far off in the west I saw clouds a-com'n. I knew if I didn't get this white man's dog team out of there and it rained, it would be there for eternity. I opened my Abe Lincoln tool kit expecting a miracle—and there it was—a chainsaw file. The chain had rounded off all the teeth on the top drive gear. So voila, I just filed the grooves deeper.

Then I noticed the bearings were going out on the top shaft, dry as a desert wash in July. Grease I did not have. But, fear not, like Mother always said, where there is a will there's a way. *Grease,* I thought sit'n there on that disabled tin contraption. My eyes were looking at those beaver and how heavy they was. I'd have to spend the night skin'n 'em and it was going to rain. Whip'n out my knife, I resigned to my fate. I no more than started when low and behold there it was!! Grease, beaver fat is pure grease!! Well sir, I sliced off a generous amount and packed my bearings, whistl'n while I worked. Wasn't long and I was back on the trail, ever so easy on the throttle. This was survival in its most primitive form. Perhaps I shouldn't tell anyone back at the settlement. They'd never believe it no how.

JOURNEY TO THE BACKWOODS

It did rain a little that night, and I lost a little sleep over my trail into the back woods. The next couple of days I skinned beaver and fixed up the old Moto-ski. Then old Jack Frost came back for a couple of days, and I knew it was now or never. If'n I didn't get in and get my traps, it would be late summer 'fore I could.

I left home in the dark and found I was the only lonely, mad trapper to seek nature's mercy. Those times in the predawn, motoring along was a time fer think'n. What would the day bring? What would this summer bring? What would life bring? The Good Book says we know not what tomorrow brings forth. I couldn't argue with that, remember'n all the times I planned the next day, and Murphy's Law ransacked my schedule.

The trail proved to be better than I expected. The soft snow had froze hard, and I knew it would hold till early afternoon. Leave'n early had paid off. Daylight saw me at Muskrat Pond. I caught an otter there and headed up towards Bear Pond where I was greeted with some beaver. Everything had drowned going down the slide wires. My taking these wild creatures reminded me of life and death, mak'n a living and the furs that were sold and mostly bought by the wealthy. For them, it was perhaps vanity as much as keeping warm. Fer me it was beans and bacon.

I left Loon Pond till last 'cause I was head'n out and I wanted to check on the hunt'n camp there. I heard when a certain bear come out of hibernation

MARRIED FER LIFE

the first place he destroyed was that cabin. Sure enough it was destroyed!! The snow was get'n soft so I left the snowcat down in the timber and snowshoed up to the door. Bear tracks everywhere. And some had a few drops of blood near. A walk around the back told the story. Every year old bruin had crashed through the lowest window, and this year was no exception. However the boys had left Mr. Bear a spring surprise party. An old hog sticker (butcher knife) secured steadfast to the bottom of the windowsill. Blackie had stuck hisself when he jumped inside.

Then he got mad!!!

The inside of that shack was a sight to behold. Not one shelf or cupboard would ever be usable again. Every can was torn apart and what he didn't eat was scattered from wall to wall. If it was glass, it was broke. Syrup had been mixed with the pancake flour. Coffee and macaroni made a nice contrast of colors. The sugar, however, didn't find the coffee. It was across the room, what was left that is, blended into the remains of Crisco. The propane stove harbored splashes of baking grease and he destroyed them beyond reconstruction. Finally, satisfied with having sampled every bit of nourishment scattered before him and with nothing left to rip, he just tore a hole in the wall and left. No more windows fer this spring feeder. I went around and opened the door for one last look and figured the best thing to do was have a bonfire. At least if'n it was mine that's how I'd have fixed it.

That at the beginning the Creator made them male and female and said, "for this reason a man will leave his father and mother and be united to his wife, and two will become one flesh.

—Matt. 19: 4–5

CHAPTER-THIRTY

ALWAYS SAWING WOOD
Circa 1967

That summer was wet and muddy. Work was as spotty as an old pinto mare. So I filled in between jobs go'n to log'n contests. I'd been to Ashland, Maine, to see Mr. John Carney. Word had gotten to me by way of the backwoods telegraph that old John was a man to make a crosscut-saw.

I found John at the Red River camps file'n big circular blades fer slashers. John was likable from the start. You can tell he would give you most anything he had. He'd long since retired but was talked into this job because they couldn't find no one capable of do'n it. John had worked for Simons Saw and Steel thirty-five years demonstrating their blades. Few people knew the old misery whip like he did. And he could out saw anyone with a forty-two-inch bow saw. When you saw him pick one up with those

JOURNEY TO THE BACKWOODS

A load of birch veneer at No. 4 road. Possibly 1967.
It was these loads Geraldine drove while I dozed.

calloused hands, you knew instantly this was no ordinary man.

This Red River camp was a busy place. Tree length spruce was com'n in out of the woods on Mac trucks with twelve-foot-wide bunks. They brought in a railroad to haul the cut timber. Huge cold decks stretched almost as far as you could see. I was impressed.

Big loaders filled long steel troughs with a massive pendulum to which hung the circular blades that sawed everything into proper lengths. Those things cut so fast and had so much power they got too hot and would warp. So John had to hammer 'em back straight. It was an art that's about gone now. John said, "Seems like a young feller like you who understands these blades would stay, and I'd

ALWAYS SAWING WOOD

teach you." What an opportunity he offered, but youth is too restless to grasp security. Down inside me was migratory. I could hardly wait to see what was around the next bend.

There at Ashland, Maine, it was obvious that the majority of loggers were of French descent. In fact, you heard more French spoken than English. They were a cheerful lot in spite of their hardships. Those big paper companies didn't pay no more than they had to, and it showed in the living conditions of those families. Many lived in tarpaper shacks. Little children with rosy red cheeks played out'n the woods. Carefree as only little ones can be, seemly not concerned about what tomorrow may bring forth.

John built me two six-foot crosscut saws. They was the last misery whips to go through Simon's furnaces in Fitchburg, Massachusetts. A few years later old John died when his house caught fire. Everyone who ever pulled those saws he filed remembered him as a gentle man with a big heart. A gifted man who never forgot how to be humble.

The log'n shows took lots of my time but were lots of fun. A lot of us have a competitive spirit and need some way to vent our energy. This day and age people are obsessed with sports. Players are paid insane amounts of money and behave worse than animals, and orphaned kids have few role models to follow. It's about the same condition Rome was in just before it fell.

We didn't have to worry about being overpaid at the log'n contests. Maybe you won enough to pay fer gas—maybe. I got to see a lot of country, from New Brunswick to West Virginia and all points in between. And lots of great people, I saw the famous Mr. LaCross throwin' knives at a girl spinning on a wheel. He was good. Then he'd shoot targets backwards looking into a mirror. And shoot the fire off cigarettes. He was do'n all this in Frederickton, New Brunswick.

Down in good ol' West Virginia we chopped and sawed at the Mountain State Forest Festival, perty country, those mountains in October. 'Course hotels were all filled up, and we were tired. One clerk suggested we drive out of town to an old boarding house that didn't take in boarders anymore. It was our last resort to sleep in a real bed. It was quite late at night when we found the place. There was only a couple of lights on when we pulled up. A very old lady came to the door. I explained our situation and wondered if she could help. She would ask her sister, "You see, it's just us here now." A short time later they both came and asked us in, treating us like long-lost relatives. What gracious people. They apologized fer the rooms upstairs, fer no one had used them in years. We thought they were the best rooms in all the world. I was too grateful and tired to pay a little dust much mind. The bed was wonderful and the hospitality was Christian. The dear sisters let you know that.

I'd spent considerable time build'n a hot saw. The engine was a West Bend with three carburetors on it. I'd tinkered and tested and wrenched on this

ALWAYS SAWING WOOD

modified sawdust maker every chance I got. One hot sultry July afternoon I was in the garage at Mom's wash'n parts in a coffee can of gas. A bad storm was brewing off in the west. Mom never missed anything. She yelled out the back door for me to come inside. I assured her, "In a few minutes. I need to finish washing these parts."

Well, she no more than closed the door and a ball of lightning came and landed right at the base of the window, five feet from me!!! It exploded the can of gas right in my face and left me in a state of shock fer a few seconds. The first thing that came to mind for me was to get the can of gas out of the garage. Still not in total control of my senses, I grabbed the can and ran for the door. Gas was slobbering on my arm and burn'n my shirt and hide. I tossed it out in the gravel and then wiped the burn'n shirt off my arm and the hide came with it!! And then pain. Tommy Kloster pulled in just as it happened and drove me to the hospital.

Upon arriving I went to the desk. The gal took one look and called a nurse. Here she comes with a wheelchair and a large needle. "You better get in the chair," she sez. And me, I was hop'n around like I had the Saint Vitus dance. I rather loudly exclaimed I didn't need a wheelchair. There was nothing wrong with my legs. She says, "There will be as soon as you get the shot." She was tell'n the truth too. After she gave me that needle, why I didn't have no leg control or feel no pain either. They could have sawed me in two, and I'd never felt it. I was happy as a lark. They fixed me right up and the skin grew back, and I was saw'n again in no time.

Some of those contests had a few wrecks too. I saw a man in Vermont stick one of those five-pound axes through his leg. It was not good.

I always enjoyed the emcee there at the woodman's field days in Boonville. He was a professor at Paul Smiths College. A Mr. Holt or Hoyt, I believe. Anyway, he was witty and funny, not someone you picture as a professor. He actually knew about woods and log'n.

For many years there came two brothers from the state of Maine. They were the Pease boys. They were rugged men and good loggers. Whenever they came out as a team to double buck on a log, old emcee would introduce them as peas and beans. A great time was had by all.

Then there was the big do'ns in Ottawa, Canada, called the Raftsmans Festival. Besides all the log'n contests they also had canoe jousting. It went like this: There was two canoes, four men, two twelve-foot-long wooden poles, with boxing gloves fixed on the ends. Two men were in each canoe, one in the stern and one in the bow. The guy in the bow had to be catty 'cause he had to stand on top of the gunnels in his bare feet. His teammate was the paddle man. These two canoes had to steer towards each other and when they came close enough each jouster tried to knock the other off his position. 'Course if'n the opponent caused your pole to glance off, then he could knock you off into the deep. Many times the canoe tipped over. It was a lot of fun—usually.

ALWAYS SAWING WOOD

This festival coincided with the annual river drive when thousands of cords of pulpwood were floated down the Ottawa River to a huge mill there. Many river drivers would work bringing the wood down from those north woods. And they were tough, agile men ready for anything. They usually dominated the canoe jousting, of course. One fellow I shall never forget. His name was Victor. Yes-sir-ree, Victor had presence. Whenever you got close to him, you could just feel the meanness. Well, come Victor's turn, he, of course, took the gunnels and with the balance of a tightrope walker, his canoe pushed off. It was no contest. The other fellow was so intimidated he fell over backwards with Victor's first punch. Instead of gliding past like he should, Victor started punching the down man on his face as he laid on the bottom of the canoe. And gave him a broken jaw!! They blackballed him and next year put ten-inch rubber balls glued on a plumber's plunger fastened into the pole's end. I always had lots of fun there and remember the competition was keen.

The last log'n show I went to was in Elgin, Oregon. They had 106 ax throwers, and I managed to come out third. I told Geraldine it was time to give it up, so I did.

As the summer dried up, I was tell'n old Hank about the stand of virgin birch timber near Loon Lake. Hav'n to walk through it trap'n in the spring, I was quite impressed. Hank said it was the last stand of virgin timber that International Paper had. I sez, "Well, let's log it!!" But there was a problem: the

JOURNEY TO THE BACKWOODS

lake. The state boundary crossed one side right at the water's edge, and this was the "forever wild" wilderness where no machines dare tread under penalty of law. His eminence, Mr. Hank, sez, "Terrillion, it can't be done!" I figured this was just another obstacle in the life of a logger to be overcome. Besides, Mother's words again came to mind, "Where there's a will there's a way."

At any rate, my belt was drawn up'n the last notch, the wife needed shoes, and the baby needed diapers. So I went to have a look-see just what Loon Lake looked like in summer's warm embrace. The old road still had some mud holes. The timber canopy didn't let in much sunlight. As I closed in on the cabin, it was evident the boys hadn't inspected their ruins yet. If possible, it looked even worse. Other bears had no doubt looked to capitalize on what remained.

My attention was snapped away by the lonely call of a loon. Down there on the lake he was adding personal authenticity to this wild place. I sneaked up on him, quiet as a shadow. Out in the center of the lake was the entire family float'n around, Mom in the lead, three little balls of fluff close up and personal. Mr. Loon behind and off to one side. I hiked down to the outlet to see if my hunch was right. And it was. Beaver over the years had done what they do best, built a very stout dam at the end of the lake and had raised the entire lake four feet!! Having only seen this place in winter under five feet of snow, I couldn't really see anything. Now it was plain as the nose on my face. If we blowed this here dam, the lake would go back to its original setting. And we would expose enough ground on the other end for a road.

International Paper agreed to let us log the timber if indeed we could get around the lake without crossing the state line or causing mud in the water.

The next phase of my plan would cause considerable uproar. Back in the good old days you could get a powder license for about one dollar. You simply went to the town clerk, a very businesslike old lady named Mrs. Henry. You answered a few questions like, "Are you a criminal? What do you intend to do with this dynamite? Are you a member of the mob?" You know, questions like that. She wrote you out a little piece of paper and you can then buy Nitro in the stick. Boy, with today's moral climate or should I say lack of morals, this would be a disaster. The last forty years have not taught much respect fer human life. Young adults once pulled harmless pranks. Now they murder at random. Divorce and liberal schools leave a lot of children with no identity. They have very little work ethic, and again we have idle hands that are the devil's tools. Well, I've been prone to wander again. Where was I?

Oh yeah, we were about to create an uproar. Me and Hank went to Beaches Bridge and bought some dynamite along with electric blasting caps. These were safer, they said. Hank didn't want to get in my pickup.

JOURNEY TO THE BACKWOODS

Next day bright and early and filled with excitement (at least I was), we hiked into the great dam. We punched several holes in under the mass of sticks, stones and mud, filling these with high drive after I'd put caps in 'em. Hank beat me to our chosen spot about fifty yards away, behind two big spruce trees. Our commotion hadn't gone unnoticed by the loon family. They retreated clear to the other end of the lake. I knew they'd be safe there. Hunkering down I yelled, "Fire in the hole," and touched the wires to the battery—Ker-b-o-o-o-m—and the sky was rain'n rocks and sticks for several minutes. I didn't dare leave the safety of the spruce canopy right off but could hear the water rush'n out. After the sky quit fall'n I ran to the lake. Man-oh-man, the dam had disappeared. Blown to smithereens. Just below the dam was a lot of boulders that kept the water from going out too fast. I was glad for that. By the time this got to the river many miles away, it would be hardly noticeable. Down to inspect the other end. Hank still wasn't convinced. By the time we reached there, the lake had receded enough to expose thirty feet of bare rocks and mud. I says, "Hank, there's our road." The only problem was it was too slick and rough for a truck road so we'd have to skid with a wheeled skidder, over a mile. And we'd have to get it inspected first.

The next week several armchair ecologists and waffle bottom foresters were observed look'n this all over. The place got more attention than a rich widow. They finally left, and left us to our misery.

ALWAYS SAWING WOOD

And misery likes company. Every time we wanted to skid, it rained. And rained some more. We couldn't skid enough logs to keep body and soul together. Not to mention in operating expenses. This was to be a winter job, freeze 'er up into a truck road.

We tackled another job where the mud wasn't up to the engine on the skidder and closer to home.

Town was really get'n to me, so we moved into a small house near Belfort. It was a very old house that fixed up quite well. The rent was cheap and the house had woodstoves. I could tell from vast experience this old house had no insulation. Many cords of wood must be hauled to keep Jack Frost at bay. Most every night I packed part of a pickup load on my way home. The wife was sure we'd be all right. Nothing like young love to keep one's spirit optimistic.

Hank and I had rented a P&H Crane to load logs from Chet Kopacinski out of Lowville. He'd moved to Boonville and was known far and wide as Bull of the woods. This man was in his fifties, and when I met him he had a physique that would make Charles Atlas look like a clothes store mannequin.

Hank said he was working in the woods near old forge many years past with a large crew of timber beasts. Chet was among 'em. They had a log'n railroad there and had shut down when they first started use'n trucks. In the depot was a safe the outfit didn't want and thought they'd have some fun with these loggers. "Boys," sez the owner, "whoever can lift the safe can have her." Well don't ya know when ya challenge a bunch of brush apes to anything, they'll make sport of it? The boys lined up. They grunted and groaned and guffawed. Chet hung back to give everybody a shot at it. Then Chet's long raw-boned arms swelled like someone had pumped 'em up. The veins on his neck bulged three times their normal size. Everyone got quiet. The safe suddenly defied gravity. Not only did Chet lift the thing!! He put it on the back in his truck. Later when they stopped to weigh the hunk of metal security, it topped the scales at 700 pounds!!

As winter came on, Hank decided he didn't want no part of Loon Lake. I, be'n near as poor as a church mouse, came up with a plan. There was a one-armed logger in Boonville who with his sons had a good-sized logging outfit. Sez me, sez I, "They can have this good timber, and I'll work for 'em." And so I did. They unloaded a Cat that was a front-end loader, and I opened the road through six feet of snow. It was tough go'n.

The old man, I think his name was Oney, was a good logger. He had one arm without a hand, with a hook instead. If he wanted to latch onto anything, he hit it straight on and the hook split in half and grabbed holt. I was impressed. When he was welding he never used a glove, just grabbed that hot iron and had a funny little grin.

There was a lot of mud under all that snow. I only made a couple hundred yards a day. By mixing the snow and mud together, plus twenty to thirty below nights, I soon had a road like concrete. Every night

ALWAYS SAWING WOOD

I had to park the Cat on poles and clean off all the mud. And I do mean all. If'n it ever froze on in those temperatures you'd never move that Cat.

Meanwhile, back at the rented old house near Belfort, the north wind was causing Geraldine some concern. With both stoves puff'n away, it was still mighty cold in the clapboard shack. At night the toilet would freeze if you didn't flush it every few hours. I left all faucets dripping but the pipes in the cellar froze anyway. The whole mess took me back to when I was a boy at the old homestead. But there we didn't have inside plumbing so never worried if it would freeze.

It got so cold the crows couldn't even fly or caw. Finally the pipes froze and busted in the cellar. The landlord was not a happy capitalist. We bailed out. Mom took us in.

Geraldine and Mom got along good, and everybody was warm—except me. But in my line of work, being cold as a mackerel went with the territory. And besides we were log'n. Oh the joy of it all, log'n virgin timber. Even the boss was in a good mood. And payday came regular like. Not a big payday but we got by, and summer would come in the not-too-distant future.

There was another lake near our last landing. For the life of me I cannot remember its name. Anyway, there was some timber beyond it the boss wanted, but we'd have to skid across the lake. "Could you do it?" he sez. I figured I'd plow the snow off with the skidder 'cause it was lighter than the Cat. Then old Jack Frost could really freeze her thick. I cut some holes to check how thick the ice was. Only ten inches of ice!! I got the skidder pointed straight for the other side, blade down and pedal to the metal. The boss on shore said later he could hear the ice split all the way across the lake. An old early day Puritan once said life was a great adventure. I agreed with him a hundred percent!!

About the time we figured out how to make ends meet someone moved the ends.

—Anonymous

CHAPTER THIRTY-ONE

OUR GALVANIZED GHETTO AND NEW VENTURES
Circa 1968

Like the Good Book promised, "As long as the earth endures, seed time and harvest, cold and heat, summer and winter, day and night will never cease."

Brother Tom with hounds,
Tom Pepper, Blue, and a nice bobcat.

OUR GALVANIZED GHETTO AND NEW VENTURES

Not want'n to impose any more on Ma's hospitality, I wanted to move up on the Jerden Road. Andrew Lyndaker's land followed it for a mile or so. There near the open flats hay meadow stood a lovely growth of white birch on a knoll, perfect place fer a cabin, nestled in the wooded glade. But our portfolio hadn't materialized yet.

Presenting myself to Andrew, I revealed my heart's dream. I told him I'd like to build a log barn and cabin and corrals. But I guess first I'd have to buy a trailer, so as to have a place to live. I could dig a tiled well myself—I'd build the cabin while living in the trailer—would you sell me a couple of acres? Good grief!! I was going on and on in my exuberance. Andrew never said a word till I'd run my course. Andrew was easy to predict. He spoke just like I should have known he would, "Why that rock pile is no good fer nuthin' much. It'll be lots of hard work. You just go ahead and build there. You can have it." His dear wife, a little more prudent sezs, "Now Andrew, you have to charge something for it." Andrew, deep in thought for a few minutes, speaks again, "You can pay a couple hundred dollars whenever you get the money." I left there think'n this man never changes. Or if he does he becomes even greater.

I bought a log loader and bigger truck to go with a skidder. If I couldn't make any money, perhaps I could lose it faster.

Loren Pate was plant'n trees then and needed a job real bad. I needed someone to help cut and so hired him. He was a top logger, a real daylight till dark man. We moved a lot of wood together. Life was busy.

Me and Geraldine had bought a galvanized ghetto (trailer house) to put on the birch knoll. The bank wouldn't sell it to us, said we didn't have enough credit. My feelings about bankers didn't improve with these latest developments. We needed a co-signer, they said. Much to the glee of the bankers, Brother Richie, who was then the manager a Woolworth's store, put his pen to the bank note fer us. We joined the ranks of those who will from that day forward pay 12.5% interest for the privilege to fix leaking roofs, have frost two feet high on the inside of the wall come winter, tweak on the door constantly, so it'd shut... Well, no sense on going on. Some of you probably been there and done that!!

If I didn't have enough to do, I put together a sawmill, got a registered quarter horse stud and some beef cattle. The scale at the mills was making life stressful. Seemed like the harder I worked the less I made. Perhaps the old nun's words about hard labor would come back to haunt me after all. But I saw it a little different. Like I always said, there's been a whole lot more folks robbed with a fountain pen than there ever was with a six gun.

I built a sawmill right behind the house. Handy like. So whenever I got home before seven o'clock at night I could just run out the back door and saw till midnight. Otherwise Cousin Snuffy ran the head rig. He was good at it too.

OUR GALVANIZED GHETTO AND NEW VENTURES

Great neighbor Andrew had sold me a few more acres to house, all this plus a shed fer the cattle.

With Loren help'n me out in the woods, we soon filled the little mill with logs. As fall came on, mud again became our biggest enemy. It stuck to the logs and froze on. You could hardly saw one log without filing the big blade. I consulted an old-timer who was a crackerjack when it came to this millwright business. He pointed me in the right direction. So I purchased an overhead scraper saw. It had an eight-inch blade with teeth an inch wide. The contraption operated on a mercury switch. When you pulled it down it started automatically and cut a wide swath ahead of the main saw about half an inch deep. Away went all the frozen mud. What a blessing.

Too busy in the summer to put up any hay, I had to buy it, a semi-load at a time. Not just fer the beef cattle but also I now had half a dozen horses. The whole outfit ran loose on Andrew's pasture because he no longer kept any stock. Old Molly and Prince had galloped out of our lives several seasons past. Walk'n along through the old familiar places in the timbered pasture, I could almost hear Molly whinny and old Prince chuckle too. Andrew said a lynx had screamed one day when the horses were down drink'n at the spring. They came run'n up and snort'n and wouldn't settle down. That day Molly just dropped dead and a week later old Prince died too. Andrew said he wouldn't eat after Molly died. Just walked around and whinnied. Just died of a

JOURNEY TO THE BACKWOODS

broken heart he guessed. Those ol' ponies sure left me lots of fond memories.

That fall we was log'n down near Bear Town again. Mostly poplar. I was haul'n it into St. Regis Paper in Deferiet. The scaler was a nice fellow but afraid of his job, and only a couple of years from retiring. He most always complained about the red spots in the poplar pulp. You see, if you cut a log right into a limb you most always got red showing. Well, this wood we was log'n had more than normal. He hemm'd and haww'd and whined and said he wouldn't scale it. "What?" sezs me, "You ain't gonna take it?" He refused to accept it. And weren't nuthin' I could do either. So I hauled it home. They say, tough times builds character. At any odds, all this should make me into quite a character. On my way back to my mill I had time to fume. It was snow'n perty good. Before I dumped my load I noticed the wet snow had stuck to the last tier and it looked like all the other pulp I'd ever hauled. I dumped it at my millyard and took mental note.

That weekend it snowed and right into Monday. I made up my mind, if they didn't take that load I would never haul that mill another stick of wood.

Just so happened they started to receive wood at night because they was run'n short. This was a huge paper mill. The first one St. Regis ever built. And they put on a different scaler after five. Sezs me, sezs I, perhaps this man will like the looks of my wood better. About dark Monday afternoon I loaded the pulpwood for the second time and down

OUR GALVANIZED GHETTO AND NEW VENTURES

the snowpacked road I went. It was about eight o'clock when I pulled up to the scaler shack. Why you'd have thought I was king of Sherwood Forest. He scaled my load and thanked me for my wood. Yes-sir-ree, sure makes a lot of difference when a man ain't afraid of his job.

The whole thing sorta left me with a bad hole in my wallet. So I moved to a piece of timber just out of Turin. It was an old maple woods that the people decided to give up mak'n syrup. We hauled the big maple to West Leyden and the hardwood pulp to Port Leyden. The wind blowed, and it was ever cold. We fought the machinery to get it started. And then Loren rolled the skidder. There it was all four wheels in the air, looked kinda like a dead elephant. I put it back on its wheels with the loader. It's a good thing we were having fun. We might have froze to death.

When I was buck'n a three-foot maple in two one day I just missed a cast-iron spout. It was left there a hundred years before. I saved it for a memento.

Our son Troy had been born and spring break up plus tax time was drawing nigh. Looked like another spring of trap'n beaver to provide for the necessities of life.

Back in them days, weather was perty unpredictable up there in the mountains. The first of March could be very cold, as in below zero. I'd loaded all my outfit on a toboggan behind my snow sled and figured to go to the end of the road and bushwhack it from there. The snow was deep, and I made poor

JOURNEY TO THE BACKWOODS

time on the way in. I'd only been married a few years, and the wife poured forth her concern at my journey into the mountains. Not to worry, I told her as I kissed a tear-stained cheek, I'd be back in a couple of weeks fer supplies.

As I was say'n, the snow was deep, and I made poor time on the way in. There was another snow sled track from the day before, but it was almost buried. I figured it was a guy who had a cabin on private land not far from where I'd leave my sled.

It was quite a storm really, and I knew I'd never get to my campsite before dark. So I sez to myself, "Self, you might as well go up there and hole up fer the night at that cabin with those fellers." I even smiled at this great turn of events in my favor.

From a ways off I saw smoke com'n from the chimney and thought about hot coffee. I roared up in front and yelled, "Hello, the camp!" The door opened and their faces looked like something you see in a wax museum. I waded through the snow and told them of my plans and said I'd never make my lean-to 'fore dark. The proud owner of this estate offered that he was full up and nodded towards his company. I recognized him as a minister who once reprimanded me fer be'n a sinner. I wouldn't reveal the good pastor's denomination because it don't do no good to open old wounds. He just stood there like a Sadducee. Then the proud owner said goodnight and closed the door. And not even a cup of coffee. I pulled my muskrat hat down a little lower. It was get'n dark.

OUR GALVANIZED GHETTO AND NEW VENTURES

I remembered where there was part of an old log'n camp from another era, perhaps. Down the trail I made my way in the night—my headlight didn't work. Back in those days snow sleds weren't all that dependable. Usually you ran 'em a day and worked on them a day. I stopped and dug out my flashlight. It was dark as another gravedigger's night. My mind went back to a story my mother had told us kids about this good Samaritan character in the Bible. Could be these folks never heard of him. I recollect someone passed a comment once about the proud cabin owner. They figured someone would have to hire pallbearers fer his funeral. I concluded ifn' he had a heart, all it did was pump blood 'cuz it weren't fer kindness.

Yup, sure enough, the old log'n camp was there all right. The door was half tore off, porkies had chewed large holes in the floor, but it was dry, except for the snow that got down through the stovepipe hole. Not one piece of anything remained. It was a naked room. I rolled out my sleep'n bag on the plank and crawled in. Tired but thankful, hungry but hopeful. Look'n up to the chimney hole I saw it had stopped snow'n. The clouds parted and some stars twinkled. They looked friendly. Joy would come in the morning.

Sometime during the night the plank floor got to my joints. And it was c-o-l-d. I was chilled clean to the marrow of my bones. Half awake, I laid there wish'n I took the time to unpack the old Army cot on the toboggan. Look'n up through the chimney

JOURNEY TO THE BACKWOODS

hole, the five feet of snow on the roof was shining by the light of a million stars. Just then a mouse scampered across my sleeping bag—the battered old cabin wasn't totally vacant after all.

I curled up in a ball to ward off the cold and tried to force myself back into dreamland. But she was a no go. All I could think about was get'n to the lean-to and beaver pelts.

Hav'n no watch, I didn't know the exact time, but instinct told me that dawn was near. I'll just get started and maybe make Sand Lake by midmorning.

It was a true wilderness winter wonderland as I headed up the old log'n road. Just past the river I stopped where the turnoff went to Brindle Pond Camp. Lots of memories there for a ten-year-old boy. Brush wolves—Uncle George shooting one in the dark—the rest devoured it entirely. It was a summer fish'n trip forever tucked away in the backtrails of my memories.

The cold was cut'n deep there whilst I sat on that sled. I'd started to shake but never noticed till the memories left me. I was sure thankful I'd seen all this when she was virgin and pretty and wild. How progress changes things.

I pulled the starter cord, and the sled roared to life. Yup, even this contraption changes things. Man, the snow was deep, and pull'n the toboggan really made this white man dog team labor. On the steeper hills she just gave up and spun out. I'd get the Yukon trailers out and break trail fer a ways, then make another run at 'er, then the end of the road. But I

OUR GALVANIZED GHETTO AND NEW VENTURES

knew Big Sand Outlet wasn't far, so I snowshoed on and hit the ice just right. Went back and gathered up my outfit and made it all the way to the lake. She was beautiful and lonely and serene.

The lean-to was there like I remembered it. I dug out the coffee pot and made a sandwich. It was fit fer a king. And look'n down the lake, the scenery was too. The forest was clothed with new-fallen snow and was still—oh so quiet. Yes, the Creator seemed to say, "Be still and know that I am God."

I spent the rest of the day cover'n the lean-to with tarps. The only stove I had was a two-burner white gas outfit. So I cut a pile of wood fer an outdoor fire and got ready fer the night.

The sun went down in a blaze of glory. It was perty but get'n cold. I poked up the embers. Sparks floated off into the wilderness. Tomorrow, I'd snowshoe over to Big Wolf Pond and set traps. I'd not sleep much tonight.

I had two Army mummy bags, one inside the other, and figured I'd be plenty warm. Weren't no heat, but the tarps kept the wind out. Yes-sir-ree, this here life was a great adventure.

I finally fell asleep and woke up cold. I guess the temperature was thirty below. Well, nuthin' to do but build up the fire and wait till daybreak. I couldn't sleep anyway thinking about all the fur hereabouts.

Soon as it was light to see, I headed fer Big Wolf Pond. I crossed fisher and martin tracks. They too loved this wilderness setting. I'd love to trap some, but their season was past. There was lots of blowdown along the trail, the kind of spruce they like to make fiddles out of.

I never cut a deer track till I got to the lake. And then the wolf tracks were as numerous as the whitetail. The snow was so deep the deer had been living on the ice following the inlet and outlet to browse. Out in the middle I could see what was left of the whitetail that couldn't outrun the pack. I examined it closely, wish'n I'd brought some boiled traps.

I found the beaver lodge and much otter sign on the dam near the outlet. From there I continued over the mountain to follow other drainages look'n fer beaver dams. I barely made it back to camp 'fore dark.

A couple days later over near Rock Lake, a big buck tried to cross over to the Emerald Lake outlet and high centered in the deep snow. I snowshoed right up on him. The bony creature didn't have enough strength to care about this trapper. His eyes showed no fear. He just laid his head down in the snow. I could see the holes where his horns had been shed. I sat on my snowshoe tails a few feet in front of him and talked low and soft. Told him he was in a bad way and didn't look like he'd make it. I retreated to some hemlock and cut some browse fer him. Poor bugger.

A couple of weeks passed in nuthin' flat. This beaver trap'n was honest work now. Skin your catch by the campfire 'cause you need all the daylight there was to make yer rounds.

OUR GALVANIZED GHETTO AND NEW VENTURES

A couple of snowmobilers even followed my track in and looked over my operation one time. Just curious, I thought. Little did I know they emptied my extra gas and set the can in the same spot. The day I was to leave fer supplies I grabbed my can and it was empty. Like Mother always said, "It takes all kinds." I ran out of gas about three miles from my pickup. I just started to walk and along came this nice man and his wife up to take pictures of the deer. He siphoned me some gas and away I went. It sort of renews your faith in humanity.

Anyway, there was this young feller I knew who'd been go'n to college and had spring break. Sezs he needed to get away fer a spell. Well, look here, sezs me, come along and I'll show you things better than a college education and a whole lot cheaper.

He didn't know what to think of my lean-to lash up. We tied the Army cots near the ceiling 'cause that's where the heat was. I kept my little two-burner stove go'n most of the night.

We really put on the miles snowshoe'n and were tired as pharaoh's slaves come night. I'd wake up in the morning and my chest hurt. "Man," says me, "I'll have to cut back on the miles." The kid laughed and said, "You snore so loud I've been beating your chest every night so I could get to sleep."

Do you know I considered all this for a couple of days out on the snowshoe trail? Coming down a fast run'n stream one day, I heard the ice split under me. The kid was behind, and I knew he'd break through. The way I figured it, the water was only eight to nine inches deep and this was my chance. Sure enough, when he hit the spot I heard this blood curdling scream. I turned to see him paralyzed and slowly sink'n. I commenced to laugh when he yelled, "Help!!!" His face showed such terrible unbelief. How could I laugh? We even had a little fun on our trip.

Freedom is the oxygen of the soul.
—Moshe Dayan

CHAPTER THIRTY-TWO

FILLING IN
Circa 1969

Like I said many times before, education is where you find it, some in school and much in the ways of many others who have trod on before us.

My love for the forests and even with the sawmill couldn't always keep the wolves from the door. The cattle and horses needed time to reproduce, so as they'd pay off. Then the opportunity came to work on construction. Who knows, sezs me, sezs I, one may even pick up some useful information for future use.

The construction company had several bids on the big army base called Fort Drum. The job started off with pour'n lots of concrete. When it came to physical labor, concrete work was right up there, sorta like root hog or die. But my financial situation would improve. Four dollars and sixty cents per

FILLING IN

Ready for a logging contest

hour, and I received it every week. All that money, why it was almost like strike'n the mother lode.

What I thought I knew about cement work didn't amount to much. Preparing the ground, tie'n the steel, build'n the forms—they made sure we done it up right. Then the cement trucks pulled up—one right after the other. We sweat like a Turkish bath. Always got done ahead of schedule, the boss smiled a lot.

I was ride'n to work some of the time with one of the cement finishers. He frowned on my chew'n tobacco habit and ferbid me to spit out of his window. The main reason most likely was a shiny new robin-egg-blue pickup.

This here fellow happened to like his beer. Every night on the way home he stopped and got a sixpack of bottles. Tool'n along, he'd sip on his booze while I spit in a can. I cringed when I saw him toss his bottle out the window, watch'n him out of the corner of my eye as he emptied the next one and I was ready. He let fly, and so did I. He almost lost control when he observed the contrast of brown splattered the length of the box in my side view mirror.

He threatened and cussed.

I just told him that his bad choice of words didn't scare me a bit. And every time he threw out a bottle I'd color up the side of his fancy pickup. He put 'em on the floor after that. I shouldn't have even rode with anyone who'd drink and drive, even if it was only a few beers. I never could stand people who saw the great outdoors as a place to toss every piece

FILLING IN

of junk known to man. They were littering God's living room.

Unbeknownst to me, the boss checked on us once and a while from afar. He observed us with spyglasses. When it came time to put together a roof crew, he seemed to pick the most independent and carefree of us—the ones with the thickest calluses on their hands.

They were ten of us yahoos to re-roof one of the barracks a day. Tear off old roofing, replace rotten roof boards, put on forty square of three-in-one asphalt shingles, and clean up the mess. And don't be all day, sez the boss.

It was back-breaking work, kinda made us feel like pack mules bare'n all those shingles up that ladder. The foreman, Gordon Dunn, was a get-the-job-done kind of guy. He made every effort to make it a little less grueling. After a few days, he came up with a power ladder. I'd never seen one. To me it was a marvelous modern marvel. He just laid four bundles of shingles on a little platform and pulled a lever, the electric motor then shot the thing skyward. Four men were there to unload and you pulled a lever, zing! Back down it flew. Why I concluded this here contraption was almost as important as those huge glazed doughnuts and coffee that appeared every morning at nine o'clock.

The big boss showed up one morning after about two weeks and sez, "You guys been doing a great job, but it's get'n really hot, so I have a proposal. It's been taking you about a thin nine hours to do a roof, so tell you what I'm going to do. I'll pay for eight hours regardless how long it takes. I think you boys could do it in seven." I looked at Walt, and Walt grinned.

Next morn'n we started at six and was done at twelve-thirty. You never saw so much work togetherness. The Amish could have took lessons from us.

Walt Baker was the most agile person I ever knew. No one had hands so fast and coordinated as his. Walt would take four rows and charge off across the roof. The rest of us took two and we still couldn't catch him. Walt was part Indian but never mentioned it. He was neither boastful nor ashamed of the blood in his veins. And he accepted no freebies because of it. He worked harder than anyone and gained everyone's respect. He asked fer no quarter and gave none. Someone nicknamed him Runn'n Bear. If you hunted with him you could only guess where he was. No one could match his endurance or the speed he traveled.

And he loved to trap muskrats. Skin'n several hundred of these river rats fer some might require considerable time. Not so with Walt. He gave new meaning to, "The hand is quicker than the eye." If you blinked the hide was off and on the board. It was a sight to behold.

Walt passed away a few years back from cancer. He couldn't have been over sixty. I went back to visit Mom in a nursing home that year. Spring breakup was in full swing. As I crossed Black River, high water was overflow'n the banks. I couldn't help but

FILLING IN

see Walt out there stand'n in the stern of his skiff, one hand on the motor handle and roll'n a smoke with the other. As he came up river an ice flow came into view cover'n the width of the river. Walt guns 'er and lands up on the ice—leaps out and yanks the boat over the other side—jumps in and lights up. I thanked God for Walt and the unique person he was. Everyone who knew him would take their hat off to him; we'll all miss him.

So we got the roofs all done by fall and then went to remodel the base hospital. You got to remember these were all built to house soldiers in training fer World War II.

Most log'n jobs was still gripped in poverty, so I considered myself fortunate to have a job that at least could buy the essentials of life. The first thing was to gut the inside. Me and Walt was good at gut'n. And I soon learned when you're carry'n on the back end of two scaffolding planks and Walt's on the front, you better hustle and keep wide when you rounded a corner.

Hunt'n season was on and a bunch of us ridge runners was moan'n and bugle'n. We thought a two-week layoff would be a good idea. We hinted whenever we was around the company crowd. They soon cut a wide berth whenever they seen us com'n, "You're crazy. Keep away from me," they'd announce whenever we got near. Those guys worried more for their job than about the quality of their work. So we had to do the weekend hunt. It's tough when

JOURNEY TO THE BACKWOODS

you're "born to hunt and forced to work," that was a bumper sticker I saw once upon a time.

The cold of winter crept into those lonely rooms. The company came up with some fuel-fired heaters. It soon became evident that place was about as healthy as a coal mine. I began to long for the backwoods breezes, the smell of sawdust, and the independent life once more. The dreams soon vanished to reality 'cause the family must be looked after, and summer was a long way off. Sometimes, though, a man's dreams is all that can keep him go'n. When the load is heavy and the road rough and the job dirty and company men get all the breaks. Yessir-ree a man's got to have a dream.

We got the hospital done and then had to remodel a huge warehouse; they brought in bigger heaters. It kept get'n colder and snow'n. I was trap'n on weekends and enjoyed the snowshoe trail. It sorta kept life in the proper perspective.

One fine cold morning I was look'n out through a hole I'd rubbed in the frost there at the warehouse window. Outside the wind cried and wailed, and there stood about a hundred Army guys all bundled up and ready for instructions. Up comes a truckload of snowshoes. The same brand I had; the long turned up Yukon Trailers—Army issue. The best powder snowshoe ever made. Well sir, someone who looked official took charge and was show'n the GIs how to strap on webs. I went to work at my job and a while later looked out, and they was all lined up and ready

FILLING IN

to go. I was kinda expect'n trouble and I wasn't to be let down.

They took off on the run, and you never saw the likes of it. Most hadn't gone a hundred feet and were bottom side up, looked sorta like a planned comic show. Good thing there weren't no enemy about. Some of the fellers were pull'n a few monkey shines, I thought this here instructor has got his hands full. Come to find out this company of soldiers were out of the south and had never been on snowshoes before. I could've gave 'em some pointers but the government don't hire "unschooled" backwoodsmen anymore. I was sure though these boys would make it with lots of perseverance.

Well, we finally got all those buildings shaped up just before spring. The outfits then got a job near Rome build'n some big concrete buildings with four-foot-thick walls. The Air Force was testing lasers in there. It was hard work, and I noticed the company was starting to take advantage of a few of us who didn't shun hard labor. My gratefulness for the job had begun to wane. No one likes being taken advantage of.

I hung in there till late spring. One windy, cold rainy day, I was cling'n to the sway'n scaffolding about fifty feet up. I was told to grind all the form marks off the concrete. There I was, no mask, grind'n away on the cement. Then the rain would cause it to stick to me. Every half-hour or so I'd put down the grinder to rest my arms and breathe fresh air. The geese were fly'n over, sing'n their wild song. I began

JOURNEY TO THE BACKWOODS

to feel like a slave wait'n fer evening shadows. What a way to muck out a liv'n. What was even worse, not far away there happened to be a nice stand of big maple and beach. It proved too much for all my backwoods memories.

About an hour 'fore quit'n time I threw in the grinder. I strolled inside the building where all the smoochers were hang'n out. I was get'n me a drink of water when that seven-foot boss walked by and gave me that "Get-to-work-or-else look." I sez, "It's all right. It's my last day."

Go West, Young Man, go West.
—Horace Greeley
(1811-1872)

CHAPTER THIRTY-THREE

A POT OF BLACK GOLD
Circa 1973

Before I could get back to log'n, Pate ambushed me. Ol' Butch Pate was home fer a visit. He had been working in Idaho, Oregon, and Arizona.

I listened to the tales of the West, big timber, big elk, big mountains. It all came back to me. The Western magazines at Gramps's camp many, many moons ago. This was not good fer a backwoods wanderer to be tantalized with such visions of grandeur.

About then we'd heard they was to build an oil pipeline in Alaska. Butch sez, "Terrillion, let's tramp." The temptation was overpowering. "Good grief," sez me, sez I. "Think of the adventure." But how could I leave the family fer months? And the mill, well that would survive, somehow—maybe. My partner could run it fer awhile.

A POT OF BLACK GOLD

North to Alaska

The more I talked about this journey, the more the wife looked worried. She knew how I was when it came to "the other side of the mountain."

Daughter Rosie, our youngest, was only a month old. And my log'n outfit was hanging on by a hair. I was beginning to become overwhelmed with this financial struggle for survival. The hard work came with the territory, but I was get'n haggard from want of a little silver and gold to show fer all my hard labor. I concluded I'd just have to go fer it.

I started to plan our trip "North to Alaska." I got a canopy fer the back of the pickup. Built us each a bunk in there. It took a couple of weeks to put it together, all the while think'n about the family.

JOURNEY TO THE BACKWOODS

The day came all too quickly. We loaded our stuff, and Butch got in the pickup. I turned to Geraldine and could feel her heart as I hugged her close. Her tears warmed my cheek, parting was much sorrow. I kissed all the little ones. They didn't seem to understand. Life was still a game in their sincere innocent minds. Out the driveway we turned and pointed the old pickup west.

We planned to drive non-stop. One would sleep in the back as the other drove. We did real good till we hit Chicago. Then our lack of city drive'n showed up. The place was a zoo. I concluded years later that the only good thing I knew in Chicago was Moody Bible Institute. The earth did not have enough paper money to entice this lover of the backwoods to live in that hub of confused humanity.

Overcom'n that obstacle, we soon enjoyed the farmland. Fresh green shoots of corn and soybeans were a testament of American framers and their commitment to work the soil. Modern machinery had took away most of the backbreaking jobs, but the hours were just as long.

Iowa and Nebraska had plenty of cattle and pig feedlots. I knew where they all were, even in the dark. This was the heartland where honest hard work and character mattered. But the land was too predictable fer me. It did little to spark my "around the next bend" curiosity.

Somewhere near North Platte we stopped at a truck stop. It had all sorts of memorabilia about "Buffalo Bill Cody"—seems like his ranch was

A POT OF BLACK GOLD

nearby or home maybe. Anyway, once I saw them pictures I forgot how tired I was. I just perked right up. Now here was a man who lived and breathed adventure. He looked the part too. Even had hair like Samson before he ran amuck of Delilah.

The old Ford pickup rolled right into Wyoming. The landscape suddenly took on the frontier look. It got hard to sleep.

That endless stretch of lonely highway had to end at the Rocky Mountains, I reasoned. We saw a sign that said "Fort Bridger." I remembered reading once that old Jim Bridger was so illiterate he signed things with an X. They claimed someone hornswaggled him of that Fort 'cause he didn't savvy laws and legal charmers. But they couldn't take away his place in history. Illiterate he may have been, but his name and what he did fer his country are remembered and claimed now by institutions of higher learning. Kind of comical, don't ya know? Everyone wants to claim a winner as their own, even an uneducated one.

History recorded that Old Jim could ride through the country once and draw you a map that showed every creek, every knoll, every landmark. And he never lost his bearings. As an old man he lived near present-day Kansas City. One day he was overheard by someone, "I wish I was back there amongst the mountains again. You can see so much farther in that country." Yes-sir-ree, Jim old boy, I totally agree with ya.

At night when I rode in the back, the wheels hummed the tune of a wandering song as I fell asleep.

JOURNEY TO THE BACKWOODS

Swinging up into Montana we could see mountain ranges everywhere. Seems like I heard once Montana means mountains or mountainous. I believed it. I wasn't all that safe at the wheel 'cause I kept tak'n in the country. Some professor, a Walter Prescott Webb in *Harper's* magazine, in May 1957, called Montana "history thin." All of us should have such a "thin" history. Ain't likely he spent any time here on horseback or hiking or hunting. Chances are he never laid in his winter's wood and meat with his own bare hands either. Such folks live a pretty "thin" life.

All of a sudden there they was!! The Rocky Mountains. "The Mountains to the N.W. and west of us are still entirely snow covered and white and glitter with the reflection of the sun. I do not believe that the clouds that prevail at this season of the year reach the summits of those lofty mountains..." That's the way Clark described the Rocky Mountains on June 20, 1805. Taken from *The Journals of Lewis and Clark* and edited by Bernard De Voto.

All the way north of Great Falls to the west they awed me. What a creation. We kept company with those ladies in the sky all the way up through Alberta. We had almost left Montana when I noticed this pickup with a couple of cowboys tail'n us. I slowed down to see if they might have something to say. But they slowly passed us and really gave us the eyeball. Didn't take Butch long to figure out they spied our New York plates. We hadn't heard the last of grief from that Empire State advertisement. These

A POT OF BLACK GOLD

boys had probably been listening to some old squaw tales about how New York is all city.

We pulled up to the Canadian border.

'Course we had our guns along. What would a feller do in Alaska without a gun, or several? Even had our pistols. We just had to put a clip on the trigger so's you couldn't shoot it.

When we left Jasper Park we had to show them that the clips were still in place. Simple enough. Well times have sure changed ain't they? Those days are gone forever.

Once inside Jasper Park we saw lots of critters. We got to feed the Bighorn Sheep bread. The beggars came run'n right up to the pickup. They being so bold and all, I was a little cautious at first. Then I figured maybe I could bulldog one if'n I could just get my hands on him. Well sir, I had a piece of bread in one hand and tried to reach over the top of his neck with the other. I barely touched his horn, and he leaped in the air six feet. I concluded we were not bonding well. In fact, I was conceiving trouble which might eventually give birth to evil.

Butch suggested we move on.

Motoring along up the Queen's highway with the window down, I was breathing air I never thought possible. Ah!! It was ever fresh.

Here and there was a tour bus filled with tourists. A few had Asian people, and they scurried here and there with their cameras clicking away. I never saw so many cameras in all my born days.

JOURNEY TO THE BACKWOODS

We sped on past Jasper head'n west and left the park. They checked our firearms real good and everything was hunky-dory. We was percolating right on time.

Get'n on down towards McBride, B.C., they was lots of moose thereabouts. There'd been a lot of log'n in the past—in fact still was. Ol' Bullwinkle was really enjoy'n this backwoods smorgasbord. They'd logged lots of spruce to make hay meadows. With D8 Cats, all the tree length was wind-rowed to burn. What a waste. There wasn't enough mills to process everything.

We stopped in town to eat a bite and stretch our legs. Many years later while going to Alaska again to cut timber, the hard reality was as plain as the nose on Jimmy Durante's face. I had breakfast at a café that looked like loggers might fill their faces at. A very efficient Chinese cook filled my plate with fluffy hotcakes. I set to work try'n to do justice to his good cook'n. Sez me, "Where's all the loggers?" Waving the spatula around he answered, "Loggers all gone, all gone now, no more loggers, all gone." It's my opinion, (and my credentials should give me a right) that everyone got carried away at this lumber market. Loggers in their genius became too good at what they did. The mills were too big; the loggers worked too hard and had too much big machinery. Sit'n there wolf'n down those pancakes, I'd bet these folks wished that all that timber they'd burned up was still there.

A POT OF BLACK GOLD

We weren't look'n forward to Prince George, B.C. You would never know the place was a logger's paradise. I mean you're up on this hill looking down over this mass metropolis wondering how in the world will I get through this. Back in them days construction was everywhere. Detour here and detour there. We took a wrong turn but finally made it through. It was mass log'n from McBride clean to Prince Rupert. Most everyone we met was friendly. Through Smithers, Hazelton, Terrace, and finally Prince Rupert. It's called "Gateway to Alaska." I got my first look at the great Pacific Ocean. And the ferry which would take us to Haines, Alaska. First stop Ketchikan—land of eternal wet feet.

It didn't rain in Ketchikan, it POURED!!!!!!

Be'n a backwoods hideout most of my life and not be'n well read, I didn't know it rained anywhere in North America like this. Yearly average rainfall is 162 inches—PLUS—PLUS!!!! Thirty-two inches of snow. Me and Butch would get a lesson in tent camp'n.

This was quite the place. Even had some roads, all eleven miles of it. We marveled at the docks and floatplanes, the air was full of 'em. Local folks at the café said they was fly'n fishermen out to fish and loggers out to log. There was huge rafts of logs everywhere. Right in the middle of town was a sawmill and forklifts with timbers sticking out both sides drive'n up Main Street. This was my kind of place. 'Course it was town and a rough one at that.

JOURNEY TO THE BACKWOODS

I wouldn't have been a cop in that town fer love nor money.

Ol' Butch seemed kind a right at home and found out there was a flea bag hotel there near the sawmill, cheap. Well we needed to regroup and get some info on the pipeline up north. I didn't like the looks of that shack, so we mosied on upstairs to evaluate. The place smelled like demon rum and dope. There was a door ajar so I gave it a quick little push. Low and behold there's this fellar going through a suitcase, and it weren't his!! The poor unfortunate that owned it was passed out on the floor. The thief was caught in the act. He leaped past us, hand over his face, and tore down the staircase. I looked at ol' Butch and shook my head a positive no.

Out in the street the rain slowed to a drizzle. Like I said before, me and Butch would get a lesson in tent camp'n in the rain forest. Ward Cove was a campground up near the pulp mill and seemed like our best place fer a pup tent.

We could see the steam before we could see the mill. Huge rafts of logs lined up waiting their turn to be ground into pulp for paper, a commodity modern man cannot do without.

The sign said, "Ward Lake Campground." We turned off there. We weren't prepared fer timber like this. Giant spruce eight to nine feet in diameter guarded the campground. Me and Butch figured we'd like to log here. The story is told about some died in the wool timber cutter who was challenged to go up there and cut one of those trees. He hung around

A POT OF BLACK GOLD

the local logger bar one night till he drank enough courage to undertake this evil act. His fellow loggers told him there was no other cutter like him. They puffed him up to the point of no return.

There was the old stump to prove he did indeed complete the evil deed.

The cramped quarters in the back of the pickup forced us to set up the pup tent. There might have been enough room in that thing for a couple of boy scouts, but I had reservations about this miniature teepee. But we were left with little choice.

There was not a dry spot to be had fer our little shelter. So we undertook to build a bonfire to dry off the area. I concluded there was no such thing as dry firewood within two hundred miles.

A couple of campsites over, some Indians were starting a fire. "Maybe I could learn something here," sez me, sez I. The boys were split'n their wood into real small pieces. Ah-ha, that was the secret. Squaw wood, more or less. Inside those big blocks left there the wood was burnable, if split into one-inch pieces.

So in no time we had white man's fire go'n. Heap big fire. We got the ground nearby dry enough to put up the tent. Pulled the fire far enough away so's not to have a meltdown.

It was again rain'n cats and dogs.

We were asleep in a New York minute, bone tired as we was, till about three o'clock. My half asleep senses told me the sleep'n bag was wet. Sure enough, anyplace that touched the nylon tent got

JOURNEY TO THE BACKWOODS

wet. I started to laugh. Butch woke up want'n to know what was so funny? I was think'n about that old loggers say'n "It's a great life if ya don't weaken." We just hunkered down till daylight. We'd see if'n there was a silver lining behind this cloud.

Things were pretty soggy in the morn'n so figured we best dry our stuff at the laundry mat. We needed to check on the oil pipeline, our wallets were get'n a little thin.

We hung around the saw shops and places that sold rig'n to log'n camps. They didn't seem to know a whole lot about the pipeline. But what they did know didn't sound good. It was union and unless you knew someone or could buy someone, your chances were slim. We even degraded ourselves and checked to see what the unemployment office knew. They gave us papers to fill out. I had never filled out papers in speculation before in my life. Sez me, "Either you need someone or you don't."

Fairbanks seemed to be farther all the time.

We counted our paper and coins and tried to calculate the cost of the ferry to Haines, gas to Fairbanks. Then they was the other necessity called food. Yes, we had enough to get there but we didn't have enough to buy a job. I didn't like the sound of that anyway. It smelled like the mob or some other bunch of evildoers.

That evening back at the campground we sat around our campfire in a drizzle and made a decision. Butch thought we might as well get a cut'n job out at one of these log'n camps. It paid pretty good

A POT OF BLACK GOLD

and at least it was what we knew. We'd heard by way of the backwoods telegraph that log'n bosses were in and out of hotels every few days. Tomorrow we might just corral one.

In the morning we decided on a hot breakfast down at the café. We drove down around the fleabag hotel. Good grief!!

They'd had a fire in an upstairs room the night before. Someone had tossed out a moth eaten mattress in the street. People just drove around it in a sorta orderly disorder. Way up north here folks had a different acceptance of life.

We wolfed down our breakfast and hung around the lobby of an upscale hotel and collared our first prospective boss. He asked us a few questions and looked us over from top to bottom, all the while glance'n through his mail, and walked out into the street. We stood by the front of my pickup and the old boy was about to hire us, or so I thought. I noticed the changed expression on his face when he saw my plates. All of a sudden he looked at his watch and said he had an appointment. The Statue of Liberty wasn't cut'n any ice up here.

The Empire State plates had to go.

That very day my pickup became an Alaskan. We went all the way and got suspenders that said "Alaska Logger" on 'um. If'n clothes make the man, we were ready fer action.

We laid in ambush fer other camp operators. We waylaid a few but it didn't take a shrink to figure out that the word had gotten around—the guys in

JOURNEY TO THE BACKWOODS

the red truck are from NEW YORK!!! We would be informed later from a camp boss that there was no trees in New York. Therefore, there could be no loggers from there. It was enough to reduce a man to tears of laughter.

We held another council. We'd gotten wind of some cutters needed up at Haines. But we couldn't cut timber without saws. Word had it the saw shop in Haines wasn't much at that time. Me be'n a McCullough man, I marched in the shop in Ketchikan and purchased a 797 with thirty-six inch bars. Butch bought a Stihl.

And they said it didn't rain near as much up there. We bought our ferry tickets in a horizontal squall.

An old friend is better than two new ones.
—Russian Proverb

CHAPTER THIRTY-FOUR

A COUPLE OF WOOD HICKS
Circa 1973

Time fer a rest on the Lynn Canal out of Haines, Alaska.

With my pickup and saws and tools safely tucked away down in the hold of the ferry, Butch and me sat up in the forward deck. We could have been tourists had we been dressed fer it. The scenery from up there was relaxing, breath tak'n. Misty fjords

A COUPLE OF WOOD HICKS

cut into mainland mountains, mountains that split the sky. They was beg'n someone to come explore. We would love to. But the working man swims against a different current. He produces or doesn't get paid. He is too moral or proud to take grants or do-nuthin' jobs.

A person can't be in this land of rain long without be'n amazed. Where does all the water go? All streams flow into the sea, yet the sea is never full. At least they haven't been since the great flood.

Fer some reason see'n Haines from the boat fer the first time reminded me of the Klondike. We drove off the ferry under broken clouds and bits of sunshine. It was beautiful.

Haines was like most far-north towns. Pockets of never-ending construction partly 'cause of the short summer season. Side streets of gravel had healthy potholes. The town's original Indian name fer Haines was "Tehshuh" which meant "the end of the trail." I told Butch I hoped not fer us.

We wasted no time get'n to the big saw mill north of town. Pull'n up to the office with our shiny new Alaska plates, we'uns figured we were up to snuff.

Part of the reason fer our confidence, we'd heard this here mill had a big contract to haul lumber to Fairbanks. All part of the oil pipeline go'n in. Yes-sir-ree, they needed us. The big log'n boss had us fill out a sheet of paper. Sez me, "I'll fill it out if you're hire'n?" He assured me they needed cutters pretty bad. Halfway down this sheet they asked the dumb question where we attended school. Oh-h-h-h-h-h,

JOURNEY TO THE BACKWOODS

this was not good. He'd know we were from New York! Well we shall not lie. We filled 'er out, and he said come back in the morning.

Butch thought we should get a hamburger and go see all them superstitious totem poles. I didn't know one totem from another, they told some story in the carvings. Haines was like all these log'n towns in log'n country, over the door of the café a sign read "NO CAULK BOOTS." Look'n down at the door-sill I could see not everyone obeyed. Times sure have changed. Now the sign sezs "NO SHOES, NO SERVICE."

Where does society go from here?

They sure fed you a monster of a hamburger in there. My memory fades or I'd give credit to the gal who gave us our money's worth and served it with a great attitude. In my estimation, too little credit goes to those food service folks. And far too little pay.

After a tour of the town and the old Fort Seward, we found a gravel pit to spend the night. Sit'n there in the pickup with the windows rolled up, we had a contest who had the most mosquitoes on their side. And they were robust buggers too. This last frontier had frontier size everything. We leaped out and dove into the back hoping most wouldn't follow us. Perty tough get'n much shut eye with those whine'n vampires about.

Ain't much darkness in that country com'n into summer. Most loggers are used to burn'n the candle at both ends. Go'n to work in the dark and drag'n himself home in the dark. This was quite a change.

A COUPLE OF WOOD HICKS

If'n a man worked from dark to dusk here, he'd be one tired slave.

Seven o'clock found us back with "the boss." He was really look'n us over. "You boys say you've cut timber before?" Look'n at Butch he read off the sheet, "Sez here you cut in Arizona? What did ya cut there, cactus?" Butch's red hackles rose up and informed "the boss" that they had big pine in the mountains there.

He then turned his attack on me. "Sez here you logged in New York? There ain't no trees in New York. So how could you log there?" I was ready fer him. I asked him if he ever went bowling. He did indeed bowl a lot when he lived in Oregon. I then filled him in that us "ol boys back there cut the maple they made the pins and lanes from. Yes-sir-ree, right there in Lewis County, New York. Cut by a bunch of wood hicks.

He put a big chew of snuff in his lip. "You start day after tomorrow, pay is $110 per seven-hour day. Job is down at the Sullivan River. Call this number; he's the bull buck. You'll ride in his boat." We took the piece of paper and thanked him kindly. We wouldn't have thanked him so kindly if we understood the boat ride. Us cheechakos might be sourdoughs in no time.

Most of the loggers in Alaska were from Washington or Oregon. Leo, our bull buck, was from Prineville, Oregon. "Ol' Leo had been in Alaska over twenty years work'n in log'n camps. Ol' Leo proved to be a man to ride the river with. He was a timber man who seemed to be knowledgeable in most everything. And time proved that he was. As good an all-around hand as you ever met, a tough and savvy hunter, a friend to lend a hand. Yup, I liked Leo right off.

Leo had a fourteen-foot tri-hull boat with a lot of horsepower. It was a stable boat all right, but the Lynn Canal had a rough rip tide. (Current go'n out while the tide is com'n in.) The tri-hull hit those waves and beat ya to death. The job was just start'n, so they needed wood on the ground, me and Butch was the only cutters so far.

Leo had his D6 dozer dropped off from a barge. And a big two-wheel log'n arch he would use to haul the logs onto the beach, that is when the tide was out. They also dumped off some old Cat tracks. Leo buried 'em out at the edge of low tide. We then built a "stiff leg." A two-log ramp overlapped way out into low tide water. It was there we tied up the boats. We cabled the stiff leg to the buried tracks. I guess you'd call it a log'n dock. The rafts of logs would in time be tied up there too.

Before the stiff leg was built, the whole crew got a laugh off Terrillion.

Leo floated us up one morning to fall timber. By then we had two more cutters—George and Bill. Well sir, everyone bails out with tools and gas jugs. Leo asked me to tie up the boat. So I did. To make a long story short, everyone showed up at the boat at three o'clock. No, the boat wasn't gone, it was tied hard and fast right where I left it. Only the tide

A COUPLE OF WOOD HICKS

had gone out. There laid the tri-hull listing to the starboard. I was ever embarrassed.

Ol' Leo just smiled. He then realized I'd never been around tidewater before. He took pains then to show us all how you push the boat way out. A small anchor laid on the bow. When the boat was out to the end of the one-hundred feet tie line you pulled the anchor off. The anchor was tied to twenty feet of line to the boat. Thus the vessel stayed out with the anchor. Regardless of the tide, you could always pull in anchor and boat together. I told the fellers, "To err is human; to forgive divine." It was all in a day's work.

George and Bill were old Alaska loggers and had some good stories to enlighten us (or scare us). Bill said we needed a bigger boat. Seems like a few years past he'd been rid'n to work in a half-submerged craft. It sank!! No life preservers. He grabbed the only thing that would float. An empty gas can. Up in that country you will last about twenty minutes in the water. Bill said his legs turned numb a hundred yards from shore. The only thing that got him to the beach was the empty gas can. I was wonder'n why Bill missed every day the water was rough.

George said the only reason he took this job was he heard there was some cutters from New York. He just had to see these guys fer himself. George had a great dry humor.

After our rough ride to town that night, we stopped by to parley with Leo. He welcomed us right in. The first thing I noticed was a beautiful griz rug on the floor. Leo said they was a story behind this hide. Over a cup of coffee that would float an ax head, we heard a frightening tale.

Leo had been moose hunt'n just north of Haines. He'd gotten to his favorite trail, only to see someone had dragged out a moose the day before. They used some all-terrain outfit. Leo went on up anyway and planned to turn off. When he turned off the trail, his daily duty called and he took the proper position to get the job done. Squatting there he heard a snuff'n noise com'n down the game trail. Peer'n through the devil's club (thorny brush), holy smoke there was griz sniff'n along. Leo figured the best defense was stay'n down till ol' bruin got out of sight. Which he did. Hav'n finished his job, he had a funny feel'n. Turn'n around there was griz!! Twenty-five feet away. Leo picked his rifle up off the backpack and stood up, griz stood up too. The stand off started in earnest.

Now ol' griz can't see fer beans. But he's got the best nose in the meat-eat'n business. Leo knew from that distance with a .30-06 to kill this bruin out right was if'y at best. He wished the carnivore would just leave. Minutes dragged out into painful time. Leo's arms were feel'n fatigue from the weight of the gun. It gradually had settled under his arm. The brute gave away his intentions when he laid his ears back—he charged. Leo pointed and pulled the trigger. The beast roared!! Leo leaped off to the side!!

A COUPLE OF WOOD HICKS

Griz landed on the packboard and proceeded to mangle what he thought was human. Leo saw his chance, walked up and plugged the man mauler behind the ear. The first shot had hit the bear in the shoulder, broke it, but caused no great immediate harm. Leo produced the packboard. No doubt about it, a mangled mess of intended slaughter.

Anyhow, our conversation got to the crew boat. Leo agreed we needed a bigger craft. The big boss had a sorta cabin boat, a six-man outfit. I wondered what would happen when the crew got to the intended ten.

The new boat worked out well with the six-man crew. We cut our travel time almost in half. Even had a little time to fish there at the stiff leg in the afternoon. Leo usually wrenched a little every day on his Cat parked there among the fifty-five-gallon barrels. Seemed like every town, log'n and mine'n site in Alaska had a collection of these colorful metal forget-me-nots; known by some residents as "our state flower!"

Ol' Leo showed us the inside of his parts van. They was everything in there from first aid to candy bars to fan belts. And back in the corner a .30-06 pump rifle—loaded to the gills. Now that we were practically sourdoughs, we'uns knew this to be the bear gun. There could be pearls to work'n in paradise.

Log rafts began to appear on the beach at low tide. The company hired a couple of young yahoos to steel band about a truckload in bundles. All these

JOURNEY TO THE BACKWOODS

surrounded by the boom logs, which the tug boat would pull to the mill. It was a sight to behold.

The crew had grown to ten, including a burly 250-pound mechanic. The boat that once sped on plane, now slushed along half swamped. And life jackets!! The only flotation device on the craft was the engine cover. Vinyl-covered foam on plywood. The big mechanic perched himself upon it. His ample paws clung to it like an old maid's hug. He had staked his claim.

As the days passed we welcomed that boat ride about like one would the IRS. We found out according to law, the company had to at least have a shack on the job fer emergencies. We pressed Leo know'n he would talk to the big boss. Soon the plywood and 2x4s showed up. Me and Butch looked at this one room hostel, dirt floor and all, as Survival Hilton. We moved in without a housewarming.

The boys had built a couple of bunks, but we had no mattresses. Not to worry, sez me, sez I, plenty of moss hereabouts. We packed a lofty mass on each bed. We would sleep like babies.

About two o'clock I was bitten awake. Red ants!! The vermin had infested my sleep'n bag. I exploded immediately into the St. Vitus dance. The sun was just dipp'n over the rise, since it never really set, when I burst out through the door with Butch in hot pursuit. Needless to say, we spent the rest of the night into morning pick'n the red devils out of our clothes and sleep'n bags. We still weren't sourdoughs.

A COUPLE OF WOOD HICKS

That afternoon I resorted to an old Adirondack trick. I cut up fine spruce boughs and made bedding with a woodsy smell.

After our days cut'n was over and the crew left, me and Butch roamed along the Sullivan River. Eagles were everywhere, no danger of be'n endangered here. Here and there a feather, but never one from the tail.

The boys claimed they may be gold in these here hills. But I never contracted gold fever—the local malaria. There was plenty of stuff fer fools there; fool's gold.

One Sunday afternoon I decided on a nap. Butch, .30-30 rifle in hand, decided to cross the river and explore. The river was shallow and easy to wade. I watched him disappear, think'n I should have went. I may miss out on some adventure. And how.

The sun was high and warm when I awoke. No Butch. I made supper and still no Butch. I began to be concerned so hiked off towards the river. Lo and behold, there was Butch on the other side look'n like a drowned rat. I couldn't believe the river, now churn'n and roar'n along plumb white with glacier silt. The sun had melted snow and ice up in those mountains that was older than written history. I kept wav'n fer Butch to come on. And he shook his head no and pointed to the river. I figured well, guess I'll have to go over and see what the deal is. I needed a walk'n pole to steady myself in cross'n. Spott'n one close by, I bent over to pick it up. WOW!! What a bear track!! My first instinct was to take a quick look

JOURNEY TO THE BACKWOODS

around. At least the prowler wasn't in sight. Good grief. It made a man's hair on his neck stand on end. I measured it using my hand fer a rule. Nineteen inches long!! Including the claws of course.

My mind shot to Butch's dilemma. Grab'n my stick, I hurried into the river, quartering upstream. About a third of the way across I began to fight fer my balance. And then my legs went numb. Ice water of the purest form. This is what Butch was try'n to tell me with all the hand signals. I had no choice but to retreat to shore.

Safely back on dry rocks, I gave Butch the hand talk to just hold on. Look'n down the river a little ways, I saw a cottonwood tree floundering in the current. The top protruded halfway across. Convinced this was the means of rescue, I began to demonstrate pole-vaulting. Butch picked right up on the method as I kept point'n at the tree. He proceeded with much caution out to the end. Plant'n his pole, he almost went fer it. But caution be'n the better part of valor took control. Ol' Butch tossed this pole into the current and stomped back to shore. This was get'n serious, sez me, sez I.

With twilight com'n on and Butch soak'n wet and big foot griz stalk'n about, I had to do something. Then it hit me, the old timberjack skidder back at camp. The company brought it out to help put the rafts together. Just maybe.

Again giv'n Butch sign language to hold on, I raced to camp. Making sure the old bucket of bolts had fuel, my heart sank when I looked fer the key.

A COUPLE OF WOOD HICKS

The mechanic had took it out! I sank back into the seat. Look'n back towards Sullivan River, I heard the hush of the vast wilderness. Over across the Lynn Canal the snowcapped mountains shot into the clouds. Moody Mother Nature stand'n there in all her naked grandeur, I couldn't afford any moods. I turned my whole knowledge towards the Timberjack. I must get this monster started. Tak'n the side panel off the engine, I located the starter and the injector pump. Ah-ha, the pump was manual, no wires. Therefore, the key was only to transfer battery to starter. I ran into the shack and got my saw wrench, tied down the throttle, and shorted out the starter—the hunk of iron roared to life. I sprang up into the seat like ol' Roy onto Trigger. "Hang on, Butch. Here I come."

I kept to the beach, so when the tide come in, it would erase the tire marks. When deal'n with the government one can't be too careful. The boss had cautioned the mechanic operators about go'n out of the timber sale area. I was on a mission of mercy head'n out.

Butch heard me long before he saw me. Plung'n into the river I shot the rapids. It would have made a great take fer *Ripley's Believe It or Not*. Butch was ever glad to see me and jumped aboard the iron horse. We roared to safety.

Back at camp over supper Butch shared the near tragedy. Like I figured, the river was low when he went over. And melt'n ice caused the river to swell. Com'n back across, his legs turned numb and the

JOURNEY TO THE BACKWOODS

current swept him off his feet, the .30-30 rifle gone forever while Butch was rolled under. As fate would have it (I don't believe in luck), Butch was thrust upon a half-submerged log. Force'n his head above the water, the water's pressure held him there as he pulled himself towards shore. Jonah had the whale. Butch had the log. Both, I believe, were there at the appointed time.

Old Bruin never did show up. We weren't disappointed in the least. Another bloodthirsty roamer did, however. Old Lobo. We began to notice where he'd been chasing a moose out on the beach. No doubt the moose went in the water to escape ol' fang.

On our next weekend boat ride into town to do laundry, I expanded on my trap'n venture. The boys really hoo-rawed me on that. "New York, there ain't no wolves in New York."

"Maybe I'll just catch this wolf," I sez. The fellows almost fell out of the boat.

In town we proceeded to the necessary evil of wash. Toss'n our duds into the suds, we headed to get some chow. Tak'n longer than we should, I sez we should get back and do the dryer thing. Arriving at the laundry mat, we were greeted with a pleasant surprise. An Indian gal who ran the place had dried our clothes and folded 'em and done it with a smile. Ya know, there's some nice folks in this evil world. She sezs, with a shy smile, "Boys, you need bleach in your white things and wash them separate." 'Course me and Butch had saved money and lumped 'em all together.

A COUPLE OF WOOD HICKS

That weekend we needed some saw parts. The company said a timber beast named Deardorf carried saw parts. He lived at twenty-seven mile marker off the Haines Highway, a place called Mosquito Lake. Let me tell ya, this here lake was properly named. I reached that conclusion as soon as I opened the truck door. We were dive-bombed by the little blood suckers.

Mr. Deardorf and family lived in their picturesque Alaskan cabin. No electricity. A small gas generator was operated two hours in the morn'n and two hours at night. This kept food froze as the freezer was only opened once a day.

Deardorf, the timber faller, was built fer the part, just under six feet, broad in the shoulders and hands that hung almost to his knees. His shirt was hard pressed to contain his robust frame. He proved to be the man from the old Alaskan school, helpful to all. And do not take advantage of a man in need, 'cause it will come back to you. Anyhow, he got us all rigged up.

Back in Haines, driving down Main Street I laughed at a couple of bumper stickers: "Lottery: a tax on people who are bad at math." The other one was on a car from Oregon, "Alaska for Alaskans."

Next morning when the boat left, I had a couple of traps and some beaver castor. Told the boys I'd show 'em how to catch a wolf. I got raised eyebrows.

That day I left the traps buried in spruce boughs. I knew they'd take on that scent. That evening I used rubber gloves to handle 'em. I dug a small hole in the ground, put the beaver castor in there, and covered the trap. As the days went by, the boys were pleased with their snickers and who-raws.

I checked it religiously anyway and smiled a lot. Then one morning there he was, Old Lobo sit'n there in that trap look'n awful foolish, but not as foolish as the boys. I told 'em I may open a New York school of trap'n should I ever pass this way again.

Nothing great was ever done without much enduring.

—St. Catherine of Siena

CHAPTER THIRTY-FIVE

HANG 'ER UP AND DRIVE
Circa 1973

Butch said his feet were get'n itchy and wanted to go to Oregon. He had friends there. And me, I was miss'n the family perty bad. Also phone reports

Down through the Yukon

HANG 'ER UP AND DRIVE

said the mill needed help and Geraldine was having gall bladder attacks and needed an operation.

The morning we left, big boss paid us off and sez, "I'm go'n to miss you fellers." I guess in his own way he gave us a real compliment. He never did say if'n we were sourdoughs or not. I guess we weren't 'cause the boys told us what a true sourdough was—"Sour on Alaska and not enough dough to get out." Well sir, we hung 'er up.

Out on the road again, we headed fer Haines Junction and the Yukon Territory. The scenery was breathtak'n. Places like Chilkat Pass, Mount Mansfield, the Tatshenshini River, Dezadeash Lake, Kathleen Lake. We was glad we'd left early 'cause we needed to get Canadian money fer our journey. And if memory serves me right, they only had a bank there on Fridays. Yes-sir-ree, things were different in the far north.

Stop'n at a small store in Haines Junction, we inquired where the bank was. The old sourdough pointed up the road and sez, "You can't miss it. Look fer the big Mountie." Not want'n to act like a couple of tourists, we departed. About a hundred yards farther we passed a white van with side doors open. And stand'n in front with arms folded on guard was the biggest Mountie in the world. I looks at Butch and sez, "Can't be!" But there it was, the once-a-week bank of Canada. We did a u-turn and parked. There in the van behind a card table stacked with money was a banker. We exchanged paper, thanked

JOURNEY TO THE BACKWOODS

the moneylender, and left. I noticed that Sgt. Preston never blinked or moved. That guy had discipline.

Roll'n down the Alaska Highway, I saw wilderness one only dreams about. My-oh-my, mountain grandeur, lakes, and rivers, Alaska couldn't lay claim to be'n the only great land. Forever tattooed in my mind is that part of God's creation. After see'n all that, how could man ever feel great about anything he constructed?

We drove all night, the wheels humm'n another song, the song of the Northern lights. Look'n out the window, I saw the great firmament of stars. It took me back to my boyhood, lay'n there on the grass at Uncle Vinny's tak'n in a warm July night. Them were shine'n times.

About noon next day we ran out of coffee, and sandman had caught up to us. Neither of us could drive no more. We pulled off the road to stretch out on the banks of a river. Surprise, surprise, bugs by the millions also loved this lovely spot. We tossed out the sleep'n bags, crawled in and pulled the top shut. Sounded like a beehive out there. And in no time sweat was pour'n off me. This wasn't go'n to work, sez me, sez I.

No rest fer the wicked and very little for the righteous.

After a ten-minute nap in the truck, we blazed on down the road again. We managed to stay awake discussing everything from log'n to hunt'n to politics.

That night we figured on stop'n at a fuel and coffee shop out in the middle of nowhere. At least

HANG 'ER UP AND DRIVE

the map showed one. Sure enough, it was there but closed. Stay'n awake was turn'n into an endurance trial. Just at daylight I dozed off, and I was driv'n!

It had rained the day before, and the road had been graded day before that. The only packed gravel was right in the tracks. Once the tire caught the soft wet shoulder, it spun the steer'n wheel out of my hands. I woke immediately. Too late! Down the steep embankment we headed. I steered 'er straight and locked up the brakes.

Butch bolted awake!!! "Terrillion!!" he yelled as he embedded his fingers into the dash. This was truly a rude awakening. Somehow I managed to miss all the boulders. Approaching the bottom, I could see an old access trail. I made a ninety on it and headed right up to a cross road, never miss'n a lick, shifting into high, and continued on our journey. Butch said he'd never drift off again.

The wild and brave country received my total attention. About mid-morning I spotted a huge bull moose up ahead. Never one to miss an opportunity to create some excitement, I cut him off before he got to the road. The brute stood there in the ditch look'n us over. Then he went to go behind the truck. So—o—o—o I backed up. Ol' Bullwinkle just stood there look'n us over again. He decided to go around the front. So—o—o—o I moved ahead. About then he commenced to slobber and shake his head—a face only a mother could love. Butch looks over at me and sez, "Terrillion, I don't know if you've noticed, but this mad moose is fresh out of patience,

JOURNEY TO THE BACKWOODS

and he's on my side!!!!" I figured perhaps I should move on 'cause this old bogtrotter might put some dents in my truck. I thanked him fer the entertainment and drove on.

Our trip down through British Columbia was more or less a scenic drive. We did see a few more moose but only at a distance, and a lynx sat on the bank just off the road, just look'n around like he was go'n to cross the highway as soon as it was safe. Next stop Sisters, Oregon.

We found Herman, the big Norwegian, at his shake mill. Butch would work fer him a few days cut'n cedar up in the mountains. Butch had been there the year before and said he didn't recognize the place. Herman said some developers from California had bought land and were go'n to town on it. Good ol' capitalism. Anyway, Butch got a room at the local hotel and I managed to sleep three hours. I felt like a zombie. I'd been liv'n on black coffee.

That night I bid Butch good-bye and nosed the old pickup fer New York. It was that long, lonely road down into the corner of Idaho thru Utah. And Wyoming. Now I remembered the endless ribbon of blacktop.

Way up ahead I could see a hitchhiker. Back in them days it was fairly safe to give a man a lift. As I drew closer, I saw he had nice clothes hang'n on the roadsign. Well, why not I figured. Lo and behold, he turned out to be a truck driver. Sez he was head'n fer a Sioux City truck stop. I put him right behind the wheel.

HANG 'ER UP AND DRIVE

Wheel'n along, he told me his story. Seems like there was a major difference of what the trucking company said they would pay and what he ended up with. So he quit the outfit in Oregon and been hitchhik'n. Said a truck just left him off at that intersection a few minutes 'fore I come by. I thought maybe I could catch a little shut-eye. But Hills-Brothers had me so wired there was no way.

He proved to be a great driver and good traveling companion. I couldn't sleep but at least I didn't have to drive fer quite a spell. I hated to leave him in Iowa.

The rest of the journey was a desperate struggle to stay awake. I would doze off, catch myself wandering, then pull over. Crawl'n in the back, I figured now I could sleep. NO WAY!! Hills Brothers still had a grip on me. I sang a lot to stay awake. And remembered old weather rhymes—"When the windows won't open and the salt clogs the shaker, the weather will favor the umbrella maker." I finally pulled into my place five days and nights after leav'n Haines, Alaska. I was thankful to be home.

It is worse still to be ignorant of your ignorance.
—St. Ambrose (340-397 A.D.)

CHAPTER THIRTY-SIX

WHERE DOES YER STICK FLOAT?
Circa 1974

The weeks away from all that responsibility of the sawmill and log'n outfit had mellowed me out. Now it leaped upon my back once again. Try'n to operate on a shoestring. Try'n to buy timber in a very competitive market. Sell'n pulp and lumber at prices set by the big companies. I felt like the dandelion who wanted to close up before the approaching storm.

Nuth'n to do but tackle the only thing I knew. Back into log'n with the sweat of my brow.

We were haul'n a lot of pulp to St. Regis and the price and the scale weren't any better. Alaska was sit'n on my mind. The West was in my dreams. It was tough to keep my heart in my work. I was a dreamer of dreams. And then Butch called again. "Terrillion, let's tramp!" sez ol' Butch.

JOURNEY TO THE BACKWOODS

Shack where me and Butch Pate holed up on the Lynn Canal, and the wolf the N.Y. trapper caught.

Come to find out he only stayed in Oregon a few weeks and came back to New York to visit his folks. He worked awhile for his dad, but they was too much alike. Said he was go'n back to Oregon, a place called Spray. He had a promise of a cut'n job there.

Well sir, I went into a Great Depression. After see'n the great West, how was I to ignore Horace Greeley's advice. I decided to take it and proceeded to sell out.

What I couldn't sell I gave away. Except my stud horse "Jack."

My partner ended up with my diggings, the whole kit and caboodle.

Geraldine had that contained worried look on her face. I was so excited I couldn't think straight. And the kids were too young to savvy any of it.

WHERE DOES YER STICK FLOAT?

I'd bought an old single-axle travel trailer. At least we'd have a place to lay our weary heads down at night. I had some things that wouldn't fit into the trailer so stored them at Mom's. She was all concerned about our leav'n the place where we'd been born and lived. Not to worry, I told her, God would take care of us. At the time I wasn't very close to God, but I knew she'd take great comfort in it. After mak'n arrangements to keep my horse, we kissed Mom good-bye and pulled out.

We'd bid farewell to everyone we could think of. They all thought I'd lost my mind. But I was head'n where the timber was as tall as my hopes. Remembering Uncle Vinny, Uncle George, and Uncle Tony, how they'd always been my trail to high adventure back in my youth. Now the mountains of the West would be a new great adventure. Look'n over at the wife with five-month-old Rosie on her lap, I could see adventure was the last thing on her mind. The other three young-uns were in the back of the old Ford pickup. The canopy made it possible fer them to crawl around, and I'd turned the whole pickup bed into a playroom. Geraldine was not really impressed. This was it, I told myself, drive'n through Croghan. And don't look back. But I did look over at the school where the nuns had tried so hard to drum some academic sense into my head. I remembered the words of admonishment, "You'll end up digging ditches if you don't study." I smiled for a moment and then felt a bit of anger. I concluded the bullies that had plagued me there were nuthin' but mean-spirited urchins.

Indian summer was just a few weeks away. For the first time in my life I'd miss the red and golden autumn. I wanted to look back at those mountains that my boyhood knew, but I didn't.

Those Blue Mountains of Oregon had much to offer I told myself as we pulled onto the New York thruway at Syracuse. That is if we ever get there between the potty stops and the I'm thirsty stops. In the rearview mirror I could see the kids wav'n into the canopy window. I got pretty good at figuring out if it was a serious crisis or a bored one.

Then there was Chicago loom'n in the distant haze. I'd sooner face an old sow bear with cubs than drive through that madhouse again. It had to be done. So I gritted my teeth and told myself–Self, it ain't no tougher than cut'n timber. The only difference here is dangerous people instead of dangerous trees. We ran the gauntlet and emerged on the other side safe and secure.

Somewhere in western Illinois we camped at a K.O.A. I didn't consider it real camp'n but the wife thought it a safe place. The kiddies got all snuggled into bed with full tummies and Geraldine was already start'n to get homesick. I slept like a hibernate'n bear.

The journey was not to be without mishaps however. Somewhere in Iowa the pickup's rear wheel bearing went haywire. Up ahead I could see a ramp leav'n the interstate, but I couldn't make it. I pulled

WHERE DOES YER STICK FLOAT?

off down into the barrow ditch, and Geraldine gathered the children together and hid out in the trailer, lock'n the door.

I took off at a dog trot fer the nearest farmhouse. One thing I knew fer sure, you were seldom turned down when you needed help out in farm country. Knock'n on the back door, I was greeted by the farmer's wife. She invited me into the kitchen while I explained my problem. She knew just the man I needed. Down the road a piece was a junkyard owned by the handiest mechanic. She apologized she couldn't drive me 'cause she had dinner in the oven. But please call, she urged. "Sure thing," was the junk man's reply, "I'll be right over."

After thanking her warmly, I'd hardly make it out to the road when an old beat up pickup pulled up. "Hop in, and we'll go see what ya need," sez the old man with a big smile. He wheeled down the interstate till he saw my outfit on the other side. Traffic was light so he bounced down across the meridian. In no time we had the axle out. The bearing was in several pieces.

Back at his shop, he found a perfect axle match and with no delay we was put'n the part in and ready to roll. Our resources be'n rather limited I braced myself fer the bill. Sez he, after look'n my outfit over, "How's ten dollars?" I had to ask again think'n I may have heard him wrong. Ten dollars it was. My regret was I didn't get his name; he was a gracious and generous man. I guessed he would never be rich or didn't care to be, know'n he came into this world with nuthin' and would take nuthin' out of it.

Meet'n folk like I did that day renews your faith in mankind.

Out across Nebraska the wind was howl'n awful bad. With such a head wind, the gas mileage wasn't nuthin' to write home about. I started to count my pennies.

Across Wyoming the wind kept at it. Fifty miles per hour was all I could coax out of the old Ford. Once we dropped down into Utah we finally escaped the gusts.

Then it happened again. The bearing went out on the trailer!! This time the traffic out of Ogden was fierce and hardly any shoulder. The semi-trucks liked to blow my little rig clean over. By now Geraldine was fit to be tied. She again sought refuge in the camper while I tried to keep from get'n run over tak'n off the wheel.

Look'n around try'n to figure which way to go I noticed what looked like another junkyard over and down the road. With broken parts in hand I raced through traffic and managed to climb the fence into the yard.

It took me a while to find the office 'cause I came in through all the junk cars. The owner was wait'n on someone, so I struck up a conversation with a young feller who had a cast on his leg. Seems like he broke it in a construction wreck. He was look'n fer some part to fix his old Jeep.

WHERE DOES YER STICK FLOAT?

I filled him in on my sorry state of affairs. "P-s-s-s-s-st," he softly sez, as he motioned his head back to the door. We held a parley out of earshot of the counter. He informed me that the owner of this pile of wrecked steel was known to take advantage of ya if he knew you were in a bind. I followed him out in the yard. He offered to run me over where they made trailers to get new parts. He said the folks there would treat me right. And so they did.

That nice young fella then took me back to my outfit.

There Geraldine was with the kids down in the barrow ditch. Seems like a concerned highway patrolman came by several times and told her she'd be safer in the barrow ditch. And when I pulled out, I had another regret. I never wrote down that helpful Samaritan's name either. It was years later that I came to realize that Him who knows even when a sparrow falls was with us as we traveled. No doubt Mom was praying too.

We made it to Central Oregon without further trouble, pull'n into Spray one hot September afternoon. We'd made it with thirty dollars and change to spare. We would surely need a friend in the com'n weeks.

Be slow in choosing a friend, slower in changing.
—Ben Franklin

CHAPTER THIRTY-SEVEN

OLD LOG'N CAMP
Circa 1975

We'd only been in Spray a few days, and Butch sez the job he was on had sawed out. "Terrillion, let's tramp!" Geraldine gave me one of those where-now? looks.

Near LaGrande there was an awful beetle infestation. Them there bugs was kill'n nigh every pine in the area. The only way to slow 'em down was to log the trees before they could hatch out and move on.

Us loggers answered the call.

But where to live when we was near penniless? The money grew on trees over there but first you had to cut 'em down. And then wait two weeks fer a draw on yer pay. A man cut'n timber can only tighten his belt so far. Not to mention a man would feel worse then a heel to see his family go hungry.

JOURNEY TO THE BACKWOODS

Old Logging Camp in Oregon.
Rosie, Dale, Tina, Tracey, Geraldine, Troy

ol' Butch offered to float me a loan till I got my draw. Old Job of the Good Book should have had a few friends like I did.

This log'n operation was near a place called Starkey. To arrive there we headed to Ukiah, then down the winding road towards LaGrande. After many miles of beautiful timber and the Blue Mountains, we crossed a semi-open plateau. We no more than dropped down into a canyon and off to our left saw a neat cluster of old railroad cabins. It was part of the Old Mount Emily Log'n Camp. A friend of Butch's suggested we stop here first.

OLD LOG'N CAMP

The good folks there may have thought we looked like a remake of *The Grapes of Wrath*.
We felt like it.
There was only three cabins occupied full-time. One was Grandpa and Grandma Benson. Not only did they own an empty cabin they'd rent to us with no money down, but we soon found they'd become adopted grandparents.

The cabin wasn't very big, but it had to do fer now. It was two railroad cabin cars set side by side. They were fastened together with a doorway cut between 'em. One was kitchen complete with wood cook stove and living room, the other bedrooms and bathroom with no toilet.

The outhouse was out back. And there wasn't even a "monkey" ward catalog. We no more than got there and daughter Tracey had to go. I pointed her to the weathered old facilities. It leaned a little towards the northwest. I went back to work unload'n when out around the cabin she came, still holding her knees together and yelled, "I can't go in there, it smells so-o-o-bad." Well, her mother got her straightened out and a little later I investigated the problem. Un-huh, the culprit was neglect. No one had put any lime down there in a coon's age.

Be'n a couple of hours from town, I thought of beg'n from the nabors. But my pride wouldn't let me do it. After all they'd already been so generous. Then I remembered the old backwoods trick—wood ashes. Check'n the ash pan under the stove, it was full. I dumped the contents down the hole and took care of that bad smell.

We slept and cooked in the camper till I got the cabin all straightened out. Butch slept in the shack on the floor. We wasted no time in chase'n down the man who owned the log'n outfit. A Mr. Ackley.

Yes, he needed timber cutters. We'd get fifty-seven cents a log. We'd start next Monday.

The weekend gave us time to organize our saws and gear, and get to know the other camp members better.

The Woodards, next door, cut corral poles and hauled 'um to big ranches in Nevada. Mrs. Woodard was the Bensons' daughter. They had three sons still there at home and a daughter married and moved away.

They was down-to-earth folks and the best of nabors. The dad's name was Bud. He showed me around camp. The big water tank we saw down past the last cabin once watered the hiss'n steam log'n locomotive. Perched there on its huge timbers, like a nostalgic sentinel, always look'n, always reminding those who pass by this was a place of history, dreams, and hard work. It sorta made this place stand still.

He pointed out cabins owned by the "week-enders." Folks came from the settlements on Saturdays and Sundays sometimes to escape the hubbub. And the Bensons' daughter-in-law—a widow, owned that last cabin. Their son had been killed in a log'n accident. A log rolled off a truck and crushed him.

OLD LOG'N CAMP

Whenever they tried to tell of it, time had not erased the pain. They never could quite get the story out.

Up the creek and around the bend was another bunch of camp rail cars. Bud filled me in. That is the church camp. The lumber outfit had given it to all church denominations to take turns for summer retreats. "How good it is when brothers dwell together in unity." The owner had not forgot the God who created the timber in these Blue Mountains. Timber barons usually built empires and left behind stumps and used-up woodsmen. But here was a man who had his head screwed on right. Every once in a blue moon you are privileged to work fer someone of this caliber.

Monday morning me and Butch awoke in the early darkness like good loggers. Geraldine fed us the old woodsman's standby—flapjacks and eggs with lots of coffee. "Early to bed, early to rise makes you healthy, wealthy, and wise." At least that's the old fable. I couldn't ever see myself wealthy, but the rest made sense.

Up the Grande Rhonde River we drove. Log trucks were already com'n down loaded with logs. I concluded the loader operator must have slept in the cab of his machine. The side rod showed us where to cut, and we went at 'er.

The timber was mostly mature lodgepole pine. Two thirty-three-foot logs to the tree. Clean timber with hardly any limbs. Our goal was 225 logs per day. We laid our timber out nice, and the boss liked our work.

JOURNEY TO THE BACKWOODS

We started at 6:30 so we figured to quit about 3:30. Well sir, about 1:30 we saw other cutters head'n out, and we didn't pay'em much mind.

They was lots of spruce mixed in with the bug-killed pine so made it harder to fall our timber. 'Course be'n newcomers, we got stuck with the toughest spots. But we just went ahead on 'er. In due time we got a payday.

I went to town and bought a used commode from a second-hand store. Poor people have poor ways. Then a ten-gallon hot water heater 'cause it had to be 110 volt. The breaker on our pole was only twenty amps.

Put'n the john in was no trouble till I started dig'n a hole fer the barrels that was to be my septic tank.

I knew better than involve the EPA.

It was pick and shovel all the way. The wife looked on with great anticipation. The kids danced around the hole and played "King of the Hill" on the ever-growin' dirt pile. Even the Woodards next door cheered me on. I was soon to find out I had the only full-size bathtub in camp.

By hunt'n season we had all the comforts of home. We still slept on the floor on foam mattresses. No beds fer awhile.

An old oil pot burner supplied heat when the cook stove went out. Someone gave us an old overstuffed couch and chair. Kitchen table and chairs were secured cheap from the Salvation Army in town. God bless the Salvation Army.

That fall I shot a big muley buck. Then I shot at a spike elk and killed a cow that stepped in front just as I pulled the trigger. My first elk, and it was illegal.

I decided to haul it home in the pre-dawn 'cause I needed the meat and figured the fish and game made a lot more money than I did.

I hung it in the woodshed to cure, as we didn't have no freezer. The Woodards would soon have room in theirs.

Meanwhile it snowed a little, and the elk came down to the highway. Some dummy shot a calf just up the road from the camp, right in the road. I seen the whole bloody mess next morning when I went to check some coyote traps I'd set.

I knew John Law would soon descend upon my humble shack.

As providence would have it, I'd been given an old pony fer the kids. I kept her down in the big corral just beyond camp. A huge manger was across one end. I laid my cow elk quarters on canvas and covered 'um with hay (old Indian trick).

Just like I figured, next day when I was out cut'n timber the game warden showed up. And asked permission to check all sheds. He was treated with the utmost courtesy. "Sir, this and sir that." That night as I dragged my body out of the pickup, everyone rushed to fill me in. The good officer never went near the old corral. Winter's meat was secure.

Heavy snow in the high country soon shut us down. I hadn't worked long enough to draw

JOURNEY TO THE BACKWOODS

unemployment, and the winter ahead looked mighty bleak.

I caught a few coyotes and managed to keep the wolves away from the door.

The elk kept us with good meat. But the two oldest kids were go'n to school and needed things. Then we had to go to town once a week to wash clothes. The stove needed oil. I knew I had to tramp.

They needed timber cutters in John Day. I fixed up the heater in the old camper. It was the last of January and really cold, with about three feet of snow over at that job.

The family all gathered around fer a hug and a kiss. It was a long drive to John Day.

The San Juan Lumber Company was go'n strong back in them days. The office got me all fixed up and I parked in a trailer court. The place was used by loggers. They had heated bathrooms with showers. That was the great thing about a log'n town. Most everyone worked fer a liv'n. Folks were accommodating and trustworthy. A totally different atmosphere than a town that catered to tourists.

We were cut'n up near some divide. Every morning we took a crew bus from town. It held about eight of us. There was a big trunk like in the back, sorta under the rig. In there we put our saws and gas. First day gas leaked out, and you could smell it all the way to the job. We were blessed with a legendary cutter around them parts named Julius Farmer. When we got to the job ol' Julius marched right up to the boss and told him in no uncertain terms that

OLD LOG'N CAMP

there would be no gas cans hauled in the bus no more. And if they tried tomorrow morning, no one was get'n in that bus. I was impressed!!

Next morning the boss put all the gas cans in the back of a company pickup. We climbed into the crew bus. Ol' Julius sat there arms folded, facial expression of a mounted policeman. He meant business, and they knew it. He was right. Those leaky cans were a disaster wait'n to happen.

An old timer once told me the only union a timber cutter had was the right to quit. I said amen to that.

I stayed a few weeks cut'n there. But it was hard there at camp fer the wife. The old oil stove quit 'cause it had some water in the line. Woodards came and fixed it fer her.

Spring wasn't far off, and we managed to struggle through till May. The big mill in LaGrande was need'n to get back at that bug-killed timber. One day a log'n boss pulled down into camp. Sez he, "There a log cutter liv'n here we've heard about?" "That would be me," I answered him. They hired me on the spot. Seems like the boss from last year told him I did good work. I thanked him kindly.

Things in our government run in spite of government. Not by aid of it.
—Will Rogers

CHAPTER THIRTY-EIGHT

LIFE WAS BETTER
Circa 1975

A steady check does a lot to lift a family's spirits. Not to mention lifting one out of poverty. The common man needs honorable work and decent pay. That summer and fall I had both.

Life was better now than in New York.

Go'n to work about dawn every morning to do what I loved made me want to do good work. And as an extra bonus I saw elk and deer with newborn most every day. An occasional bear or bobcat would hit the road in front of the pickup. What more could a work'n man ask?

There at camp, the sunny days soon melted all the ice away. The children played under the big pine trees and paid many visits to Grandpa and Grandma. Evening left plenty of time to have a campfire to roast marshmallows. Troy played in the creek and

JOURNEY TO THE BACKWOODS

Cutting timber in Oregon

caught a few trout. There was lots of time to visit, no one had a TV, and it was here we learned the value of reading, almost totally lost today among the Internet of information.

Sometime that summer "ol' Butch" came to visit. He'd been work'n somewhere near Prineville. He wanted to buy my camper, so I sold it and bought a mule named Skinner. I had plans to go elk hunt'n in the mountains come fall. I'd pack Skinner, or so I thought anyway.

When I went to look at this mule, the owner led me out to a round corral. There stood old long ears watch'n our every move. The man had a lasso 'cause he said Skinner didn't like be'n caught. He assured me once your hand was upon him he was ready fer work.

LIFE WAS BETTER

Round and round the corral ran Skinner.

It was all too obvious. The owner couldn't rope fer beans. But after several empty loops the noose finally settled over the sorrel's neck. Skinner froze. This was a good sign, I figured. The man worked his way down the rope, all the while tell'n Skinner what a good mule he was. I wasn't so sure.

He'd gotten about five feet from Skinner when mule let out a terrible snort and took off. Round and round they went. 'Course the man lost his foot'n and was be'n dragged, mud and manure fly'n in all directions. The owner was a gutsy fellow; I gave him that, and he hung right on. In a soft voice, interrupted by the spraying of mud, he called, "Whoa boy, whoa now." Me, well I just jumped in the middle of the corral and watched this catch that had gone Western.

After several passes I figured if'n I didn't do something that poor man would get dragged to death. I made a move to intercept the mountain canary. Be'n smart as all mules are, Skinner didn't like the odds and stopped.

By then even the mule was breathing hard. He stayed put this time while we approached. The man said, "Oh, ya don't look him in the eyes." Seems like he forgot himself awhile back.

One thing Skinner had go'n fer him was his looks. He was one good look'n mule, slick as a cow pony and nimble as a cat. In spite of his nonsense I liked him. I bought him. He loaded good when I threatened him with a stick.

JOURNEY TO THE BACKWOODS

Once in the trailer, the man told me he'd bought him last year in Bishop, California, mule capital of the world. On the way to Oregon by way of the deserts of Nevada he let Skinner out fer exercise. Not a good move. Skinner pulled the lead rope out of his hands and ran off. It was then he realized why the mule had the name Skinner. If'n ya held onto the rope too tight, you lost the skin off yer hands. It took him two days to catch the run-a-way. I was hav'n second and third thoughts now.

Back at camp Skinner fell in love with Penny the pony. The mountain canary would really sing if'n ya took Penny out of the corral. It was a comical racket.

Towards the end of summer Butch came again and brought a friend from Madris, Oregon. They had an old car that was on its last leg. The transmission was go'n and all it had was first gear. They went into town and bought another car and now had to get rid of the old one.

Up the road from camp a couple of miles was an old rock pit. We used it fer a dump. Butch decided this should be the last resting place fer the old jalopy. The pit on one end was deep with a sheer drop off about fifty feet. They pointed the old bucket of bolts straight fer the cliff. Wired the throttle wide open, tied the steering wheel in place and then reached in the window to pop the thing in gear. The gravel and stones flew as the wreck raced to its tomb. She shot off the cliff and landed in a great crash. We all whooped like a bunch of cowboys at a rodeo.

LIFE WAS BETTER

With idle time on his hands, Butch could be dangerous. The boys hung around a few days, and we made plans fer our fall hunt.

The grass was perty tall around camp so I let Skinner out to graze. However, with his reputation to be caught I put a long chain on him with a pronged wolf drag. This way when he tried to get away he'd get caught in the brush. Everything went fine till Butch showed up.

One evening Skinner was feed'n down along the main driveway. Our cabin was up on a knoll about fifty feet away. Butch was lean'n up against the woodshed with his arm rest'n on one of my spare tires. I heard Butch say "Skinner," and I looked to see the tire bound'n at a high lope right at the mule. Well sir, he took one look at that leap'n black demon and took off in a cloud of dust, chain fly'n high. He hit the chokecherry along the creek and never slowed down. The heavy wolf drag's prongs were now straight. Up the mountain he went, snort'n every other jump. He soon disappeared in the brushy timber draws. It's never a dull moment with Butch around.

I didn't see Skinner fer days!! 'Course I went to work every morning and was too tired in the evening to go hik'n up on the mountain. I figured Saturday morning I'd go look; perhaps he was tangled up somewheres. Friday, while I was at work the wife spotted him about a hundred yards up on the hill. I then devised a plan. Knowing his love fer the pony, I took her out of the corral and made believe I was leave'n camp. It was more than old Skinner could

JOURNEY TO THE BACKWOODS

stand. Down the hill he came, bray'n all the way. Once around the corral I just led the pony right back in, the mule close behind.

Early fall came, and I worked a lot with Skinner. He never warmed up to me though, and I could see me chase'n this critter all over the backwoods. About then I ran into an outfitter named Shorty. He was rid'n a gentle old black horse who obviously needed a rest. I noticed Shorty was a real mule man. So I worked a trade, Skinner fer old black. He sezs it's a deal.

I seen Skinner a few times after that, Shorty always had him last in the string. Said he was one of the best mules he ever had. But he always kept him in a small corral and roped him.

That fall Brother Tom came out and went elk hunt'n with us. The Woodards went too and Butch. We camped about ten miles back in the Minium Wilderness. Tom got a bull, and Butch got a cow. We had a great time.

About then we had a near tragedy at the cabin. Bud Woodard and one of his sons was over one night fer a visit. I was think'n of sell'n my Remington rifle, and he wanted to see it. I always left it in the gun rack in the pickup. He sent his son out to get it, and I warned him I always had one shell in the magazine. He came back in and handed it to his dad who bolted it, aiming at the wall, and pulled the trigger. "Bang!!" right through the wall. You could hear a pin drop after that fer what seemed like an eternal silence. It shook up everyone. I never let anyone handle any

LIFE WAS BETTER

of my guns since without check'n them myself. We hear of so many hunt'n tragedies every year. Guns are dangerous. Handle with care.

Butch had left to stay at a ranch near Monument, Oregon. Old Ray, who owned the outfit, was a friend of Butch's. I got an invite over to hunt mule deer—I left the next day.

Ol' Ray lived alone on his little spread and turned out to be quite a feller. Part cowboy, part logger, good mechanic, a fair rancher, in other words just a good all-around hand. And I might add a top-notch rattlesnake catcher.

Well sir, ol' Ray invited me right in to sit down and said he'd pour me some cowboy coffee. I turned to sit at the table and froze. There fer a center piece was a rattler in a gallon glass jar. Ray barked, "You know, I never did like to eat alone!!" All I could think of was guess who's com'n to dinner.

Anyhow, Ray had this here viper there fer six months and gave it no water and one live mouse. The snake killed the mouse but never ate it. Said he had to fish the deceased rodent out with a clothes hanger. And very carefully, he added.

Ray had a thing fer rattlesnakes.

He said they'd get under the planks in the floor of his shop. Then when he'd crawl under a rig to work on it, the varmints would crawl out and keep him company. Some company!!

Then he acquired Mickey. Mick was half heeler and half lab and all muscle. Quickest doggone dog in the West, and that ain't no exaggeration either. He

JOURNEY TO THE BACKWOODS

trained Mick to grab the rattler's tail before it could coil whenever he tipped over a plank. Mick would snap the reptile out where they couldn't get away and ol' Ray would put a cowboy heel on 'em and take off their head and tail with his knife, all in that order and faster than you can read it. They pretty well cleaned out the snakes around the buildings. There on the shelves was proof, a large jar full of rattles. Ray was sure proud of his dog.

Once while out building fence, Mick came to Ray with a young turkey in his mouth, unhurt and in good health. Ray had big plans fer this bird. He took it home, put it in with the chickens, and they raised it. The next year Ray got a handsome Tom and before long he had sixteen wild turkeys roost'n in the barn. That fall I was awakened by their throaty gobblers. Past the window they'd parade, all sixteen of 'em.

The following year the sneaky coyotes got every one. Ol' Ray was perty upset. So that fall I went over and trapped some coyotes, little consolation fer the loss of his beautiful birds.

That same summer the turkeys disappeared. I stopped by to visit Ray once in a while. I was so impressed with Mickey, I told Ray I'd like to have him if he ever decided to get rid of him.

Mick didn't get along well with Ray's cow dogs. Fact of the matter was the place was in a constant dogfight. After break'n up one of those fights one evening, Ray was really mad. Yell'n at me to "Load up that dog before I shoot him." Ray went stomp'n

LIFE WAS BETTER

into the house while I proceeded to load Mick. When I went to lift him into the pickup, he bared his teeth at me. This wouldn't do, sez me, sez I. Know'n Mickey could jump over anything, I took his favorite bone (the one that caused the fight) and tossed it into the back. In he leaped, and I slammed the canopy top down.

Back at camp I opened the canopy just a little and gave Mick a piece of meat. He sniffed it real good and with one eye on me he gingerly took it from my hand. Mickey soon forgot Ray's place and went with us to Alaska and New York and Montana. He was a great dog.

I sure enjoyed those trips over to Ray's place. The hunt'n was great. But most of all, the hospitality was unsurpassed. And the knowledge I gained from ol' Ray beat a college degree many times over. And as usual it was a whole lot cheaper.

After hunt'n season I had to go back to work. There's the bumper sticker again: "Born to Hunt—Forced to Work." A lot of us hardcore hunters felt that way.

However, jobs were tough to come by in the dead of winter. I finally landed one up near Toll Gate, in five feet of snow. Boy, was it tough going. I had to shovel down to the ground 'cause we were only allowed twelve inch stumps. Then the exhaust from the saw about asphyxiated me. And then, when the tree started to fall, get'n out of that hole was a sight to see. I finally devised a plan. I'd wait fer the tree to get about halfway to the ground, and then leap up on the butt. I was soon catapulted out in the clear. I earned every copper penny.

January brought sad news. Geraldine's dad passed away.

The summer before when work was good I bought an Oldsmobile station wagon. But now I hadn't got a paycheck yet from the Snow Belt. Usually it took a month, and I needed eight hundred dollars fer the trip.

The banks in LaGrande wouldn't consider it. When it comes to borrowing money, loggers are in the same class as migrant farm hands.

Someone on the log job suggested I try the bank in Elgin. Oh well, what did I have to lose? I entered think'n I had about as much chance as a dragonfly on a pond filled with pike.

My experience with banks would cause Frosty the snowman to shiver. Thus confidence in the banking world was at an all-time low. And I was tired of arguing till I was blue in the face.

The girl at the desk directed me to a smiling fellow over in the corner. Somehow his smile looked sincere. He looked me in the eye and had a good handshake.

I just laid it all out fer him and told him unless he loaned me eight hundred dollars I couldn't go back fer the funeral. He looked me up and down and leaped to his feet. I leaped to mine, expecting to be shown the door. He reached fer my hand and asked when could I repay the loan? Caught off guard like that, I sputtered perhaps early summer. He had

LIFE WAS BETTER

me set back down and went to get the papers. It all happened so fast I could hardly believe it.

Sometime in early summer I walked back into that bank and paid in full. The man recognized me as soon as I walked through the door. Somehow he knew I'd come. And he in a loud voice wanted the other people in the bank to know who I was. Apparently he'd been jeered fer loan'n me the money.

As I sat at his desk, he said he very seldom judged anyone wrong. 'cause he once was a used car salesman and had to give it up. We both had a good laugh.

We made our trip of sorrow to New York. In Wyoming we ran into a terrible storm. Snow was pelt'n us on a horizontal plain, driven by the gusts of an icy wind. Somewhere near Rawlins the oil light kept com'n on. I deemed this quite serious and dangersome. There was hardly any traffic and abandoned rigs in the ditch everywhere. Once I got out to check the oil. The door was almost ripped from its hinges. The dipstick said full, and I didn't know what to think. However, it was all decided in Cheyenne—the road was closed till morning.

I got a motel room fer the family and Mickey. At a garage I learned something about cold and wind I never knew. The temperature was so severe the oil had got so thick it wouldn't run back down fast enough. Thus every so often the pump had air and the light would come on. That solved, we arrived on time to pay respects and comfort the hurting.

JOURNEY TO THE BACKWOODS

We visited everyone we could reach and phoned the ones we couldn't. It was nice to see everyone, but I knew there was nuthin' to hold me fer it had lost all the joy it once held. Most of all we missed Mom. She didn't seem to understand why I had to wander all over the West.

When I got back to Oregon they'd shut the Snow Belt job down. I had to sign up fer unemployment. They gave me an awful time because of leaving fer New York before the job shut down. I always hated those places and years later, even when I was entitled to it, I refused to claim it. Instead I learned to trust in God fer work, and He never let me down.

The next summer Butch wrote from Alaska of all places and got me all worked up. Before I could react, he left. Just as well, I'd planned a trip to New York to get my horse and pick up the rest of our stuff.

I'd sold Grandma's lot up on the river back in New York to Brothers Richie and Tom. I figured that I would never move back there anyway. Many years would pass when the property would cause a great argument between them, and I would regret sell'n it.

We spent more time in New York than I had planned. That's the way those things usually work. I did some hik'n up around some of my old hunt'n and trap'n grounds. Yes, I remembered where I shot my first buck. And the spot I got the big ten pointer, my first wolf and fox, the otter and mink. I hiked over in Julius Brouty's flats and recognized where I'd caught those muskrats. There along the back-trails of my memories again it seemed like yesterday. Still, I'd outgrown the country. There was "no trespassing" signs everywhere. I guess everyone wanted to have their own little woods to themselves. I reckon it was their choice.

Mom didn't make it any easier this time either. I think it was Abe Lincoln who said, "No man is poor who has a godly mother." We said good-bye to everyone and took one last look at that "tin tee-pee" trailer house and cabin I sold Bob and one last look at the barn and sawmill where I'd worked like a galley slave.

Jack the horse gave one last whinny to the mares in Andrew's pasture and westward once again we drove.

Driving across the United States with the horse proved a little bit of a challenge. Be'n a stud horse besides, you just couldn't leave him out anywhere. We found a stable in Iowa where he got first class accommodations fer the night, and again in western Wyoming.

Each day I let him out at noon to stretch. I decided to drive the rest of the way without an overnight layover. True to form, we had just entered Oregon, and it was the middle of the night when the state police stopped me. They wanted to see all my papers.

I felt like an illegal immigrant.

Geraldine was scared to death like we'd broken some unknown law, and we'd end up in the crowbar hotel. The officer said I didn't have no brand on this horse. Well, I informed him, in a nice way, you didn't need one in New York. He really gave me the go'n over. Finally, after a talk on his radio, he decided we weren't part of Butch Cassidy's wild bunch. We arrived at the camp without further mishaps.

We settled back into our golden times there in the golden West. I went to work cut'n north of Union, Oregon. The timber was good, but a shyster owned the outfit. He paid us less than he said he would.

Then I cut myself in the rear end of all places. The saw kicked back, and I was on steep ground, my glove hung up in the trigger. What a mess!

At the old sawbones office, he commented over the years he'd stitched up a lot of loggers but never one in that area. Somehow I wasn't proud to be the first.

I had a week off, and my mind got to wandering back to Alaska. And Old George, I decided to give him a call.

His oldest son said he'd moved off to Afognak Island just off Kodiak. Said he was cut'n timber there. It all seemed so far away.

We finished up the job near Union, and I took another over near Heppner, Oregon. It was there I learned about a loader job near Palmer, Alaska. The pay was good and even had a house.

The wanderlust gripped me again.

Big plans began to materialize. We had someone who wanted to buy the cabin fer a little more than we paid. I bought another horse, a mare. I'd haul the

LIFE WAS BETTER

horses with the pickup and Geraldine would drive the car with a little two-wheel trailer I'd built, loaded with our earthly goods. She stated "What was we get'n into?' With much excitement I sez, "Life on the last frontier." She had sort of a frightened look.

Grandpa and Grandma Benson gave us our first Bible. I wasn't into reading it right then, but somehow Grandma knew someday I would.

She well knew that the "Word of God is alive and at times sharper than any double-edged sword." But she never tried to carve me up with it. She was the perfect example of the mature Christian. She was pray'n when prayer mattered more than preach'n. They were of the Baptist persuasion. Drowning Bear, a wise old Cherokee, would have had a whole different view of Christians had he known Grandma. He once commented on the Bible: "It seems to be a good book, strange that the white people are not better, after having had it so long?"

We saw Grandpa and Grandma once more. Years later, they stopped by to visit us in Montana. We miss them dearly. Word came to us shortly after that she died in California of cancer. I knew she had gone on to Abraham's bosom. And when the last trumpet blows, we will see her again with our Savior and walk those streets of gold together.

If your ship doesn't come in, swim out to it.
—Jonathan Winters

CHAPTER THIRTY-NINE

HEAD'N INTO THE MIDNIGHT SUN
Circa 1976

Look'n back, I've concluded I was a glutton fer punishment. But at the time the adventure of the whole affair overcame my good sense.

The biggest problem turned out to be the bugs. They loved horseflesh. Somewhere near Fort Nelson, B.C., they proved to be too much.

I spotted a campground with lots of grass and figured we'd make camp. The horses could just be put out on picket. The mosquitoes about carried me off while I was unload'n the ponies. They was some small logs nearby, so I tied 'em to those. I wiped them down with diesel fuel, think'n that would deter the pesky bloodsuckers. It didn't even faze the torturous buggers.

The wife and kids jumped back in the car to escape be'n 'et alive. I was unpacking the tent when

JOURNEY TO THE BACKWOODS

jack horse tried to run off—log and all!! That did it, I opened the horse trailer door and them Cayuses jumped in. There had to be a better way.

I remembered a little store nearby and inquired about a barn. I was told a Mr. Kennedy up the road had a small rodeo grounds and he had barns. I headed there with high hopes.

The ol' boy was everything you'd expect there in the far north, friendly and helpful without fault. "Why certainly," he sezs, "put 'em right here in this box stall." He even had it fumigated, weren't a bug to be found. And gave 'em a bucket of oats. I was grateful beyond words.

We headed fer the nearest bug-free hotel.

Next morning when I picked up my horses, the good nabor wouldn't accept a copper penny. Sez he was glad to help out. We sure met some nice folks way up north back in them days.

But bugs wasn't the only problem we ran into. Somewhere in southern B.C. we spent the night, and I put the horses up at a big ranch. The cowboy was helpful and put my horses up and he wouldn't take a cent either. However, he must have noticed they didn't have no brand. Next morning I only got a few miles when an official look'n car pulled me over, a brand inspector. He sez you just can't go hauling horses around without a brand. I had all my border papers in order. I laid everything out on the hood of the truck. "Looky here," sez me, sez I, "I'm so legal it scares me."

He didn't laugh. He didn't even smile.

HEAD'N INTO THE MIDNIGHT SUN

No loophole could he find. Everything was up to snuff. He was a nice fellow, I think. Just took his job a little too serious.

The miles and the scenery just passed by. And what scenery it was, my, oh my, the mountain ranges and rivers and lakes. And wildlife most people only see in pictures. It was a rugged land. Cascading waterfalls boiling down over boulders. It was breathtaking.

Time and weariness stopped us at a place called Laird River. There was gas pumps and a café.

Tired horses needed out. Jack was first. I had Geraldine hold him while I backed out the mare. Jack, wanting to eat the lush grass, moved and stepped on the wife's foot. And all she had on was sandals. Of course she was in bad pain. The nearest X-ray machine was at Watson Lake, it would have to wait till next day. And big rain clouds were looming not far off.

The com'n rain chilled the air enough to keep the bugs down. The horses had a corral near the café. We pitched the tent and soaked Geraldine's foot in warm salt water. It swelled and got black and blue. The tired family went to sleep not far from the corrals to the beating of heavy rain.

Next morning everything was bright and beautiful except Geraldine's foot. We loaded the animals and kids and drove off, thanking the good folks at the café fer the corrals.

We'd been told just up the road and to the right was a nice campground. We passed it, and I never

JOURNEY TO THE BACKWOODS

thought about it again until years later. I heard a rogue bear had killed some people there. They have some wonderful camping spots in Canada run by the government. But no one had a gun, so could do nothing as the unfortunate people got mauled and killed. At that time I had my guns along, but they were "sealed" with a clip at the border. Sealed or not, no bear was go'n to eat anyone if'n I had my say.

Watson Lake had a nice little hospital and X-rayed Geraldine's foot. The good doctor said the foot was swelled too bad to see if anything was broken. We paid our bill and got a room fer the night. I don't remember where I put the horses up there.

Somewhere up in that country I was reminded to drive carefully. I saw a truck and horse trailer down off a steep bank rolled over. The Mounties were there and a wrecker. I couldn't stop to see, but it looked bad, some of the horses were dead. I couldn't tell about the driver.

Then on a desolate lonely stretch of road I spotted a herd of horses race'n right at us. Out of the woods they charged. Fer fear they'd collide with my truck I slowed down into second gear. Once out in the road they sped ahead of me like the devil himself was on their tail, single file on a well-worn trail just off the gravel. I shifted gears and tried to leave 'em behind. They ran on, manes waving in the wind. The faster I drove the faster they ran, kick'n up almost as much gravel and dust as we did. After a couple of miles, however, one by one they conceded to the greater horsepower.

HEAD'N INTO THE MIDNIGHT SUN

My only consolation was they'd escaped from some outfitter. I drove another hour before I saw a gas pump and café. I needed coffee.

A grizzly character was sole owner and inhabitant. While he poured my coffee I told him about the band of Cayuses way back yonder. Not even look'n up he sez, in a laid-back sort of way, "Ya, them horses ain't hard to find this time of the year. Whenever they hear a car com'n up the road they fall right in so's the dust and wind will blow the bugs off."

Yup, I concluded, them were smart critters.

By and by we stopped at a beautiful lake and picnic area in the Yukon Territory. A nice breeze was com'n off the lake keep'n the bugs away. Snowcapped mountains in the background. It was sure enough to make a man's burdens roll away. I thought it should remind a weary pilgrim of the Promised Land.

I became so mesmerized by the beauty of the creation I plum forgot my stainless steel Thermos bottle. Last I knew it was sit'n there on the picnic table.

Alaska!! Land of the midnight sun. We crossed the border, and the road got immediately worse. Potholes like moon craters. We maneuvered our way to Tok.

The small Alaskan town boasted more dogs than people. I believed it. The curs were everywhere.

We secured lodging fer the night at an old hotel. I liked the setup 'cause I could see the horses from our window. I had 'um tied on a high picket line out back.

JOURNEY TO THE BACKWOODS

It was a beautiful evening. Twilight's amber had been swallowed by evening shadows. The bugs were somewhat less; probably busy harassing the wolf dogs around town. Before I was taken in sleep I noticed the sky had blossomed with a million stars.

The next morning Jack was gone!!

I leaped out of bed like the place was on fire. Jump'n into my clothes, I bolted down the stairs with shoelaces fly'n about most dangersome. I ran down to the gas station. The man in charge took one look at my cowboy hat and sez, "You look'n to find a horse?" I assured him I was indeed. He told me during the night he'd been awakened by what sounded like hoofbeats. He calculated that it was a dream till he asked some other folks a bit ago.

They'd seen the black horse racing north with sled dogs in hot pursuit. I visualized that pack of mutts ripping my pony to shreds. I'll shoot the lot I told the gas station owner as I left. Just then I heard a commotion down the street. Lo and behold here came a Good Samaritan lead'n my horse. He had a pocket full of rocks and pitched one at the wolf pack every few steps. They kept their distance.

By then half the town had gathered to see a horse. The Johnny-on-the-spot wrangler sez, "The horse came right to him probably fer safety." Sez he figured the horse came from this direction, so he'd find the owner somewhere in town. I told him how grateful I was, and he figured it was a good way to start the day.

That day we arrived at our good friends, John and Linda Shue in Palmer. It was good to sit in a real house again. John had built a log cabin and was maintenance man for the Pioneer Home there. They had two sons, good boys. John was from Port Leyden, New York. They insisted we stay in their fifth wheel trailer till we got settled.

Next day I called the outfit to see where and when I needed to start load'n train cars with logs. The news cut like a wind off the nearby glacier in January. They said I was due yesterday and they hadn't heard from me. I'd lost the job.

I didn't take the news well.

Murphy's law had blind-sided me before. But this time it really caught me off guard, what with the family and two horses and a dog. I felt like someone had took the rocks from my brook, and I'd lost my song.

I figured the only thing I could do was call ol' George on Afognak Island. They had a radio system set up there you could call night and morning.

Well, George talked to the boss and got me a cut'n job. I went down first. In several weeks the company told me they had a house on Kodiak Island, and we could rent it for five hundred dollars a month plus electricity. However, I'd have to stay in the bunkhouse and only go in on weekends. At least the family would be closer.

But what would I do with the horses?

Well, Linda found pasture there near Palmer. I'd leave 'em there.

JOURNEY TO THE BACKWOODS

John sold the old pickup fer me. We'd go down the Kenai and take the ferry in Homer, the car and the little pull-behind trailer with our earthly possessions. I'd miss that old Ford pickup. It had carried me to Alaska twice, all over Oregon to Maine. Many a woods road she took me down and took me home. The only time she left me to walk was there in Iowa. Not bad fer 176,000 miles on the same engine, transmission, and rear end. Funny thing about an old truck like that, it was like losing an old friend.

Appreciate adversity.

—Anonymous

CHAPTER FORTY

TO THE ISLAND OF MONSTER BEARS
Circa 1976

Geraldine was not look'n forward to this boat ride. Once I saw the round-hulled ferry, I wasn't too sure myself. Oh it was big enough all right. But driving down the pier to get on, I couldn't see any ramp door be'n lowered. Even Noah's ark had a load'n door and the pier ended just as high as the deck, and I saw the first car drive out right on top. Good grief!! Surely they weren't go'n to lash our rigs onto that deck. All of a sudden the car disappeared down through a hole. Ah-ha, sez me, sez I, them fellers had it all figured out. Must be a new sort of ferry.

Little did I know ignorance was not bliss.

We drove right out on that table like the man directed. And down we went, a giant elevator.

We all gathered up in the forward lounge for a bird's eye view of the journey. And what a view it would turn out to be!!

TO THE ISLAND OF MONSTER BEARS

Ol' George, log cutter extraordinarie,
Afognak Island, Alaska

The captain steered us for open sea, destination Kodiak Island.

The first hour, the kids had a grand time. I took them out on the deck, wind in our faces. Geraldine refused to go out and enjoy the vastness of it all. She told me a hundred times to hang onto the children, her voice overflowed with fear, perhaps Mother's intuition.

Back inside we had lunch while we sat on velvet cushions. This was grand treatment—deluxe accommodations, all of it marvelous fer a backwoodsman.

JOURNEY TO THE BACKWOODS

Back up we went to the forward lounge where I took a toasty nap and awoke to the sound of something break'n—dishes maybe.

Someone was "raising Cain."

What was this rock'n and roll'n my half asleep senses awoke to? I looked around and there sat Geraldine with white knuckles gripped to the seat. And her face was even whiter. The scow was really buck'n and pitch'n and roll'n. I glanced at the bow and breakers were com'n right over. Geraldine wanted help to go to the powder room. And I could tell by the way she held her hand over her mouth she didn't need to powder her nose. We made good use of the seats as supports till we could grip the handrails. I turned my attention back to our offspring.

They were crawling around on the floor. So I joined right in and made a game of it. Like Mother used to say, "Too young to know the danger."

I could see why this vessel was round hulled. If'n the thing was V built it would break in two with such a storm. The old tub just rolled with the punches. This violent storm was just another one of Mother Nature's fits.

After about an hour Geraldine still hadn't come out of the rest room. I started to get a little concerned. I crawled over to the women's door and asked a lady go'n in if she'd check on my wife. She came out and told me not to worry. It was just seasickness.

Geraldine never came out till the journey was over. Ten hours of it and sick every minute!!

TO THE ISLAND OF MONSTER BEARS

I don't remember how many hours we got banged around, but I longed to see land. What few ferry people I saw were quiet as mice and grave as owls.

Finally—finally Kodiak Island. As we walked of onto land I remembered they weren't no Viking blood in this child's veins.

I learned later it was the worst storm of the year, and the ship took such a beating it had cracked and had to be nursed back to Seattle or somewhere fer repairs.

We proceeded to the log'n office, and the clerk led us to our house. It was a comfortable place on a quiet street over looking the bay.

But there was RATS in the garage!!

Mickey was then pressed into service. Whenever I heard any rustling out there I'd throw the side door open and softly say, "Sic 'em, Mick." Ol' Mick sure put the fear into them Norwegian devils. We never did have one in the house all the while we rented there. Geraldine was paranoid they'd bite someone during the night.

The outfit gave me a couple of days to get settled. Next morning I went to the bank. Entering through the doors I wasn't look'n just where I was go'n. Too busy sort'n through my check stuff, I bumped into a curb. I looked up and there it was: a life-sized Kodiak bear. Whoa!!! A ten-foot monster, paws outstretched and a head the size of a backhoe bucket, little beady eyes. Mounted standing like that I noticed the round patch holes on its torso. Seven. I counted 'um twice

JOURNEY TO THE BACKWOODS

just to make sure. Theses things took a lot of kill'n. Man-oh-man, those claws looked like butcher knives. The back of my neck felt a little weird.

Time to head out fer camp rolled around. I gathered all my plunder together, survival gear: black wool longjohns, Filson coat and pants, caulked boots, and my .357 pistol. Hardhat, of course, and cut'n tools, headed up by my old McCullough chainsaw. I delivered the whole kit and caboodle in the morning to Kodiak western flights.

Kissed all the family and crawled into the "goose." Gee, I never had to take a "goose" to work before. And sit'n there wav'n out the little round window, I noticed the water was only inches from the glass. I kept look'n at the floor to make sure the thing wasn't leak'n. The powerful motors roared to life. We were soon skimm'n across the water at a high rate of speed. As the plane's whole belly was in the water it took some time to break the suction. And we were airborne. I think I liked the Beaver floatplane better.

Every man ought to be inquisitive through every hour of his great adventure down to the day when he shall no longer cast a shadow in the sun.

—Frank Colby
American Editor

CHAPTER FORTY-ONE

THE LOG'N CAMP
Circa 1976

Danger Bay soon came into view. It didn't seem like thirty minutes of flight time to me. The log'n camp looked peaceful, nestled there by the pebbled beach. The pilot slid us down into the bay as smooth as a gentle breeze.

As we approached the beach, suddenly the plane's engines really came to life. We roared right up onto the land. This thing had wheels. In the water and in flight they'd been folded right up into the body. If only the old schoolmarm could see the education I was get'n.

Here came a pickup bounce'n down to meet us. Some choker setters had come in too. "You must be the cutter," sez the pickup man. I nodded that I was and told him I was "rabid with the obsession to fall timber!!"

THE LOG'N CAMP

The "Goose" coming in to pick me up

Abusing the pickup, he spun beach gravel fer thirty feet. I could tell driving was not his profession. Come to find out he introduced himself as the side rod (supervisor). I was glad I hadn't commented on his driving. We coasted up in front of the bunkhouse.

He said cutters on this side and rigg'n crew on that side. I would soon learn that though we were all the same skin, we were a segregated lot. Most everyone didn't like cutters 'cause we worked shorter days than everyone else. Mother used to say, "Jealousy is big in the world."

The cookhouse, of course, was the main camp attraction. The cook was Leroy, a passive, quiet man who seemed to be scared to death of loggers. The grub was good and plenty of it all the while I worked there. A few of the men complained because they felt they had to scare the poor man. I appreciated Leroy and told him so many times. And although years later in bigger camps I ate somewhat better, this place was the best assortment of food I'd ever had. I couldn't afford to eat like this at home.

That afternoon I met big Ike. He came in drive'n the cutters in a crew bus. Ira (Ike) lived over on the next island and had been here twenty-five years. Married to a local Indian woman. He was built a lot like these bears. And was a likeable cuss, he was the bull buck.

And it was good to see ol' George again. He had his own trailer in camp for his family. Said the cheap outfit wouldn't let cutters have company housing so he had his own floated in. We made plans fer some serious fish'n and hunt'n.

Next morning as dawn came slowly out of the east, I tossed all my gear into the "crummy." Stuck my peashooter into my pack along with my lunch. I was ready. The road was surprisingly level hav'n been built from blasted rock. To the untrained eye, this looked like it had been put through a crusher. Not so. The drillers and powder men knew how to shoot the pit so's to make little bitty rocks outa boulders. Like good loggers always said, "More than one way to skin a cat."

Everybody but me and George got dumped out at their place of toil. Ira had agreed to let us partner up. Timber fallers most always team up in twos fer safety reasons. If'n one got hurt the other was in hear'n distance to come to his aid. And you shut

THE LOG'N CAMP

your saw off after work'n up a tree to see if your pard was saw'n. If'n his saw wasn't run'n after a couple of trees you hiked over his way and gave him a holler. Your very life may depend on the old fossil.

This timber was Sitka spruce and limby. Us cutters called it "grouse ladders" 'cause a bird didn't have to fly up in it. He could just walk from limb to limb. This spruce was very tough material. Highly sought after by the Japanese for many uses, it made the best piano backs in the world. And fine Cello wood also. The limbs were even tougher than the wood and dangerous if one was wrapped around bent double. You learned to savvy just where to cut the skull crusher. And you learned quick. Or they'd be tak'n ya out on a stretcher. And a volcano erupted!!

That is in 1912, somewhere over on the Kenia and spewed ash twelve inches thick over the Kodiak Island region. This here ash laid on the limbs and moss covered it over, year after year. The old eyeball grinder was in the air every time you fell a tree, but was so fine ya never saw it. Weeks later I began to notice my eyes watered a lot.

I heard a choker setter tell one evening that the dust was ruin'n his contact lenses. Well sir, the old school mar'm would have been proud. I put 20 and 20 together and came up with the problem. After that whenever I was fall'n into a breeze I'd close my eyes fer a few minutes.

The fine dust was so bad on bars and chain that the company furnished them pus files. The stuff was

JOURNEY TO THE BACKWOODS

like valve grind'n compound on steel. And when it got wet and froze, oh brother!! But this was summer and the salmon were run'n.

First day off, me and George loaded our poles in his new pickup. He said he wasn't go'n to be stuck in camp, so he had a new Chevy floated out with his house. Clever fellow that George.

We chose a place called Portage Lake and would fish near the outlet. A huge bear trail led the way.

George had brought his rifle, said he didn't trust my peashooter. Once I saw a bear's hind footprint in the mud, I lost considerable trust myself. I could have laid three pistols in the hole. You couldn't see over twenty yards fer the brush. There was no doubt, the brutes were eat'n salmon, the trail smelled like rotten fish.

Those bear knew where to fish. The trail hit the stream just below a fish ladder. They'd put in this contraption so the salmon could go splash'n up over the falls. Well sir, just below there was a pool full of nice sockeye. Old Burin had 'um all riled up fore we got there. They'd bunched up in midstream. We couldn't get 'um to bite any of our lures. But I finally hooked one on my treble hook by chance. The fight was on. I forgot all about the bears. Up the creek, down the creek and up out of the water. Sez me, sez I, this was worth twenty bucks in anybody's money. After a bit I dragged him to the rocks. What a beauty!!

Then George hooked one and after a brief struggle he lost it. I started to rib him when a small

THE LOG'N CAMP

floatplane flew over. George sez it was the game warden when we heard the plane land on the lake. Sure enough, pretty soon here comes super sleuth. Look'n all official like, he strolls down where we was sit'n. "You know it's against the law to fish within so far of a fish leear?" Cool George, in his quiet way sez, "What's a leear?" The warden stabbed an authoritative finger at the ladder and sez, "That's a leear." George let silence reign supreme for a few minutes and asked, "What's it fer?" The fish cop got a knowledgeable look on his face and sez, "Why its function is to assist salmon up over this falls." George let silence be golden again and then sez, "That's funny, we been here fer an hour and several fish have leaped the falls and not one has used that thing." As if on cue he no more than spoke when a shimmering sockeye flashed over the falls. All three of us witnessed the spawner. The warden was feel'n merciful that day I guess or felt out maneuvered by cool George. At any rate he made it known that we now knew what a leear was. And best be fish'n elsewhere. He wasted no time in get'n airborne again.

Pack'n our salmon out that afternoon up that bear trail gave me the willies. George sez if they charge, give 'em your fish. Back at camp I gave my fish away be'n I was in the bunkhouse.

Every two weeks, weather permitting I got to fly the mail plane back into town. It was a precious two days with the family. The three oldest in between jump'n up and down told of school and read'n, rite'n and 'rithmatic. We always went down town to see

JOURNEY TO THE BACKWOODS

the same few stores. It was a good walk together. Evidence of the abuse of alcohol wasn't hard to spot. Whiskey was by the gallon jug. Out at camp I took an occasional drink to be sociable. Till one night some of the crew got so drunk they ended up outside with guns a blazin'. Fortunately their aim was as bad as their tempers, and no one was hurt. More and more as I witnessed this it reminded me of Dad. And how we all went without because of the booze. I got so I didn't care to drink at all.

The 4th of July in the log'n camps is no less than a week off. Most are two. The boss got tired of my ask'n fer a home guard (family trailer) and he said to have the family come into camp fer a week. George would let us stay with them.

Things got perty exciting at the house in town. The goose was to whisk us away. Geraldine got that fearful expression again. I gathered all the kiddies down at the plane dock. Momma had no choice but to come along. The cargo was loaded, and so was we. The water was up near the windows again even higher this time. The kids looked out in awesome wonder. The engines roared, we flew along the waves. And we was way past the buoy and still in the water. I noticed the pilot working the lever over his head and had an angry look on his face. After think'n we were go'n to camp without lift'n off we did leave the water. The plane ever so slowly left the ocean farther under us. The pilot still looked angry and was peel'n someone out on the radio. He circled camp like they always did to alert the pickup

THE LOG'N CAMP

person. And to my surprise headed back to town. It was a rough landing.

The plane had hardly stopped, and he bailed out with long strides stomping into the office. As I was get'n out I heard him yell, "Who weighed that freight?" Seems like someone forgot to weigh the cargo. And we were dangerously over loaded. He didn't sit down at camp 'cause he feared for a crash and wanted it to happen next to town. The ol' boy was in the right. Ruffled feathers and all.

We had to wait till morning.

Our flight was picture perfect the next day. The family didn't know quite what to think of the log'n camp. The weather was co-operative even if the black flies weren't. Troy caught some rock bass right from shore. The kids had great wonder as we explored the shoreline. Starfish and crabs were met with shrieks of delight. Horse clams spit streams of salt water at faces of discovery. Low tide was a child's fairyland.

Get'n my hands off the power saw fer a few days didn't hurt my feelings a bit. My ears were hurt'n fer the first time after years of absorbing that racket. It didn't help matters any by pull'n out the baffles in the mufflers. It gave me more horsepower. I just loved to roar them big trees off the stump. Geraldine had picked me up a pair of earmuffs made fer shoot'n; I needed to use 'em whether I wanted to or not.

The week passed all to quickly, but fog set in and planes couldn't fly. The family had to leave, so they sent out the company tugboat. The kids thought it

JOURNEY TO THE BACKWOODS

another adventure. Mother didn't think so after her ferry ride and spending most of it sick to her stomach. They cast off with much regret and fanfare.

Camp life returned.

Nothing great was ever achieved without enthusiasm.

—Ralph Waldo Emerson

CHAPTER FORTY-TWO

BEARS BEYOND BELIEF
Circa 1976

The company was mov'n a lot of timber. Trucks hauled big loads to the end of the road, there to be loaded on huge barges by a monster Manitowoc crane. Ocean go'n tugs towed 'em to Homer. There they was sawed into timbers before being shipped to Japan. All this when they was still some common sense in Alaska timber industry. Now they ship the logs in the round and thus have taken away a lot of American jobs. Greed and graft in Washington, D.C., has no patriotism.

Our cut'n areas started at the road and worked our way along ribboned boundaries. We usually had to walk alone to wherever quit'n time found us the day before. After a week or two we had a trail of sorts through the muskeg and devils clubs and alder. We had to work at these trails to make 'um usable.

BEARS BEYOND BELIEF

I soon discovered I wasn't the only one walk'n in and out. Bear tracks began to appear in the mud, and mine disappeared!

Danger was now my constant companion!! The scary thing about these brown bears was half the time they didn't know their next move. And even scarier, the other half of the time I didn't know their next move either.

Stand'n there in the drizzle'n rain sizing up those incredible prints made me reconsider the .357. The pride of Ruger didn't do much fer me.

That night in camp we struck up a lively discussion on bear protection. That day another cutter had watched a big brownie come up his trail after he had his saw run'n. Yet another cutter, who had recently been fall'n timber out of Sitka, told us about a narrow escape from the claws of death. "I was cut'n the last bit of timber near the side of the unit. My partner had left about an hour before 'cause they weren't enough room fer us both. All of a sudden this pile of teeth and claws come charge'n up out of the brush. I had just shut my saw off to head out. One look at that thing, and I figured my life wasn't worth the price of a cancelled postage stamp!!" By then everybody was on the edge of their bunk. And to make matters worse, he fooled around roll'n a smoke. He'd told the thing so many times it was old hat to him.

"Instinct caused me to fire up my saw be'n it was the only weapon I had. The beast stood on his hind legs, and I almost wet my pants. Those critters at ten yards will put the fear in ya now. I kept horse'n on the trigger, but the fool beast just stood there. So I started fer the road all the while a-gas'n on the trigger. I thought I had 'er made. He came down on all fours and stood there. Then charged me again. I had that old Homelight wound to the limit. He stayed between ten and twenty yards and followed me right along. The road wasn't far but all I could think of was this saw is go'n to run out of gas. The rigging crew was just sett'n the yarder and I knew they kept a .30-06. That fool bear followed me right along. The yarder engineer heard my saw, looked over and figured he better do something. Usually I wouldn't trust my life to a rigg'n man but that ol' boy could shoot. Saved my hide he did!"

That did it. I figured all that .357 would do is aggravate these giants. Next morning I devised another plan. I started to carry my .30-06. And so I walked in and out with a great sense of security. It was somewhat of an inconvenience because of my other gear. But I made up my mind these salmon snatchers wasn't get'n me without a fight. I knew my -06 was the medicine these bruins needed.

Till the sow chased the crew bus!!

It happened like this. Roll'n up the road one morning we had a different driver, another cutter 'cause Ira took his boat and went home fer a few days. If'n you drove you got ten bucks a day extra. Anyhow, we popped over a hill, and there in the road was two cute little cubs. The driver lays on the horn and stepped on 'er. The baby bears took off across the road right away. About then mama hit the road

BEARS BEYOND BELIEF

and headed towards her offspring. The crazy driver lays on the horn again and before you could blink ol' sow swapped ends. Here she came fer the crummy. By then the driver had enough sense to stop.

Let me tell you, a GMC suburban don't feel so big with one of those Kodiaks bear'n down on ya. The hair on the back of her neck stood up a foot. Her lips were curled and rolled like last week's lottery ticket. There was a lot of snap'n and gnash'n of teeth. We threatened our wheelman that if'n he didn't back off he'd never drive again. He took it seriously. Give'n some room, the old sow backed her way to the woods, cute cuddles stay'n close behind. As a parting show of authority, she stood on her hind legs just before she entered the woods. The old girl had my respect.

I walked those trails every day and observed the concealment of the brush. I couldn't see over fifteen yards. I decided it would take something like a 458 to save oneself from be'n abused and overwhelmed by the king of bears. I didn't want to be found one day in a pile of bear dung.

Then I came by another plan.

I started to carry an extra gas jug fer my saw. I always had an extra gallon come'n out at night. In the other hand I carried a trusty Bic lighter. If a man-eater charged me he'd have a trial by fire. This one thing I thought I knew, bears didn't like fire. I thus carried that jug the rest of the year.

Along towards October when nature had exhausted summer, we got our first snow. About four

JOURNEY TO THE BACKWOODS

inches of wet stuff, all stuck to the heavy limbs of the spruce. It was not a happy bunch of cutters slosh'n up the road of misery that morning. We'd be like drowned rats inside of two hours. Be'n out in the woods all yer life, you learned not to quarrel with the weather. So while Ira drove and jaw'd with Mike in the front seat, the rest of us dozed. Our dreams were about sunshine, lay'n in a hammock tied to some huge yellow pine. Then Ira slammed on the brakes.

"It's that same bear," he assured the crew. "What bear?" we all yelled in one voice with every face gawk'n out a window. There it was, printed in the new fallen snow, the largest bear track north of Seattle. Ira further assured us it weighed 1,800 pounds.

Now we all knew Ira took an occasional nip in the evening but never till quit'n time. So we'uns just started to figure he was put'n the shuck on us newcomers. At any rate, he climbed out, so we figured the coast was clear. And it looked like the monster had been up to high jinks—he'd been drag'n something, or so we thought. On closer examination we discovered it was his hair drag'n in the snow. We all gathered round with our mouths in a fly catch'n state. I ran to the crummy to fetch my log'n tape. The ruler didn't lie; twenty-two inches long with the claws and eleven-and-a-half inches wide. Yup, it was—it really was. No one made a motion to track the thing down into the brush.

Back in the crummy we was all wide awake. Some started to prod Ira on how much he really knew. He starts off tell'n us that there bear hide would square eleven to twelve feet according to the width of the track. He went on to tell us how he knew that bear personal like. A few years before, the Fish and Game came to him ask'n where the biggest bruin was on the island. They knew none of their biologists had a clue. At the time Ira was guide'n bear hunters hereabouts.

They set out bait.

'Fore long Mr. Giant was com'n fer the handout. They had a helicopter just over the ridge wait'n, and when the time was right they swooped down. After a brief chase they tranquilized him. The chopper was equipped with hang'n scales. Hoisting the mass of flesh up, the scales tipped 1,800 pounds. And that's how he knew; we had no reason to doubt him.

The day was even more miserable than we thought. It started to rain, which caused the brush to be even wetter, if it was possible. I found an extra heavy limbed spruce near my strip and brushed it with another tree. Once the snow came off I decided to eat my lunch under it. Sit'n there with my lunch box open and shake'n from the cold, I remembered that ol' drawing again. The one in *Loggers World News*. It showed a bunch of cutters hunched around a skimpy excuse fer a lunch fire. The rain was a-pour'n down while they munched on soggy sandwiches. Under the sketch it read, "A picnic every day!!"

I had to smile about the ol' boy find'n some humor through the dreariness of the circumstances.

JOURNEY TO THE BACKWOODS

Off to my side I heard a rustle. Glancing over, there was a pine martin root'n about in my lunch, so close I could have touched him. He seized a piece of meat and beat it. Figure'n he'd be back, I slid it closer and stuck my hand under the lid. Sure enough after a few minutes he peaked around the tree. I kept my face straight head while track'n him out of the corner of my eye. When he climbed back into the bucket I quick shut the lid. But no use, there's not many critters faster than a martin. He blew out of there before the lid slammed shut. I couldn't help but laugh. He came back fer several days to an entrée. The little beggar stayed just as tame even after my several attempts to box trap him.

Then George shot a bear.

Not a huge one but an average-sized male. They hung it down in the shop and skinned it. The thing stunk like they all did there—rotten salmon—phew!!! George sez he shot it twice in the heart, bang-bang. Then the thing came after him. He leaped back into the pickup and went back'n up faster than he'd been drive'n forewards. The enraged beast chased him a hundred yards before drop'n dead. Sure enough, there was the two bullet holes, two inches apart, right through the heart.

I decided not to shoot one fer the cost. The outfit in town that sent the hides south charged three thousand to complete the job. I didn't have that kind of money. Someone had a fox farm back in the thirties on Kodiak. Once the price fell through, they just turned 'em loose on the islands. I trapped

BEARS BEYOND BELIEF

a few. Then the grader operator in camp stole some on me, so I pulled my traps. "It takes all kinds," Mother used to say.

When the weather got bad—in the fall it was always bad—crab boats had to wait out the storms there near camp. After a few days the boatmen needed to wash their clothes. The boss let 'em use our machines, and they came bearing gifts. Bowls full of picked King Crab meat. Well sir, I never had the stuff before so just dove right in. Perty tasty it was. And perty rich too, I realized too late. About midnight I awoke with an urgent need to find the commode. I spent half the night there. And besides the problem on that end I noticed I had breath like a buzzard's. I didn't quit the stuff entirely after that, but well, let's just say I became a conservative.

As fall started to turn into winter, the weather came in a howl. My subconscious was tuned to the window near my bunk. I usually wake at 5:00 a.m. Breakfast was at 5:30. The wind whistled me awake and caused me to moan. As any timber cutter knows, you don't cut timber on a windy day 'cause if'n you do, you won't live to collect yer dough. One can only stand so many days hang'n around camp. And not get'n in regular to see family was give'n me the itch. Another cutter, Tennessee Crocket, who was a direct descendant of Davy, was ready to tramp. He talked me into it. We quit together.

The boss was wait'n fer us when the plane landed in town. Said he'd give us a raise if we stayed. Ol' Tennessee told him he thought the outfit was a cheap one, and he didn't work fer cheap outfits. I agreed.

JOURNEY TO THE BACKWOODS

Geraldine was overjoyed to hear we was leave'n. She just found out behind our rented house was an old Russian Orthodox graveyard. The steep hillside sometimes washed out a bone or two. This woman across the street from us was give'n all the info free of charge. She didn't like loggers.

I had this book at the time that gave every sawmill in the West. So we decided to try for a small one in Cody, Wyoming. I called, and they needed good loggers.

Then Butch called.

We decided to meet him in Seattle just before Christmas. We'd fly from Anchorage. Now all I had to do was get the car there and the horse trailer that was still at John's in Palmer. And my horse? What would I do with my ponies? I concluded it was go'n to be a lot harder get'n out of here than it was get'n in. At least we weren't rid'n that ferry out.

The ship'n company assured me that the car would be put in a container and hauled to Seattle—no problem. We paid the fare.

All the loose ends were tied up. With our personal baggage, we waited at the Alaska Air building. The size and layout could hardly qualify for a terminal. However, it was adequate to provide passengers' needs in the mid-seventies.

I watched the 727 come in fer the landing think'n this here runaway looks perty short. The pilot had put on all the stops, so it looked like to me anyway. The plane was fast approach'n this huge pile of dirt and rock which ended the runway. At the last minute the pilot braked just the right wheel and the thing did a 90 to pull up to the building. No doubt the man at the controls had landed here many a time.

The handful of folks wait'n to board was motley look'n Alaska types. We fit right in, dog and all. Old Mick gave a soft growl behind me and caused me to turn around. A couple of fellers came in, each drag'n a deer, four feet tied together. When they got to the counter, they just stuck 'um through the scales to be loaded like so much baggage. The gal just swung the carcasses around and never batted an eye. Only in Alaska.

Our flight stopped at Homer—a gravel runway with a one-room shack, and on to Anchorage. The Shues picked us up fer a short stay over at their place.

I had no more idea than the man in the moon what to do with my horses if'n I couldn't sell 'em. Had it not been fer the Shues I'd have been in a pickle. In a few days Linda Shue found a buyer.

From the telephone, arrangements were made to load the horse trailer at Sea-Tac. It would arrive, so they said, same time as our car in Seattle.

The Shues' hospitality allowed us to hang out, giv'n enough time for our car and trailer to arrive in Seattle. The day they were due, we waited to board a DC10 at Anchorage. It was snow'n, and our flight was delayed, not from a wintry standpoint.

There was a moose on the runway.

Once the delay was ran off into the forest of birches, we took to the friendly skies, dog and all.

As iron sharpens iron, so one man sharpens another.
>   —Proverbs 27:17

CHAPTER FORTY-THREE

BIG SKY COUNTRY
Circa 1977

As we circled Seattle and got below the clouds, I could see a little green grass where everything hadn't been paved over. Safely we had arrived back to the lower 48. We called a cab to deliver us at a motel where Butch awaited us. "Terrillion, let's tramp," was Butch's greeting. Geraldine envisioned another wild-goose chase.

With the wife guard'n the little ones and our plunder, Butch took me to get our car. It had arrived safe and sound at the docks. The horse trailer, however, wasn't due to be unloaded fer a couple of days. Back to the motel.

A busy highway ran close by our place of confinement, and keep'n the children busy and out of the road became a monumental task. And Butch, bored to death, picked on Mickey. Ol' Mick would

JOURNEY TO THE BACKWOODS

Left to right back, Tina, Geraldine, and Dale
Left to right front, Troy, Tracy, and Rosie

growl like a bear but never bit him. And I had to take the canine out a couple of times a day to do his job. We were as out of place there as a mud hen in a chicken coop.

Two days came and went, and they weren't any closer to unload'n the trailer than before. And a lot of our personal stuff was in there.

Butch had done some research in my tramp catalog. And he thought Missoula, Montana, would be a better place to winter than Cody, Wyoming. So I made arrangements to send my trailer via Garrat Van Lines, and we left the hubbub behind.

It was cold and snowy in Missoula. And the stench from the big pulp mill was not too inviting. The place might be nice to visit, but this was one old woodsman who wouldn't find a lair thar abouts.

BIG SKY COUNTRY

We scanned the paper and found a trailer east of Bonner to rent. It wasn't much, but we'd get by fer now.

While I waited fer my trailer and cut'n tools, me and Butch went seek'n land. This ad in the paper told of twenty-eight acres in the Seeley Swan area. The old realtor gave us perfect directions and warned that it snowed in that country. He spoke the truth, the whole truth.

Three feet of nature's white wonder awaited us.

A lodgepole pine thicket complete with elk tracks. It was love at first sight. We stomped around with our map of sorts and agreed the place was out'n the woods. Just the way we liked it, and easy to divide up. I figured Wyoming wasn't the place fer a timber cutter.

We made the deal. $1,000 every three months. It would prove to be a struggle fer me. Butch, be'n single, would end up pay'n more but would take eighteen acres. I'd keep ten.

Geraldine wasn't in no hurry to see the snow field we'd bought. I assured her I'd have a cabin up as soon as the snow melted. She finally consented to have a look. Struggling through the winter wonderland, she wanted to know if it always was this deep. I told her to look on the bright side. The kids could slide here fer months.

By now Butch had got itchy feet again. And wanted to tramp off to California. We'd found work, but the price didn't set well with him. Montana

JOURNEY TO THE BACKWOODS

wasn't noted fer pay'n its loggers a fair wage. In the years to follow, I learned this to be the painful truth. Idaho would have been a better choice, but fate had decreed our residency. Fer better or fer worse, it was here we'd settle.

The trailer arrived with our necessities, and I went to work way down the other side of Drummond in a place called Jens. We left the highway and ended up on top of a range of mountains. It was colder than Antarctica. The wind howled and moaned, and the trees were froze solid. You had to cut a deep face so's they didn't barber chair.

The trees were Douglas fir and hard as a bone. The growth rings told the tale, some so close together you couldn't count 'em. One of the locals quirped, "Them's petrified trees!" We huddled around our lunch fire and swallowed our frozen sandwiches. The campfire, be'n the greatest philosopher on earth, brings about the chew'n of the cud. I shared with the fellers what old Jim Bridger once said about a petrified forest he'd found. "Petrified trees stand'n up with petrified birds in 'em, a-sing'n petrified songs." Yes-sir-ree, old Gabe spent many a winter at the Rocky Mountain College learn'n how to tell a story.

We sure did have some roar'n lunch fires. Weren't no shortage of wood. Sometimes we'd set a huge stand'n snag on fire, and it would burn fer days. Com'n up the road fore daylight ya could see the hillside aglow. The only problem with those old larch or fir—they burned so hot ya had to stand back and turn around often. Sure felt good when it was thirty or forty below though. It was hard to get back to work after such comfort.

Work'n in those conditions causes me to wonder how we stood it. Many times I went out way 'fore daylight to put a coffee can of diesel fuel under the motor. And once it was burning you checked it every few minutes to make sure the motor didn't catch on fire. It's not something you look forward to at 5:00 a.m. This backwoods journey had a few potholes. Look'n back, some of that misery I wouldn't go through again fer all the gold of Ophir.

I remember how many times the truck finally started and the radiator froze up, the air be'n so cold from the fan. Sometimes I got a mile or three from home and the steam commenced to fly. I stood out there with the hood up not dare'n to touch the radiator cap, that old blister puff'n and vibrating like a steam engine. I'd get to think'n Mother was right. I should have went to work fer the government. I could've became a summer time shade tree scenery inspector. After all, who knows more about trees than a timber cutter.

But it would be impossible to attend college and get in a forestry class, taught by someone who knew a whole lot less than you did.

Anyway, there I was, prowl'n around the old bucket of bolts, wav'n my arms about like a preacher who had the fire of Hades on the run. You didn't stand around long fore you was frostbit and shiverin' like a jackhammer, just wait'n fer a good Samaritan to come along and give ya a ride. Someday I knew my ship would come in. I hoped it wouldn't spring a leak.

But just like the Creator promised, spring finally came. I went up and cut the right of way into the building site. Troy usually went along to make sure "Dad didn't get hurt." It was hard fer me to keep track of him 'cause I was so used to work'n alone. A man fall'n timber gets so involved in his work it's just "me and my old McCullough." We couldn't hear nothing above the snarl of those things.

Some of them old timers I worked with were a hard-headed lot. Kinda reminded me of me. They were as deaf as a stump. Hav'n put straight pipes on in place of mufflers. We was as independent as a bunch of rove'n cowboys.

I hired a man with a dozer to push out the stumps and shape up the driveway. Sure was a good feel'n to drive up to the cabin site.

By then I was broke and needed to hit the tall timber trail again. Somehow or another I located Butch, and he was cut'n fer helicopter log'n. The money was good but the ground was steep'r than a cow's face, down the river out of Headquarters, Idaho. Potlatch Company had a big log'n camp there and was cut'n white pine. Sad it was, all those beautiful pine was die'n from "blister rust."

I'd bought a Mazda pickup to cut down on expenses and loaded up. Leave'n the family again, as necessary as it was, didn't come any easier. This log'n was tough on everyone.

BIG SKY COUNTRY

The scenery down through the Locksa helped a little but would not replace the time lost from the treasure of family.

Destination: Pierce, Idaho.

Log'n town, U.S.A.—that was my first thought drive'n down Main Street the first time. Stop'n to get gas, I saw a feller in a tee shirt which said, "Earth first, we'll log the other planets later." Most loggers didn't like to take life too serious. Tomorrow ya might be mashed under a log. Plenty of good men from this area had their lives cut short in such a manner.

I found Butch down at the cutters' camp'n spot. He was liv'n in the old camper he'd bought from me. On the premises was part of a shack, one of Potlatch's old camps. It was the "Hilton" in which two other cutters was holed up. Toss'n my bedroll in, I made it three.

Butch introduced me to the cut'n boss, Monty Colby, saw boss extraordinaire. Monty was a middle-aged cutter who just became a bull buck. He was one of the few bosses I ever had who never lost my respect. He was thoughtful, fair, pleasant, and knowledgeable. He'd paid his dues and earned this position. I think he was originally from Maryville, California. He worked all over the Northwest and the log'n camps of Alaska. In the years to come, I would work under him many times. If'n he had enemies, I never met them. When the helicopter outfit had a tough job and couldn't hire enough experienced men, they put Monty in charge. Those of us who knew him would answer his phone call.

JOURNEY TO THE BACKWOODS

Once the paperwork was take'n care of I met the crew—and what a crew!! A happy-go-lucky look'n bunch of roughnecks. Tough jobs called fer tough men. And when the go'n gets tough the tough get go'n. Early in the morning.

We hit the floor at 4:00 a.m. Pat had a hotplate so we could make cowboy coffee. It was chilly there in the mountains at that time of the morning, with even some snow up high. But down on the river it would get sultry and hot by eleven.

The 12E chopper came into our park'n spot even as the day was break'n. Two men quickly ran up with their gear and fastened it to the carrier. They wasted no time climb'n in and were whisked away.

I had to wait till last.

Monty gathered me up finally and instructed me as to the in's and out's of safely fly'n to work. I wasn't exactly look'n forward to this mode of transportation. My first trip was sort of a white-knuckle affair.

I'd already heard the pilots were ex-Vietnam vets and could get a little hairy. But that morning was as pleasant a ride to work as ya could ask fer. And the pilot, see'n I wasn't too sure of this contraption, flew us near a magnificent waterfall. In behind it was several mountain goats, what a picture!!

We started into a heavy timbered draw where someone had fell a "heli-port." Didn't look like no land'n strip to me.

We just rotated down onto two big trees that laid side by side. We climbed out sort of slow like so's the pilot could adjust fer lost weight and balance the bird. Someone has said rules were made so's we didn't have to make decisions. This was once in my life I tried to follow the rules.

The cut'n of this pine was a dangerous proposition. Many of the tall pine had already died. They stood like giant rat-tails stick'n out of the green trees. Potlatch had only bought the green timber still alive. The problem was we had to fall all those dead snags before we could cut the green trees. If you brushed those stand'n widow makers, they were just as apt to come back and get you!! Thus your dear wife would become a widow. And not only that, but the crew hook'n the chokers to the long line on the big chopper feared fer their lives as well. The terrific wind created by the big bird would blow 'em down. Many of these snags had been dead awhile, and the roots were rotten. It kept ya on yer toes.

Better a live dog than a dead lion!

Like I was say'n, this place was a goat farm. Ground so steep sometimes when you fell a tree it turned endways and took off—ya never saw it again. But ya sure could hear 'em go'n, crash'n down the mountain. I must say it was rather excit'n and right up my alley.

One such snag, on a rather hot day, went clear out of hear'n. I was afeared the thing might have made it all the way to the road. That afternoon when they flew me out I spotted it. Lodged in some rocks on a ledge right over the road. Half of it stuck out into space, and drive'n down the canyon after work

JOURNEY TO THE BACKWOODS

I kept look'n fer it. I came around a corner and there was the job superintendent right in the middle of the road. I couldn't stop in the gravel road. He wheeled fer the ditch. I missed him by a millimeter. He wasn't stuck, so I kept right on bore'n down the road. He didn't care fer me after that and was an oily-tongued fellow, tell'n Monty how he narrowly escaped death because of some crazy cutter that Monty had on his crew. Those project managers always seem to have a PR problem with the cutters.

We cut out the quota by the end of June, and the outfit headed fer California. I had jingle in my jeans or as the old timber tramps would say, I was flush. I opted out and decided to go home and start my cabin.

The family, of course, thought it was all peachy-dandy. Ya don't get much accomplished in life without some sacrifice. And it certainly was a sacrifice be'n away from the family. But now I had the money to pour the floor fer the cabin. I hired a couple of young lads who lived near us out of Bonner. The plan was to pour on the first of July.

I was glad to have the knowledge and where-fer-all to complete this task. A man does a lot better in life if'n he has jack-of-all-trades knowledge. A work'n man can't well afford to hire everything done.

By and large the only way the work'n poor could have their own place was to build it themselves. Now-a-days the price of land, dumb governmental regulations, and bureaucratic appointees make it all but impossible.

Anyway, 'fore I get carried away on that, I best get back to the cabin.

We put up the forms fer a slab floor. Time and money was what I had to deal with. Dale Conley, right there in the Swan Valley, had two cement trucks. Ready mix was thirty-five dollars a yard, he'd be there in the morning. We were ready.

But I wasn't ready fer the driver.

The truck pulled in right on time. Climb'n out of the cab was Dale's wife and eight months pregnant!! But I needn't worry, she was cut from that same bolt of cloth that Mom was, the pioneer woman.

We unloaded in no time and she took off fer the other truck. Seems like Dale was get'n the cement ready while she drove. She kept com'n back regular as clockwork, and I was work'n myself to death. Those young lads had never poured concrete before. Run'n that screed back and forth, I was almost do'n it by myself.

The old sun climbed in the sky, and I was sweat'n like a politician the day 'fore an election. We poured the house floor, 50 x 35 and then the shop 16 x 24. I was sure glad to get that over with, and we headed fer Holland Lake to take a dip.

I recollect it was just before dark. I slammed the pickup to a halt and raced fer the water. A nice fly'n leap, and I was breathless. I hadn't considered the snow still up near Gorden Pass that fed the lake. I might as well land into a bed of ice.

Right after the Fourth I hauled in the material to nail down to the floor. In order to nail to concrete ya had to do it while it was green. We still bent plenty of nails.

I'd been driv'n the back roads look'n fer logs to build with. It just so happened they was an outfit log'n right behind the house on Owl Loop Road. They had a pile of big Larch snags on the landing, and each log for the cabin was selected as a friend. The man in charge wasn't the easiest to deal with, and I really had to horse trade the feller.

Next thing was get'n those fifty footers to the site. I hired a happy-go-lucky trucker out of Potomac named Butch Mikesell. He said he was game. It took us awhile to load, they was big. And then he was spin'n come'n up the driveway. The logs hung so far out the back, they was knock'n over trees as he turned the corner. I should have took a picture of that monster load. It's a good thing he didn't have to go down the highway look'n like that. John Law would have had a heyday.

We set them in place with the self-loader. Then I managed to get the ceiling on between rainstorms. Usually it didn't rain that much in July, but it did that year. It soaked up the particle board, it buckled. From a distance it looked like a bunch of sand dunes. I sawed a bunch of cuts here and there and nailed the tar out of it. I put felt paper on the ceiling, and I ran plumb out of money.

Hi-ho, it was back to cut'n timber I go.

It happened there was a cut'n job just out of Seeley Lake, off the left of Jocko Pass. The timber was spruce and lodgepole, nice size wood. I had moved the family to Seeley Lake so's to be closer to the new place. Against my better judgment I'd rented a trailer in town. It was all I could afford. Liv'n in town didn't set too well with me, my hounds even thought it was the pits. I had got two hounds from Rod Houppert back in New York. My plan was to raise hob with the resident mountain lions.

I enjoyed go'n to work there near Elk Meadows every morning. We was get'n $1.10 per log. By ten o'clock every day I had 125 logs and the skid'n crew followed me around like I belonged to 'em. They started to get in squabbles over who would skid my cut'n. Some of the cutters just dumped their trees helter-skelter and it was very hard to skid. No matter what a man does in life, he needs to take pride in his work. Not be proud of himself, but the pride it takes to do his very best.

That job had some nice dead lodgepole pine. Big ones. I should have bought some and had 'um hauled to our new place. Like they say, hindsight is 20-20.

The boss there didn't like his cutters to quit till three o'clock. So we sat around and had a visit and took a nap. No sense in cutt'n anymore 'cause he'd have cut the price. He was on down the road a piece with the skid'n crew. So we had to pass him on our way out. He never asked us what time we quit, and we never told him. He was get'n what he agreed to pay fer. And we was get'n what he agreed to pay. We cut that job out just before hunt'n season.

JOURNEY TO THE BACKWOODS

I had been able to get the roof on weekends, but knew I'd never finish it 'fore winter. Besides, like I was say'n, hunt'n season now took top priority.

Butch was com'n over first part of November. He wanted to hunt Muleys out of Lincoln. I worked on the place till he arrived. About all I could do till spring.

I'd bought an old square front-end Jeep wagon. It was a gem of a hunt'n rig. That thing would go where mules feared to tread.

We were typical dyed-in-the-wool hunters. Got up in the middle of the night. Hav'n never been over there, someone I'd worked with said go to Alice Creek. We stumbled across it near daylight and fresh snow greeted us, the bucks were in the rut.

We drove till we hit a likely-look'n spot. Butch went left, me right. It had quit snow'n but I could see old sign in the previous snow. I stalked down along a ridge keep'n my eyes peeled. I came to a draw and looked like trails came together, so I figured to set a spell.

A goofy squirrel spotted me and of course turned into the forest crier. "There's a man here, hey!! There's a human here!!" Good grief, the thing sounded like it would wake the dead. Past experience had taught me, do not move even an eyelid, for after ten minutes or so the red squealer would tire of it and sneak away.

The clouds showed signs of move'n off. Head'n east, I had scraped a spot under a big tree and felt tired. Hunt'n season always seemed to cut into my sleep. I dosed off.

When I woke there he was!!

One of the biggest Muleys I would ever see not thirty yards away and look'n right at me. He was plumb gray in the face and looked older than Methuselah, his neck about the size of a drum. Just stare'n he was, hypnotized like only that age-old urge of nature could bring about. When he turned his head I knew he was gonna make a move. I shot, nuthin' happened. Instead of run'n he turned and glared at me again. I shot again, nuthin' happened.

Perhaps I was still asleep and dream'n. Surely he should fall over at any moment. He didn't. So I shot two more times, one near the tip of his shoulder, the other at the bottom. He just wandered off like I'd never been there.

I sat there awhile in disbelief. I'd had some problem get'n the -06 to hold a group, but it had done me right so far.

Butch hadn't seen hide nor hair of any, so we started out slow. I stopped about a hundred yards from an open side hill to shoot at a rock. I emptied the gun twice and couldn't get closer than ten inches from it. Adjusting the scope didn't seem to help. I pulled the bolt and looked down the barrel and there the problem was plain as day. Huge skips of rifling were missing and pitted, it was like stare'n down a drainpipe.

Back at home, I took it to the gunsmith in Seeley Lake. He filled the barred with solvent and told me to come in tomorrow, which I did. The next day when I looked down the bore it was as smooth as a 12-gauge. In the can was a mess of crud. He said the barrel had been corroded with military ammo and had finally gave up.

I had him install a 270 barrel on it. It now shot like old Betsy of Davy Crockett fame.

Back up in the Swan, we hunted the wily whitetail stalk'n the game trails. All of uncle George's instructions soon took over—move slow—move quiet—stop often—know the habits of your game.

Season after welcome season Uncle George would come down the back trails of my memories, causing a tear to fall on the forest floor.

I settled fer an average 4 x 4. I considered whitetail meat surpassed that of "painter." That's what the mountain men of old called mountain lion. It was their word fer panther. They considered it fine fare.

After shoot'n one myself, and fry'n up the back straps, I tossed it out to the hounds. 'Course if'n a man's famished fer meat, he might consider it great cat cuisine.

I started to hunt that cat there near the cabin and chased him two days over across the Clearwater Loop road. The thing was wear'n me out, so I took a day off.

Next day be'n Saturday, I called Steve Niles to join in the chase. Loaded up the old green Jeep, and the hounds were ready to hound the cougar.

We picked up the track where I figured he'd cross. The dogs were off on a high lope, the woods ring'n with the music of the chase. I took off, full cry after 'em. A couple hours later, Susie dog came back feet all bleed'n. She just backtracked to the Jeep. Her son Duke was hot on the trail, the snow kept get'n deeper and deeper. By and by we caught up with Duke. He had this side hill all tracked up. He kept run'n around and would bay every once and a while. We was stand'n under a big fir tree, and I sez to Steve maybe he's treed close by. I looked up, and there he was!! Glaring down at us. I dispatched him with my .22 mag rifle. He was a big cat.

Naturally, I never read all those rules regulations properly so we dragged that thing fer hours, way into the night. I thought we had to turn in the carcass when all that was required was the skull. These hunt'n regulations have gotten way out of hand.

In Loving Memory

Of

STEVEN ALAN NILES

My brother in the Lord, Steve; great friend, great companion, great hunter, great timber cutter.
I will see him again one day.

Welcome one, Welcome all.
Makes no difference if you're short or tall,
Poor; rich in millions.
Everyone's welcome at the Terrillions.
> —Some of my first writings and
> posted over the door at the cabin.

CHAPTER FORTY-FOUR

CUT'N TIMBER
Circa 1977

The season of the hunt was now part of memory, so it was, "I owe, so off to work I go."

Jim Fara, there at Seeley Lake, was log'n fer Champion down the east side of Rogers Pass. The backwoods telegraph reported Jim was a square shooter, the timber wasn't the best, some more of that petrified forest.

Ol' man winter was start'n to blow in a great deep freeze. The drive over to Lincoln and beyond saw lots of deer on the road. Travel'n that there route 'fore daylight was more hazardous than cut'n in the wind over there. Wind, the likes I never saw.

Ya sure didn't have any problem get'n those treees to all fall the same direction. Once ya got yer back cut in, why the wind just sorta snapped 'um off the stump. This was another one of those jobs that could be quite dangersome. But it all went with the territory. It became mind over matter.

The drive was almost too much after work'n that hard all day. The heater in the Mazda wasn't the best, so I decided to rent a cabin in Lincoln fer the month of January.

Rent'n that trailer in Seeley Lake left me with little worry about the family, or so I thought. Geraldine could walk to the store if the car didn't start. I settled into the settlement of Lincoln, and it got even colder.

The Alberta clipper started off near zero, then ten below, then twenty-five below, then forty below. It was back to the chopper mittens 'cause yer hands froze in any kind of glove. Jim was have'n a struggle get'n the Cats go'n every morning. I ran an electric cord out my cabin door to plug in my pickup. By then I'd made enough money to install an engine heater.

The morning came when the thermostat at the gas station sez fifty-one below. The little rice burner hardly had enough power to get the gears all move'n. And the heater or should I say lack of heater, barely left me enough defrosted windshield to see out of. To the pass I thus rolled, never able to get into high gear.

Part way up the pass I could no longer see adequately. I pulled over side the road and waited on the defrosters. It unthawed two inches, then three, then four. I was peer'n out when what did I see a little sign that told it all, "coldest recorded spot in

JOURNEY TO THE BACKWOODS

the Continental United States: seventy-four below zero!!!" I believed it.

Down on the job Jim had somehow got one of the Cats go'n. I'd learned enough about Jim Farra to know that if'n anybody could do it, he could. The old D6 was smoke'n like a locomotive.

I knew my old McCullough would start and it did. I horsed it a few times and bang, she set up. Then Jim went to lift the blade on the Cat and BANG—the ram busted right in two. I looked at Jim, he was look'n at me. The rest of the crew was look'n too. Jim sez, "It ain't fit fer man or beast out here. Let's go home till the weather breaks." I needed the money, but he was right. My other saw was older and would probably suffer the same fate.

At the saw shop in Lincoln we discovered the piston had busted into several dozen pieces. The heat from the combustion and the severe cold wouldn't off set each other. I made it home just in the nick of time.

Geraldine said she didn't have no hot water. So I opened the door to the crawl space and what did I find? Hot water spray'n in all directions.

Look'n on the bright side it was only thirty-five below there at the Tin Tepee. It proved to be one of those happenings of Murphy's Law that ya never forget. Like they say, "Every cloud has a silver lining," and I was confident this too shall pass. This town cloud would carry us to our silver lining cabin, our homestead.

CUT'N TIMBER

The rest of the winter over at Rogers Pass blended into a normal log'n operation. This ranch we were on was all new roads. I took special note of all the mule deer. I was quite sure I'd be work'n fer Jim next fall.

Along towards spring I started drive'n back and forth again. One night I came home, there poor Duke dog was bleed'n bad out of his nose and acting awful sick. I called the vet and he diagnosed it as strychnine poisoning. Apparently some town nabor was try'n to kill my hound dog. The vet didn't give me much hope but said, "Dump a quart of warm milk down him." I also mixed a bottle of Pepto Bismol antacid and gave him the works. He pulled through all right. This live'n here in the settlement was enough to try the patience of Job.

Spring couldn't come fast enough fer me. Problem was, there was four feet of snow at the new place. And the road over on Jim's job was break'n up. We had to give that up till summer. Out of the blue Butch called with a grandiose timber tramp.

California, here we come!! I needed money to do all the inside work at the homestead. And I knew from vast years of spring breakup there would be no jobs fer two months. By now, Geraldine had come to realize be'n married to a woodsman meant, don't fence me in. She probably wondered what it would be like to be married to a desk hound.

Gather'n together my gear, I cast a doubtful eye on the old McCulloughs. They'd served me faithfully they had, but were get'n to wear the look of an ol'

JOURNEY TO THE BACKWOODS

logger. It was like sell'n an old friend when I released one to the custody of a man in Milltown. He promised it would only cut firewood fer his house.

I took a big step and bought a Stihl. Mr. McCullough had changed the design of those great cut'n machines. They no longer appealed to most loggers, sorta looked like a hobby thing. And it bothered me he would spend part of his fortune buy'n the London Bridge and ship'n it to Arizona. I always thought all those big saw manufacturers might have considered a retirement fund fer loggers. At least pitched in and started one. It was the woodsman who made 'em rich in the first place. But alas, they gave no more thought to the ol' timber beast than most of the lumber companies who became wealthy. Capitalism was alive and well.

Butch drove and towed his new camper and brought along his new wife. It was quite a journey but left us plenty of time to straighten out the world, the forest service, and most government bureaucracies. We surmised they didn't hire old woodsmen anymore 'cause we'd straighten 'em out pronto.

We ended up near Weaverville, California, and found a trailer court that seemed to fit our style. I don't remember fer sure, but seems like Evergreen Helicopter was fly'n the logs with a sky crane. It was a monster. Reminded me of a gigantic preying mantis.

We drove up along some river to the landing, and about a dozen hardheaded timber cutters soon appeared. They was fly'n us up on the mountain with

CUT'N TIMBER

a Huey 500 chopper. That thing flew faster than a secret amongst some womenfolk.

First order of business was to fall a five-foot sugar pine. The saw boss hiked me over to this sugar daddy and sezs, "Fall it." It was steep, which wasn't a big problem, but the three draws that came together was. I had a sneaky suspicion that this was a pre-cast plan. With only one decent place to put it, I fired up my new saw. After Alaska, what was a little ol' sugar pine?

The sharp saw sliced right into the big beauty and saw dust flew in every direction. These big trees were sure a challenge to fall and made me thoughtful. Sometimes I sensed Mother Nature's moods at times like this and they were solemn. Years later near Unity, Oregon, after a burn I cut a yellow pine that was there before Columbus. The rings on the stump told the truth. That tree had seen the red man out hunt'n with the most primitive weapons, long before the horse came into that eastern Oregon country. Seen the first white man as he trapped his way into history, the first homesteaders with their teams of oxen and their hopes and dreams.

The big sugar pine came crashing down. Then it hit and broke and broke again and again. My heart sank along with the tree into the loose shale. I never had a tree break up like that. I felt ever foolish, of course, with the boss look'n on. "Did you ever cut sugar pine?" he asked. I assured him I hadn't. "Well, you have now," was all he said as he walked off. Yes-sir-ree, just like I figured, a set-up

JOURNEY TO THE BACKWOODS

job. He knew no man alive could fall that heavy pine without it break'n up. This boss needed watch'n I concluded—you could always tell what kind of bird yer deal'n with just by the song he sings.

They was some good timber cutters on this here job. One was a big red-headed, red-bearded chap who looked to be straight off a Viking ship. His authenticity was finished with fearless liquid deep blue eyes.

The Huey 500 whisked me and Big Red every day to our place of toil. The pilot was one of those left over from Nam. He flew like he was still try'n to out maneuver the Cong.

Ya know, when it comes to aerial acrobatics, I ain't no Sky King, and every time we took a breathtake'n dive, my Viking friend's knuckles turned white hold'n onto the seat. I didn't figure that old boy feared anything. And then, down near the landing, where he delivered us to the pickup every night, ol' Updraft just had to zip between two GIANT sugar pine, with about two feet to spare on either side. I tell ya, the big Norseman put dents in them there metal pipes that held the seats in place every time we roared betwixt them stately trees.

I'd been keep'n an eye on the expression of Big Red's face and could tell this one night was curtains fer ol' Updraft. We climbed into the chopper at the end of a hot, sweaty day and Red was awful quiet. He reached over with a huge paw and latched onto ol' Updraft's arm and sank his fingers in, DEEP! Sezs Big Red, "Say, friend, ya know those two pines down there you seem to have to fly between?" I could see water come'n from Updraft's eyes, and he nodded in the affirmative. The tone of Red's voice commanded attention!! He continued, "You all just leave me off before you pass through tonight, and I'll cut 'um down!" That's all he said, and say, we'uns had rides after that like us boys were on a sight-see'n tour. Why, ol' Updraft became downright upright. Yes-sir-ree, I bet the old boy was soak'n his arm in Epsom salts fer quite a spell.

Summer was heat'n up like it always does in California. The job was near sawed out, and my thoughts was on the family and the homestead. I'd made arrangements to take the bus home from Redding on Sunday. Butch would deliver me there, but after one last good deed.

There on the streets of the settlement one day, Pat Conway ran across an old adventurer. Age had forced him out to pasture, and he didn't like it. He'd once been a rugged fellow. You could see it and sense it. His hand was still steady but a life of mining the hard way had done in his knees. The search fer the golden rock had took him clean to South America. All he had left was a shack up near the river and a box full of memories.

Sunday morning a bunch of us, guided by Pat, surprised the ol' boy. You could tell he didn't receive much company. He seemed beside himself as he hobbled about make'n us coffee. I never drank Java like that. If'n it wouldn't float a ax-head, I guarantee ya it would bob one up and down. We sat and

JOURNEY TO THE BACKWOODS

listened to a life full of adventure. A primitive life it had been but no regrets. Somewhere down old Mexico way he'd married a Senorita. She died young. He didn't elaborate as his voice grew sad. I remember just before he talked about her, he was reliving a time of bandits and gunplay.

We noticed he cooked and heated with wood. And his pile was down to a few oversize chunks. Pat made a motion that we should all cut some wood. We all seconded the motion. Fer the next few hours we did what woodsmen do best. We cut wood, lots of wood. The old boy made sure we got plenty of help from "Hills Brothers."

Afternoon shadows cut us off from our good deed. The old miner said he'd like to pay us but didn't have much money. We assured him a day of his company was pay enough. As we left him lean'n on the woodpile wave'n and smile'n, I thought we should have paid him. What a gem fer young people to discover, but no one was out prospect'n. How sad.

Monday Butch hauled me to the bus depot. Come'n down out of the mountains I could see Redding off in a heat wave. May in that neck of the woods was not like anywhere I'd been. Pull'n into town there wasn't hardly a soul to be spotted. The sign on the bank sez 106 degrees. At the counter I asked fer a ticket to the mountains.

Some people make enemies instead of friends because it is less trouble.
>   —F. C. Mc Kenzie

CHAPTER FORTY-FIVE

GOOD-BYE TOWN – HELLO HOMESTEAD
Circa 1977

Why is it those buses have to make so many stops? I was sure glad to get home. Absence makes the heart grow fonder.

Our Montana homestead

GOOD-BYE TOWN – HELLO HOMESTEAD

I wasted no time in get'n my big white pine boards. I'd spoke fer 'um the year before, they was come'n from near Lolo. Eighteen inches wide and sixteen feet long, you don't find white pine like that anymore. A feller named Steve and his dad had a little mill down that way. Fer the life of me I can't remember his last name. Anyway he delivered 'em, and I set to work.

All the inside walls and the end walls were rough full size 2x4 studs. I bought 'em from old Pete Rovero. He'd once had an outfit log'n his place and had set up a stud mill. They was piles of timbers, much was no good, exposed to the weather. He told me to dig down in the piles and pick out the good ones. I could have 'em fer twenty-five cents a stud. That was music to this poor man's ears.

The walls finished off fast with those huge boards. Every time I cut one of them beauties, it seemed almost sacrilegious or something.

Geraldine and the kids came up with me often now. She had peeled most of the rafters. Her brother Carlton, who had recently moved to Missoula, came and helped sometimes. The children made the most of all the room to roam. When they tired of their bikes, the woods offered endless entertainment. It's amazing how quickly children can find things to do out of doors, while in town they had to be constantly entertained. Mickey, the dog, found every squirrel cache, while the kids squealed with delight as they helped excavate the find. Mr. Bushy Tail sat nearby on a limb and scolded at this new intrusion.

JOURNEY TO THE BACKWOODS

I didn't savvy wire'n and plumb'n much, but I managed to get it all done. The only code I knew was the code of necessity. However, I got a feller from the big sawmill to come and hook up the main box. When he threw the switch, it blew the breaker that ran the kitchen area. In no time he discovered that I'd wired a box wrong. I explained to him the only thing I knew fer sure about electricity was you received a bill every month fer life.

The year before when I had started, the sewer system was one of the first things I'd done. After renting a bobcat with backhoe attachment, I discovered how hard my soil was. It was a challenge. That little machine bounded around as I fought the hard-pan shale. I think a badger could have showed me up.

Get'n the cabin semi-liveable to move into by July would be exactly a year since I started. I had been to every bank in Missoula to apply fer a loan. After try'n several, I was feel'n more like a soap salesman than an American build'n his dream. First off, be'n a logger was only one notch over a seasonal fruit picker. Then, I kept get'n the "Why, that's a depressed area up there." Not near as depressing as these banks in Missoula, sez me. I didn't have to go far from one to the other. There seemed to be one on every corner.

I'd about gave up; one last try. The Missoula Bank of Montana was the name written in stone over the door. They directed me to a Linda Hensley, loan officer, it said on her desk. At least her smile seemed

GOOD-BYE TOWN – HELLO HOMESTEAD

sincere as I explained our dilemma. I needed money to purchase metal roof'n, matched lumber fer the ceiling, plumb'n supplies, and insulation. She said she understood our predicament, but we had no well dug. And banks didn't loan money very often on land with no water supply. I told her I had just bought a trailer with tank and pump to haul water. I couldn't tell if the look on her face was unbelief or shock. Funny how folks in the settlements take fer granted turn'n on a faucet or flipp'n a switch.

I'd told her how all the other banks had said it was a depressed area up there. She thought it was funny 'cause a lot of the bank people had summer homes or spent a considerable part of their vacations in the area. She said she did herself. Perhaps that's why she decided to give me a personal loan fer five thousand dollars. That's all I needed, 'cause a man can get bent in the shoulders from carrying a mortgage. We moved in thirteen months from the time I started the driveway.

Like I said before, there was lots to do yet but even part of a house in the woods beat a mansion in town. Duke and Susie, the hounds, bayed with delight. Mickey renewed his harassment of the pine squirrels. The kids could be as noisy as true kids at play. And Geraldine had her very own nest to arrange anyway she wanted. Me, well town was behind us, out of sight, out of mind.

Now that the house was liveable I built a woodshed. It would not go well to spend a winter without one. I had poured the cement fer the garage when I

JOURNEY TO THE BACKWOODS

did the house. But knew I hadn't the time that year to put up the building.

Even though it was July, I could visualize fall and the hunt. Brother Richie, his brother-in-law and Butch had wanted to go into the Bob Marshall Wilderness elk hunt'n. I'd bought a couple of mules (Shorty and Dorsey) and an old dude horse from Virgil Burns. 'Course then I needed corrals for which I had plenty of lodgepole timber on the place. By the time I finished 'um, the old sock was plumb empty.

It was time fer Butch Pate disease again. You know, the itchy feet fungus tramp. Ol' Butch had finished up in California and was back in Idaho, down on the river out of Headquarters, same place as we was before.

I found it hot over there, really hot. Down where we crossed the river we heard from the Potlatch crew a funny story. One sweaty, stifling afternoon when they crossed the bridge, there was a bear in the river, totally submerged except his head.

The big log'n show days were coming up, and it was the buzz about town. If'n you didn't compete in the saw'n and chop'n events, you were at least expected in town to celebrate.

I decided to partake of neither. I had given up the log'n shows and the party life. I just wanted to cut timber and make some money to take home to the family.

The woods that summer had more bees and wasps than anytime I ever remember. You could fall

GOOD-BYE TOWN – HELLO HOMESTEAD

a tree and be limb'n away, engulfed in your work and you didn't see the enraged insects till you were had. You instantly dropped your saw and raced to safety. Then while you rubbed the welts, you sneaked back to observe the hive of activity about yer saw. There it laid right where ya dropped it, still faithfully purr'n away. My favorite retrieving method called fer a long vine maple pole. Without my ax I'd been in a world of hurt. I left a stub of a limb to hook the handle with. Again, sneak'n up to the mad hornets, I'd snatch the saw and streak away.

Ol' Butch had a run in with the dive'n devils that left him with one eye swelled shut. He was sure a sight fer sore eyes. Anyhow, this sting'n event took place a couple of days before the log'n show. Butch sez it weren't to cramp his style and did his level best try'n to drag me along. I told him if anyone needed me I'd be at camp. First night of the big do'ns Butch was make'n the rounds of the local hangouts. Between waterholes he met a surly fellow who was look'n fer anyone to vent his bad disposition on. Butch turned out to be in the wrong place at the wrong time. Next morning ol' Butch couldn't see out of either eye.

The heat was tough to take on that steep ground pack'n yer saw and gear up the draws and over the rocks. A good paycheck kept us go'n but it was a dangersome place. One fellow out limb'n a tree over a rocky outcrop fell and ran a stub into his gut. He hung there till his cut'n partner came to check on him 'cause he didn't hear his saw fer a spell. He survived but never cut timber again.

JOURNEY TO THE BACKWOODS

Good pay or not, I was glad when we cut that job out. It was so hot ya could fry an egg on the hood of the pickup. Head'n fer home when I dropped down into Orofino, the seat was so hot I couldn't sit on it. I held myself up pulling on the steer'n wheel till I was up the Lochsa River. I reached home just in the nick of time again.

Geraldine was haul'n water from the spring down the road. I hauled the tank to Beaver Creek and filled up. The shallow well I'd dug down in the draw only had water winter and spring. We needed a real well, but couldn't afford one. It called fer extra funds and would be my next year's priority. Ya just had to put up with these inconveniences on a homestead.

With elk season just around the corner, plan'n the hunt was a major project. It required a lot of gear to go into the Bob Marshall and stay two weeks. That's unless you wanted to live like a coyote. And I had somehow outgrown and survived that stage in life.

Everyone showed up on time, a few days early. The bugle season started September 15th, and we needed to get to Lena Peak on the 14th. It was sorta a shot in the dark 'cause we'd never been in there before. Virgil Burns was to haul in our extra stuff with grain and extra saddle horses fer some of us. We didn't get much sleep the night before, and Virgil always gets go'n in the dark. I don't know what it is about these hunt'n trips, but a feller is supposed to rest and relax. Our trip in had the normal small wrecks. Some pack needed a rock or two so's to

GOOD-BYE TOWN – HELLO HOMESTEAD

level things up. The weather was perty as a picture. Nice camp'n weather, though, usually made fer poor hunt'n.

We camped opposite the big slide below Lena Peak on the creek. The mountains' display of nature's grandeur was outstanding. All hands made short order of put'n up the wall tent, build'n a hitch rack, and gather'n wood. We finished all the chores and turned the mules and ol' Rebel loose to graze before dark.

By and by we sat and relaxed and listened to the murmur of the creek. We sized up that slide and the best way to hunt the stands of lodgepole scattered across the mountain. All of a sudden out from one of those stands runs a big griz!! He been there hid'n whilst we made camp. All the commotion must have finally got to him. He sure crossed that slide in record time. Big 'ol chocolate bugger he was. He'd reach a ripe old age if'n he stayed clear of our camp.

That night as the campfire threw our shadows out beyond the circle of light, we planned the hunt. Probably Washington crossed the Delaware with less preparation. We needed all the help we could get, fer we'd seen little fresh sign. And we needed a storm but it didn't look like any soon.

I planned to tie up the stock every night so's they wouldn't wander off. They'd spent most of their life in these mountains and knew where the barn was. Carl Eksdedt always said, "Better to count ribs than try to count tracks."

JOURNEY TO THE BACKWOODS

A couple of hours 'fore daylight I fed some kindling into the sheepherders stove—right from my sleep'n bag (old trapper's trick). Within minutes the tent was comfy-cozy and everybody out and about. Back in those days of yore it was bacon, eggs, and pancakes and lots of black coffee. Calories mattered little when you were young and never stand'n still.

Daybreak was creep'n over the rise as we all made our planned departure. The horses had their pellets and refused a drink. Mother always said, "You can lead a horse to water, but ya can't make him drink."

Richie took the mountain straight up. The rest of us sought the more moderate haunts of the great Wapiti. The first thing I noticed was no shortage of the forest crier clan. It seemed like every good place to sit and watch one would appear out of nowhere to announce my presence. I put my scope crosshairs on 'em and thought how I'd like to blow you into fragments. Who wanted to betray his watch though just to thin out ol' bushy tail?

The weather remained uncooperative. We saw a few deer, and Richie saw a cow elk. He couldn't believe how big those things were. The elk never saw him and passed within a few feet of him. Richie said he'd climbed right to the top of Lena Peak, up that steep slide. 'Course we didn't believe him. Said he left an apple core right on top of some old boards. Next day I followed the pack trail up there and sure enough. Right there on the site of the old fire lookout was the apple core.

GOOD-BYE TOWN – HELLO HOMESTEAD

After about a week grass got perty scarce around camp. They wasn't much to start with. Against my better judgment I left the stock loose one night and had old Rebel hobbled and belled. The musical tinkle of the horsebell drifted me off to sleep.

In the morning nary a ding-dong could be heard. How fer could a hobbled horse go anyway? She had headed out towards home with the two faithful mules tag'n along.

Just west of Pendant cabin was some other fellers camped. One stayed in camp all day while the other hunted. He sez during the night he was awakened by a horse bell headed out. They'd put some poles up near the pass on the way in to stop runaways and figured mine might be there. The good nabor even loaned me a horse to fetch 'um with. Sure enough, there at the blowdown patch was the deserters. The mules seemed to say, "We were only following her."

Years later on another Bob Marshall hunt down Gorden Creek, I rode "Boss." He was a small gray gelding I'd picked up at the sale fer the kids, barely twelve hands high and not over six hundred pounds. But what a horse! Anyhow, me and Steve Niles was head'n in and met a couple of cowboy types ride'n big strong horses. They paused 'side the trail to observe me thunder'n down the trail on Boss. A smirk appeared on one and he sezs, "Yer almost afoot, ain't ya?" I sezs, "This here is my elk hunt'n horse, and we'll be head'n out in a few days with game." He

JOURNEY TO THE BACKWOODS

didn't look convinced. Steve was rid'n a three-year-old bay I had raised.

We camped with some boys from New York who'd been packed in by D. K. Mitchell. Some were friends of mine: Russell Hunkins, reknowned hunter; Charlie Woodruff, reknowned wing shooter; BowBow Bill Ellis, great companion; and others I've forgotten. They had camp all set up and a great camp it was. A finer bunch ya never would find to hunt with.

Opening morning we all split up. I climbed way up above camp before daybreak. Just after light I heard a shot from where Steve should have been. There was lots of sign but I saw not one stinky bull. Back in camp at eleven I was pour'n a cup of coffee when in walks Steve with a bloody liver. That was him that shot, a nice 6x6 bull.

Congratulations were in order. I'd made a wood trade with the owner of Holland Lake Lodge Dick Shaffer to haul out our meat. Steve hiked down to their outfit on Cardinal Creek. We'd meet him next morning. The packer came and packed the meat to their camp. They hadn't seen any big bulls.

Third day I told Steve, let's ride down the trail and look fer sign. We'd rode several miles and seen fresh tracks but tracks make poor soup.

On the way back we rounded a corner in the trail and there stood a rag horn bull!! I bailed off Boss, yanked my gun out of the scabbard, handed Steve the reins and got winter's meat. On the way back to camp we ran into, of all people, the cowboy

GOOD-BYE TOWN – HELLO HOMESTEAD

who carried the smirk. He was guide'n other hunters and hadn't got no game. I hated to elaborate on our hunt, but I took a few minutes to fill him in. I wheeled my elk horse thundering on down the trail. Justice is sweet indeed.

Back to the other hunt, the weather stayed so warm we gave it up. That year in that area we concluded elk were about as scarce as hockey players with teeth. And at the homestead, the hole in the woodshed needed attention. Then there was the root cellar to finish. Old man winter wasn't go'n to cut us any slack. Coyote trap'n was at hand and general hunt'n season. What a great way to finish out a great year.

Andrew Garcia once wrote a book calling his time in early Montana, "A Rough Tough Trip Through Paradise"

CHAPTER FORTY-SIX

FOREVER OUT'N THE WOODS
Circa 1978

Old man winter blew in. We were expecting him, we were ready. General season had treated me right. The freezer held a rag horn bull elk, and a huge buck.

Vegetables were buried in the root cellar now covered safely with snow. The woodshed overflowed, and the daily task of fill'n the woodbox fell to Troy. He sometimes accused his Mother of emptying it just so he'd have to fill it. Everyone took turns on the supper dishes except the hunter.

As the snow piled up, cut'n jobs became scarce. There was one job down on Glacier Creek log'n nice lodgepole pine. Old Rammell and a young lad named Keith and myself took it on. We at least hoped it would buy beans to go with the wild meat. The outfit we was work'n fer was to get paid by Plum Creek

Lynx at our homestead in Montana, early '80s

Timber. But before that, the sawmill in Seeley Lake had to scale and pay the other log yard in Condon who had the contract. It was a job that wears heavy on gloves and temper.

It took a Philadelphia lawyer to keep track of the money trail. A month went by with no payday. We lived on credit at the local store. Five weeks, six weeks and still no paycheck. We were run'n out of beans. Two months and I was get'n a little upset to say the least. The buyer fer the log yard in Condon showed up one day to check on things, and I gave him a piece of my mind. The snow was up to my

FOREVER OUT'N THE WOODS

belt. I had to shovel every tree before I cut it. Some mornings it was thirty below zero. It was hard to force a smile. The Good Book sez to pay a man before the sweat is dry on his brow. There was plenty of sweat on my brow every night and no pay to show fer it, nine weeks and finally a payday. By then I owed it all to local stores and gas pumps. If'n anyone had a conscience, it didn't show up. Along in March face'n spring break up I made a hard decision. Alaska again. I mustn't leave the family penniless, only one thing to do; sell my good horse. I'd got him in a trade from Sam Camphouse over near Fort Shaw.

A bunch of us decided to share expenses and drive to Prince Ruper, take the ferry to Ketchican—ol' Butch of course, Pete Walters, Steve Niles, Mike Kampnich, and myself. The work would surely be demanding and dangerous, but we would have many a laugh along the way.

I'd bought an old Ford station wagon the summer before. We piled gear on top and piled in. Leave'n the family hadn't got any easier neither. We took turns drive'n and never stopped till we came to the ferry at Prince Rupert, B.C. Once the car was loaded we stretched out on the forward deck. Those forced marches can really tire a feller out.

The sights and sounds of the harbor didn't keep me awake. Two and half days in that car called fer a much-deserved sleep. I missed the beautiful British Columbia coast with its misty fjords, the quiet fish'n villages, and all the marine wildlife. The ship's horn woke me in Ketchican, land of the midnight rain.

JOURNEY TO THE BACKWOODS

The place had changed considerably since my last trip. The town was plan'n a dam and hydropower to furnish cheap electricity. They'd been run'n the settlement on diesel power, if you can imagine that. Those engines had exhaust pipes big as trees.

First stop, Gilmore Hotel. We ran into a friend of Butch's, Delvin Deardorf, topnotch timber beast. He too was look'n to get hired by one of the log'n camps. The hotel had work'n man's rooms. It was clean and comfortable, though old. We ate two meals a day at a café just down the street. Daily we made the rounds of floatplane offices, restaurants, and bars, try'n to run down some camp boss. The local unemployment office was your typical government paper shuffle'n bureaucracy. You sit there fer hours and gnashed yer teeth, feel'n like some beggar and wishing to be like old Elijah and disappear in a whirlwind.

Butch landed a job with Reid Timber and got Mike on. Reid was well liked and ran one of the best camps in Alaska. I knew the bookkeeper fer L.O.G. and finally got to talk to him at Cape Pole. He hired me and Delvin. Delvin had worked fer that outfit before, and they was glad to put him back on. They didn't want to hire Steve and Pete 'cause they'd never cut in Alaska before. I argued they had to start sometime, so give 'em a chance. Well they had another camp at Bradfield Canal, steep and big boulders everywhere. He finally agreed. We were glad to leave town, not to mention we were broke.

The Beaver floatplane gave us a pleasant scenic ride to Cape Pole. There was even a little sunshine splashed upon the many islands. My, there's nothing quite so grand as view'n Alaska from a plane. Snowcapped mountain peaks jutted into the clouds. The vastness filled you with awe and wonder. And some fools say it all started with a big bang, some fools indeed. Our able pilot buzzed the camp, and we floated in just in time fer supper. No lack of good food here either, I noted. With full bellies we retired to the cutters' bunkhouse. Delvin knew the layout, he'd been here and done that. He dug out the saw file'n vice fer those of us who hand filed and several boxes of old saw parts left over the years by flee'n timber tramps.

Bunk house life fer those of us away from family was barely tolerable. Delvin's sense of humor helped pass lonely evenings while the eternal rain beat upon the shanty, to bed at 9:00 and to sleep at 9:03. The physical exhaustion we experienced from cut'n timber on that broken ground didn't leave no one toss'n and turn'n. It may not have been the sleep of innocence, but it surely was the sleep of the deserving.

The timber was mostly big hemlock. Many trees were so root swelled and hollow you could crawl under 'em. One be'n so dangersome if'n I was to cut it, it would have meant almost certain death. Another old cutter on the crew, Don Harwood, told me to have the road crew blow it. I watched as the powder monkey carried a whole box of high drive down to do the job. Smoke belched out from all sides, then the boom was heard. Then the big old fool killer just sat down and keeled over. From my safe perch it looked just lovely. Ol' Harwood was get'n near the end of his cut'n career, but what he lacked in strength he more than made up in savvy. He taught me many helpful tricks. Some situations left a feller dig'n like a badger fer safe ground.

One near-fatal incident involved another bad hemlock. I was forced to saw footholds in its huge root swell, in order to get high enough to cut on the main trunk. I knew it was hollow so had an escape route picked out. As the tree started to fall, the root swell crumbled. Yank'n the saw out, I pitched it and ran fer dear life. The ancient monster was come'n over sideways as I leaped onto what I thought was a moss-covered rock. It turned out to be a rotten log and one leg broke through. My leg stayed, and my body kept go'n causing considerable pain, not to mention the tree just missed me. Thus ended my stay at Cape Pole. It was time to go home anyway.

Home sweet home, where a man could rest and nurse a bum knee. I should a drawed workman's comp. But I never drawed it once. I'm pay'n fer it now.

After a month or so, I could get around almost good as new. It gave me time to start my little shop with hayloft in the back. With summer came the opportunity to fish and take the kids swim'n. A man misses too much work'n away from home. But there are some things we have no control over, so we make the best of them. We must try and be content with what we have and live life the best we can with the

FOREVER OUT'N THE WOODS

time and place give'n us. Someone once said, "Today is the tomorrow you worried about yesterday."

The children sure enjoyed their summers there out'n the woods. We never had to worry what they were do'n or who they was hang'n out with. That is, until they got in high school. Which in time became a great concern of mine, but one I could do very little about. We had no freedom of choice.

A helicopter outfit was to fly logs near Swan Lake, about forty minutes north of the homestead. I was delighted to get on in spite of the steep, brushy terrain. It took us to our physical limits again, and I slept as in a coma. One evening about midnight, as I was deep in this incoherent state, my wife shakes me awake: "Dale, the dog near the garden is barking!!" My response was "Uh-huh?" I in my sub-conscious state. She again shakes me and tells me the dog sounds afraid. The word *afraid* caused me to bolt upright in bed.

"Afraid of what?" I asked. I'd tied Ben, a half hound, half lab near the garden to keep deer out. He wasn't much good fer nuthin' else. I did my best to convince her that he was do'n his job and tried to collapse back into my coma.

She wouldn't let it rest though, so in anger, (it's never good to act in anger) I raced out of the house in my birthday suit. Head'n fer the garden I was yell'n threats at the mutt when a loud crash stopped me cold. It came from just behind the horse trailer, sorta in line of my direction. This was no deer sez me, sez I. No whitetail breaks down lodgepole like that. Fer

JOURNEY TO THE BACKWOODS

some reason known only to inner self-preservation, the hair on my neck suddenly stood on end. My old green Jeep was face'n that way so I reached in and pulled on the lights: WHOA!!!

There stood a griz right where I'd have been had I kept run'n. The dreadful beast intended on have'n me fer dessert. I didn't linger there once he hissed and growled. Jessie Owens couldn't have beat me to the house. I grabbed my rifle and wasted precious minutes load'n it. By then Geraldine was in a state of near hysteria and didn't think I should go back out there. I assured her I would shoot the beast, but first I put on my pants.

The dog was now bark'n frantically, think'n I was come'n to save him. I figured if'n I turned him loose he'd show me where the old Purina Chow feeder was hide'n. I cast the flashlight about on my way there but couldn't spot the bugger. Once loose the cur ran fer the house!! Look as I might, no bear was in sight.

Before I left fer work next morning I made sure Geraldine kept the kids close to the house and left Mickey out all day. In my semi-conscious state that night I forgot to let Mick out, or he would have led me to the guilty party.

I called Guy Shanks, our local warden, to report the incident. That evening he showed up with the live trap. Guy was a game warden who possessed plenty of common sense. It was a trait not found in many government employees. Anyhow, we baited it with leftover dog food and bacon ends. We stood and admired how the bruin had opened the door on the trailer. There in plain sight was a muddy paw print where he'd opened the latch. This was no ordinary bear.

Several nights passed. The old thief came back once and cleaned up the ground where he'd spilt the bag by the trailer. But he never entered the trap. We concluded this here bear had been in one of these things before and would not enter another. Guy came and hauled it off and sez, "If you have to, do what you have to do." He put human life over the animal. These days, Fish and Wildlife agencies do their best convincing city dwellers we humans are in the way of nature. They use up taxpayer's funds go'n around to schools and indoctrinating the children. Wolves are good. People are bad.

That bad bear, have'n worn out his welcome at our homestead, showed up down at the nabors' ranch. They were raise'n a few hogs there along with the cattle and he paid them a visit one night. A loud commotion down at the hog pen demanded an investigation. There the culprit was run'n off with a four-hundred pound pig in his jaws. Seems like by the time the owner started to blaze away, the barn yard bandit was out of range. However he did drop the squeal'n porker. That must have put the fear into the naborhood prowler, 'cause he stayed clear of us after that. I did see his track up on Barber Creek road in the fall though. He was drag'n a mule carcass away that had been dumped out. Old long ears had gotten killed out on the highway.

JOURNEY TO THE BACKWOODS

When the job in Swan Lake ended Mother Nature was start'n to announce Indian autumn. That job had helped me pay off the land. We owned our homestead: that is, as long as we'uns paid the land taxes. Ya see, we never really own our homes 'cause as soon as you fail to pay the taxes, it belongs to the government. That's what happened to a lot of folks in the Great Depression. It's not what our founding fathers had in mind.

Anyhow, this looked like the fall we could dig a real well. I'd called Leo Krause down at Potomac, and he said he'd be up in November. Mr. Krause came highly recommended as an honest man and one who knew water inside and out. The news left the kids in a great state of delight 'cause the part-time well had the pump way down in the draw and only operated when you hiked down there to turn it on. In the dead of winter it became a dreaded chore, sometimes at night, and dad wasn't always there to do it.

Be'n between jobs again, I took full advantage of my "free time." Gather'n winter's wood turned into a family affair. Off to the woods we took a lunch and a saw. I'd sold the horse trailer and bought a '56 Ford one-and-a-half ton truck with stock racks. It was a lot of work to fill that thing, but it taught the kids how to work. And we traded extra wood fer used wash'n machines, gas down at Mel Nelson's, and we acquired more than one horse to boot from old Sam Camphouse.

All this out'n the woods cured Geraldine from extra camp'n. Someone once asked her why we

FOREVER OUT'N THE WOODS

didn't go camp'n more? Sez she; "I camp 365 days out of the year right at home."

Hunt'n season was in full swing when the well driller showed up. Old Leo had one of those ancient cable rigs, in my estimation still the best way to drill fer water. These modern day rotary outfits are fast—sometimes too fast. When yer look'n fer small sources of water, sometimes you have to develop 'um a little.

Poor old Leo was almost deaf. All them years of listening to that hammer'n, pound'n driver had taken their toll. Mr. Krause produced two brass rods bent at a ninety to "witch" fer the best place. I don't why they called it "witch'n" fer. Like find'n water was a devil's trick; not hardly.

Old Lucifer has nuthin' to do where water is or ain't. There was no hocus-pocus about it. Find'n water works on some folks and some it don't. Probably has more to do with body chemistry than anything. Leo went to walk'n around and over near the garden and the rods crossed and one commenced to bob up and down. After a bit it quit. Leo was quite certain we would have life's liquid somewhere near sixty feet. He then invited me to try. So I backed off and started same place he did, when I got near to his spot the rods suddenly crossed like before, and took off bob'n. At near forty it quit. Mr. Krause took a piece of lodgepole and drew an x, to mark the spot.

I don't remember but seems like it was fifteen dollars per foot. He got five-hundred dollars setup fee and would settle fer that if'n he drilled under forty feet. Leo drilled and I hunted and trapped. Coyotes were bringing a good price. Near dawn ya could hear his tenor note, that haunting, mocking, lonesome call. Mink and beaver started to show up on the boards also. The trap line yielded more than prime fur. Days spent out'n the woods renewed the simple life between self and nature, follow'n the ways of the wild creatures. Yesterday's worries and cares were quickly lost in the solitude of the forest. One's mind is at peace as it tries to digest all the greatness of creation. Though the songbirds had fled to southern winter hangouts, the season still had plenty of company. And new-fallen snow told me of their habits. Those rabbits told the hunter and trapper where his game could be taken. Wild animals usually only alter their go'n and come'n because of pressure from man.

By and by Leo hit water at thirty-four feet. We gathered around to see the mud he pumped to the surface. It was a small vein like we figured. He spent considerable time pump'n and dig'n around to develop the well. When everything settled down we had eight gallons per minute. Not a lot, but enough. We had enough money to purchase a pump and I found a used pressure tank. Barry Seaman came up with his back-hoe and put in the line. We were get'n plumb civilized there at the homestead.

Can't quite recollect fer sure, but that may have been the fall of the big bull. It was the last five days of season, it was. We had gotten about seven to eight inches of fresh snow and elk commenced to show

FOREVER OUT'N THE WOODS

up down on Beaver Creek. Friday morning found me track'n two big bulls that crossed in that storm. I was stalk'n through the lodgepole like a Seneca scout when just ahead, BANG! I froze. How could someone be ahead of me? I'd seen no other tracks. Nuthin' happened so I trailed aways and there the guilty party was, two of 'em in fact. They was hunter orange from head to toe. One was wav'n his arms about and mumble'n. They spotted me and the arm waver volunteered his story. "I shot the thing in the neck and it got up and ran off, and it was huge." He tried in vain to get his arms as wide as that bull elk's rack was. They hadn't seen the other bull so I wasted no time in pick'n up the trail.

All day I tracked 'em, they hardly stopped. That night, as I sat and listened to the larch cracklin' in the stove, I felt robbed. Them fellers had just stumbled into those elk. Still, they had as much right there as I did.

Day two with only four days left, I picked up the trail again. They'd settled down some during the night and fed a little. Then headed up into the high country much to my dismay. The morning was cold and a savage wind was wail'n down off the Mission Mountains. Just when I figured they were heading fer Sunset Peak, they turned south. The trail was perty cold and obviously they were still not ready to hang out. As the day wore on, up one hill and down another, I marveled at the stamina possessed by the great Wapiti. In spite of the cold, I was drenched in

JOURNEY TO THE BACKWOODS

sweat and welcomed the trickle of a little spring, one of the many that fed Beaver Creek.

I rested a spell and tried to guess where these two old bulls would end up. Uler Creek seemed likely, steep and partly inaccessible, fer now only a guess'n game. The tracks beckoned and drew me onward. The boys in orange weren't kid'n when they tried to describe how big the antlers were on this pair. Whenever they approached two lodgepole about three feet apart, they detoured around 'em. The trail stayed cold except where they'd urinated, and I sniffed the scent long before the act was discovered. Late afternoon found me too weary to continue on. I reluctantly headed fer the barn.

The warm cabin and a good supper, the kids discussing school, Geraldine's words fer the day, and my mind stayed jailed upon Beaver Creek. Those were the biggest elk I had ever hunted. And unless they slowed down, the hunted would outlast the hunter.

Next day, still leg sore, I picked up the trail. The pair seemed to not really want to head way up high like I figured they would, but instead circled back and kept pass'n through old elk sign. A rub here, a rub there. They'd bedded a time or two but hadn't stayed long. By noon the tracks were still cold. I decided this wasn't my year to have the big one.

Back at the homestead I admitted defeat. I laid on the couch fer a toasty nap. As I dozed off I remember think'n, Lord, I give up. Soon in dreamland, what did appear but those elk. I snored on and on (according to the wife) and suddenly in my dream I heard a voice as plain as old Moses once did. "Those elk are near Colt Lake." And I saw the tracks cross'n the road near there. I was suddenly wide awake. There was no get'n around it. A dream, yes, but I heard the Voice. It was now two o'clock. No matter, with the vision control'n me I grabbed my gun.

The old Jeep bounded over the rocks as I gazed at the western sky. Not much time. What if someone else was at the gate on the Colt Lake Road? My fears were unfounded fer I had it all to myself.

Adrenalin took total control as I trotted up the road. Up ahead where the vision had mapped out the spot, I could see something had crossed. And it was the two bulls!! No time to tarry. I followed as fast as I could. But they soon turned up the steep slope on the east side of the lake. Less than two hours of daylight forced me on without a rest. Some old skid trails were grown over with alder. They hadn't slowed the elk down or me neither. Once on top of the ridge, the old fossils done a lot of feed'n and sign was fresh. I slowed down to a stalk. Then some deer peeled off the south side, and if they snorted it would all be over. The few precious minutes ticked by with no sound. I was safe. Step by slow step, just like Uncle George had taught, I slipped across the ridge. And there he was, bedded down half asleep. He was a majestic animal, huge brown antlers with ivory tips, much more than a trophy.

Admiring this one, my mind went to his pardner. Perhaps he was bigger? Now isn't that how a true

JOURNEY TO THE BACKWOODS

hunter thinks? There I stood, greedily scan'n the brush while the biggest bull I'd ever seen in season laid not fifty feet away? While I was try'n to make up my mind, the elk at hand suddenly looked up the hill. 'Course, there I stood big as life, complete with the thoughts of a fool. His reaction was not as drawed out and as foolish as mine. As he leaped to his feet I shot him in the neck. Down he went and up jumped the other one from the alders. My, oh my, he was just as wide but heavier. And he left with his huge horns clattering on the trees. I could hear him fer five minutes.

To the business at hand, the downed bull was paralyzed. His eyes watched my every move as I walked around to finish the job. He knew what was coming. I could read it in his eyes. Many hunt'n seasons have come and gone, but I still think about that afternoon. I can't help feel I should have learned and retained much more than I have.

It was the same bull shot three days previous. When I skinned him out there in the neck was a .30-06 ball, already cocooned in gristle. It had passed through without hit'n any bone or the spine. Just like the fellow in orange so excitedly explained, "I shot him in the neck, and he just jumped up and ran off." The rack was 6x5 and a fifty-six-inch spread.

It was dark 'fore I got the hide off so he could cool proper. I knew the road was straight down the mountain so strap'n my rifle to my back I dove off the hill. Hold'n my hands in front of me kept me from poke'n my eyes out. Stumbling along, I suddenly ran smack into something. A loud crash brought back memories of the big griz at the cabin. My heart stopped, then pounded like a hammer. Perhaps this one hadn't hibernated yet and smelled the kill. And smelled me!! After dress'n out the bull I was as rank as any stinky elk. You can't imagine how helpless I felt as I pulled the rifle off my back, and I couldn't see the length of the barrel. To my surprise the beast took off, and I could hear the pleasant clatter of horns on alders again. The old elk had thought I was his companion because I smelled like him.

I called Steve Niles that night and gave him the scoop. If he helped me get out my bull, I'd put him on the other one. Well, he did and I did. He chased that one fer two days at a lope. Even got a couple of shots and a little hair. The old gun he had was long ago worn out and so was Steve come Sunday. He'd ran so hard he'd lost about fifteen pounds.

What would life be if we had no courage to attempt anything?

—Vincent Van Gogh

CHAPTER FORTY-SEVEN

THE NITTY GRITTY
Circa 1980

By and large, my desperate devotion to the hunt left us in somewhat financial straights—again. With no prospect of work nearby, I commenced to trap in earnest—a lynx here, a coyote there, now and then a mink or beaver. Not much, but they kept the wolves from the door.

I was determined this would not be another winter of discontent like last year. No more two-months' paydays, or company store situations. Even after a year I was hard pressed keep'n myself from become'n bitter. Some people have no idea the hardships they impose on others. So forget'n what was behind, I looked fer a better year ahead.

Christmas sorta crept up on me. The tree in the live'n room had little else but the stand under it. Geraldine had her annual look of fear that the kids

JOURNEY TO THE BACKWOODS

It snowed at the Montana homestead.
Geraldine on the cabin roof.

wouldn't have a happy Christmas. My prime fur hang'n in the shed must be sold now to rid the house of old bah-humbug. I must make a trip to Great Falls to the fur buyer. Put'n up a nice bunch of fur is lots of hard work. And the more a man puts into it, the more attached he gets to his pile of hides. And of course he most always feels he's get'n offered less than they're really worth. This was a good year fer prices but was near the last. The next year started a decline that has never stopped.

After the first of the year, me and Rammell got a cut'n job over near Ovando, another one of those re-log projects. The company had no business log'n timber in an area that had been logged just a few years before. 'Course my opinion meant nuthin' and what did I know anyhow? Those guys all had degrees in forestry from the university. Therefore, they held all knowledge in such matters. Anyhow, another one of those Alberta clippers imposed ol' man winter upon us.

There seemed no shortage of chilly winds to waltz the snow on ahead of the Mazda pickup. Up and over the snow banks it sifted off in a beautiful arch that would inspire postcards.

Once the mercury hits twenty below and a wind chill push'n it beyond reason, it takes a hungry man to force himself out of the pickup at daylight. The Mazda helped, 'cause the heater was about as cold as the timber company and get'n worse by the day.

The morning came when I picked Rammell up and the heater quit entirely. I drove to work with the window down, one eye out to see where I was head'n. I don't know who started it, but we got to laugh'n. I told Rammell someday we'd get to die and wouldn't have to do this anymore. That morning we stopped at the Cenex store in Ovando, and it was thirty-six below—in the shade. Up on the job our Stihl saws kept frost'n the carburetors. We built a roar'n fire to thaw 'um out. It was a good thing we loved our work.

One of them things that made cut'n timber a great job was the independence. If'n ya were good at what ya did, even the boss seldom bothered to come around, which suit me just fine. To stay safe fall'n timber, yer concentration must not be interrupted. We needed to be left alone to our job and our dreams.

JOURNEY TO THE BACKWOODS

As the winter wore on it was evident we'uns were cut'n ourselves out of a job. The price was way short of fair, so we had to cut a lot of logs to make 'er pay. At least we got paid every two weeks. An old timer around that Ovando neck of the woods told me about some of the old bachelor loggers who once worked fer the ACM Company. They sold the mill in Bonner to another outfit, and the old loggers sorta retired. Too wore out to work and no retirement, they sometimes lived on canned dog food. Not much of a legacy fer a big mining and lumber company to leave behind. Fer the local hard work'n folks they left little besides stumps.

Like I was say'n, we cut ourselves out of a job. The lumber market was get'n soft and didn't look like much chance of work in Montana or Idaho. The backwoods telegraph brought word of big job and big timber near Klawock, Alaska. I had to take the family, somehow, some way. Mother always said, "Where there's a will, there's a way."

All the past disappointments of try'n to find housing fer a log'n family in Alaska came to mind. Be'n told us timber cutters weren't "key" personnel caused us to rely on ourselves. An old logger in California once said, "Ain't nuthin' ever been got that hasn't been gone out after." So I went out after a camp trailer.

The ad in a Missoula paper said, "Thirty-two foot aluminum Spartan trailer, $1,000." From winter's work, sale of Martin hides, and income tax return, this journey may become a reality.

THE NITTY GRITTY

We found the trailer owned by a sweet old lady. Her husband had recently passed away, and she cared not to be concerned with renters. The old Spartan was a park model, meaning it had no holding tank and needed electricity to run the furnace. I couldn't find anything near as good fer the contents of my wallet. I bought it.

The humble hovel was really built. Looked like a forerunner to the great Airstream. Solid birch interior, all aluminum shell with rounded roof. If'n anything would shed the downpours of southeast Alaska, it would be this camper.

I made over the rear bedroom, four bunks fer the kids. Me and Geraldine would make do with a double bed. Everyone had lots of blankets. The '73 Jeep Wagoneer would be adequate to pull our home away from home—if our meager funds held out.

We were to meet Butch, Ed Cooper, and Gary Gills in Ketchikan, then take another ferry to Hollis on Prince of Wales Island. I calculated number of days versus number of miles plus number of dollars. Two days 'fore we left, I got pneumonia.

I was sicker than a dog, but it wasn't a dog's life. Steve Niles was back in Montana and stopped by to wish us well. Lay'n there on the floor near the stove, I didn't feel well. He said I didn't look well either and was in no shape to be head'n fer Alaska. I guess I wasn't, but somewhere down inside I managed to gather enough strength to load up and head out. Loggers are noted fer be'n hard-headed.

JOURNEY TO THE BACKWOODS

We got a late start. By the time we headed up Lookout Pass, night was swoop'n down. The damp March evening began to rain like cats and dogs. The wipers couldn't hardly keep up. About a mile from the top it got worse, and the radiator blew out!! I could smell it before the steam showed up. As I pulled off the road, Geraldine wanted to know what we were go'n to do. Get'n out in that down pour wasn't something I should do in my diseased condition. But it had to be done. My drenched flashlight confirmed my fears. The top core had separated from the flues. And the engine was bathed in anti-freeze. Back in the Jeep, I knew I had to come up with some old logger trick. Traffic was light, and no one stopped, and no one had yet heard of cell phones. The wife and kids all looked at Dad, and Dad needed to come through.

I left the hood up to cool things down. I figured if'n the engine got cool enough I could drive to the top and coast down to civilization. After fifteen to twenty minutes I cranked it up, but the belt was so oily the alternator wouldn't charge. No matter. The Jeep throwed gravel as we climbed fer the top. She was heat'n up perty good by the time we topped the pass. Without the engine runnin' and no way to charge the battery, I dared not use the lights except if'n we saw a car come'n. Snow banks became my guide, and I had no trouble keep'n the kids quiet, since the incident was a bit worrisome. Where-oh-where was the highway patrol when ya needed 'em?

THE NITTY GRITTY

By and by the road leveled out some, and I let 'er roll. The battery now dead left me no choice but to pull over on the shoulder. This was a four lane and I couldn't believe the light traffic. Then, over off across a meadow on the old highway shined another one of those miracles that appear by divine providence. A motel!! Gather'n up the crew and a suitcase, we ran through the rain. The owner thought this quite unusual but welcomed us right in, rain-soaked clothing and all.

Next morning the owner gave me a number of a small garage and tow service. He proved to be an honest, hard-work'n mechanic. The old radiator was shot. He found another at a salvage yard and fixed us up fer ninety some dollars. He was another one of those guys we should have kept preserved in an address book. He was another great American.

Our breakdown had cost us over a day and would cause us to miss the ferry schedule at Ketchikan. We'd called and left word with the people who was house set'n fer us, to inform Butch if he called. Which he did. We motored up through British Columbia without further incident, and took the ferry at Prince Rupert.

The hustle-bustle of the port and the Inland Passage fascinated the children. Geraldine, however, was no more impressed than she was on the trip years earlier to Kodiak Island. She kept her little brood huddled together at all times lest one jump ship. Those ferry rides up through the Inland Passage, to me, were always a great relaxing float trip.

JOURNEY TO THE BACKWOODS

No big ocean swells or rough seas. Small villages were observed in their quiet, serene, misty settings. Tug boats with huge log rafts in tow tugged at my spirit and stirred my soul. Stand'n out on the forward deck with the wind in my face, the scents I sniffed were of adventure.

Before the day was over we drove off the big boat. From past timber tramps, I knew where the ferry dock was to load fer Prince of Wales Island. Butch or Cooper was nowhere to be found. We'd missed 'em like I figured.

Then more bad news, they had caught the last trip of the normal ferry before it broke down. The outfit had to press into service the old Chilcat tub less than half the size of the other one. And ya couldn't drive on and drive off. Ya had to back down the ramp, around a corner or two, to load. It looked like a Maalox moment.

As it turned out, I was the last to load. And be'n my turn I didn't like the suggestion to wait till the bigger ferry came back on line. The deck hand wondered out loud if it was possible fer me to back all the way down there. Sez me, sez I, it's just an everyday challenge fer a logger and I started down. He was a good man with hand signals as the silver and yellow rig rolled on down. The trailer started onto the boat when in my rearview mirror I saw him waving his hand like a traffic cop in Calcutta. He came run'n up all excited to say there was a pipe stick'n up out of the trailer that wouldn't clear the upper deck. Lock'n up the brakes, I rushed back

THE NITTY GRITTY

to view the problem. Yup, there it was, a steel vent pipe lack'n a foot from go'n under. "Now what will you do?" he asked, in a subdued voice. "No problem." I sez, "Ya got a hacksaw?" He disappeared and quickly returned with the tool. I had climbed from the upper deck to the trailer roof and by now had acquired an audience.

The Captain and a host of passengers had gathered to see what the hullabaloo was. In five minutes the piece of pipe fell with a clang onto the ferry floor. The ship's mate shook his head as I parked precisely in my allotted spot. The ramp came up, and we were on our way. Later, I ran into the captain who confessed, "I saw you starting to back down that ramp, and I headed for the aspirin bottle." He smiled and shook my hand.

The little vessel bobbed long towards the village of Hollis, Prince of Wales Island. The sea was sane and peaceful, Geraldine didn't spend much time in the ladies room. However, she'd dosed herself with Dramamine and slept a lot, so I watched the kids most of the day. She'd prepared sandwiches and drinks and homemade cookies, so everyone fared well. Up above the wheelhouse Old Glory floated in free air against liberty's sky. It was a glorious day to be an American.

Low tide greeted us at the ferry dock in Hollis. It didn't take to long to size up a potential problem. The ramp on the Chilcat wasn't near high enough to reach the pier used by the larger ferry. I glanced up where the captain was carefully steering the craft towards the gravel beach. Deck hands heaved mooring ropes at men on shore and secured us in place. Down went the ramp—on gravel and uphill to boot!! The ship's mate glanced nervously at me and sezs, "Last on, first off." Look'n at that waterlogged beach I sez, "Only in Alaska." The ol' say'n, "Lead-follow—or get out of the way," came to me as I pulled the four-wheel-drive lever into place and eased down that slick ramp. Jeep Corporation should have been there with cameras roll'n. What a commercial shot. Up the tide flat we crawled and clawed, the Quadra-track no spin shift'n the power to the tire with the most traction. I knew if'n we spun a hole, I was done fer. But the faithful Wagoneer clawed to the top and landed on the road. And down the road we went, headed towards Klawock.

It was special to drive on a real road again. And this one had big timber along it. Sitka spruce, hemlock, and cedar. Very green moss clung to limbs bearing witness of a rain forest. Small patches of muskeg soaked in water grew only scrub brush. Seemed like a creek crossed the road every hundred yards. A hundred-fifty-plus inches of rain a year makes fer lots of water. I tried not to think about the days I had to toil in it.

The long cool shadows of evening had enveloped the land when we came to the log'n camp. There parked along the road was Coop and Butch. They hadn't got hired yet, so the outfit wouldn't let 'em park in the trailer spots. There we was, a bunch of

THE NITTY GRITTY

trailer tramps look'n fer a holt and look'n like another remake of *The Grapes of Wrath*.

It was a poor place to camp fer the night, but we made the best of it. The worst part was that we couldn't run the furnace without electricity so towards morning, I turned on all four burners on the gas stove. It helped, but I had to leave the top vent open, sorta like a stove pipe. Yes-sir-ree, poor folks have poor ways.

Next day we got the kids enrolled in school, found the laundromat, and drove around look'n fer a camp'n spot. A few miles out of Klawock on the way to Thorne Bay, we found a pull off.

Butch, Coop, and I spent half of each day try'n to catch up with the log'n boss. He seemed to think we had a case of smallpox 'cause he disappeared like Houdini whenever we tried to collar him. Be'n somewhat of a shifty character, someone nicknamed him Mr. Nobody.

Our cupboards were begin'n to look like Old Mother Hubbard's after several days. The canned elk and deer meat were proving to be a real blessing. Me, why I never tire of wild game. The children and the wife, though, started to hint of spaghetti and other delicacies. And they began to dream of a pan of brownies.

Us cutters began to turn our attention towards a right of way through virgin timber to the town of Hydaburg. At least the man who had this job didn't hide from us. We tried not to show too much joy when he hired us. He needed four men, however, as we needed to work in teams, so Gary Gills teamed up with me.

Butch and Coop started on another right of way near Craig. That left the Hydaburg road to Gary and me, and we were glad to go to work. A lean hound needs to hunt.

We could drive to the river, and the new road was to start on the other side. The road crew had laid a long walk log across fer us to cross on. Every morning at daylight we tipsy-toed across over an ever-rising current. To fall meant drowning. We had no radios or any other communications of any kind. I told Gary we'd best be careful. If'n we had a serious accident out here, we were done fer.

The pounding rain and melt'n snow soon overflowed our walk log. On this particular day it was a foot out of the water in the morning and three feet under at day's end. Me and Gary stood there soaked to the hide, and twilight was to force some kind of a decision. The road crew was build'n a camp only a few hundred yards across the river, but with the diesel generator go'n they'd never hear our plea fer help. And they couldn't see us.

We needed another bridge. Out of the right of way and up the river a couple of hundred feet was our only hope. One big spruce that might just reach across the river, maybe. I'd packed my saw out the mile from our labor that night 'cause it needed some work. Otherwise we'd have had to walk way back there and get it. Anyhow, I took extra care in face'n up this tree of salvation. It needed to land in the water all at once to keep the one end or the other from float'n down stream. Timber!! It landed perfect, water flew in every direction.

Then it happened!! The strong current began to take it downstream, still lay'n crossways of the river. Me and Gary looked at each other, teeth chatter'n. The rain had started come'n horizontal in squalls off the bay. Our hard hats had to this point, at least, kept our heads dry. Now water ran off our noses like a small faucet. I felt the urge to laugh, but this was no laugh'n matter. The spruce had rolled with the current and the biggest limbs were now on the bottom. And miracles of miracles, those heavy limbs caught on the old walk log. We whooped fer joy as we slushed to catch up with the bobbing bridge. I leaped on the butt and went first, as visions of a hot shower, hot supper and a dry bed danced in my head. As I neared the other shore I could see the top lacked about six feet from reach'n the bank. When the top got too small to walk on, I throwed my saw and knapsack to safety.

And I took the leap!! Restricted by my soak'n clothes, I didn't quite make it. I landed up to my waist in snow-melted water. I grabbed frantically fer the huckleberry brush and hung on like my life depended on it. That lowly brush was priceless. It held. And I dragged my saturated carcass out of that swollen river.

Gary was now about halfway across and close'n fast. I motioned him to wait. No need of him go'n through what I just did. I cut a small tree, whacked

JOURNEY TO THE BACKWOODS

the top out, and tipped it out onto the walk tree. With both of us now on the bank safe and sound, we stared up to the road. There stood the road boss glare'n down at us with the shovel operator at his side. When we got with in earshot he yells, "That's a salmon stream. You can't fall no trees in a salmon stream. We're in big trouble if the fish and game see this."

By then we'd made the road and told him we didn't care who seen it. That there should have been a bridge there by now anyway. And we asked him if'n anyone in the Native corporations who controlled all this, cared that we made it out alive. He didn't answer so we got in the Jeep and sped fer home. Somehow we might keep from get'n pneumonia. Loggers get a bum rap. They're discussed and cussed, "Rid the earth of 'em." The morals of loggers are many notches over the morals of politicians. Even then, we elect them and trust 'em with our future laws.

Camp'n out the way we was, we had no run'n water, hot or cold. We'd learned the school opened up the gym every night, showers and all, with endless hot water. It was lovely. And I'd get a return on my tax dollars.

The school in Klawock was mostly Indian children and many were very racist, no doubt learning it from their parents. Troy seemed to be the one who ended up with their hatred. It would have been too much fer him if'n not fer a teacher named Mr. Swenson. He alone saved the day. He was funny, witty, and best of all, children wanted to learn in his class. Troy had a hard year till we moved up there. Now he came home to the trailer after school and was all excited and laugh'n at something Mr. Swenson had said or done. Oh, those are the kind of dedicated teachers we need.

About then Mike Kampnich showed up. Remember he came up a couple of years before to cut timber? Reid Timber Company had given him his chance, and he had become a skilled timber faller. He confessed the first few weeks were touch and go. He'd beat a box of wedges into nubs. Like Frank A. Clark once said, "If you can find a path with no obstacles, it probably doesn't lead anywhere."

Anyway, Mike was wait'n fer the log'n camps to open up too and needed a place to stay. We didn't have much room but he said the floor was all right with him. I was glad to help him out. Years later he repaid me ten times over. He never forgot, and I haven't either.

By and by someone undercut the price we were cut'n the right of way for on the road to Hydaburg. We had to pull out, and I went onto the job with Coop and Butch. It was another right of way to a large tract of timber. They said the area would produce twenty years of log'n. Five years later I went back there to cut, and it was all gone. Greed is a terrible disease.

Well sir, we finally got hired by the big log'n outfit and got to move the trailer into camp, right next to the diesel generator. Twenty-four hours a day,

JOURNEY TO THE BACKWOODS

we would endure the drone from that Cat engine fer two months. I had a sneaky suspicion that spot was fer cutters only.

Look'n on the bright side, we had electricity and furnace and run'n water. Across the road was a stream where the kids could play and catch a few trout. Many kids from camp went there as sorta a get together spot. One evening Troy come run'n to the trailer all worked up, "Dad, Dad! Ronnie's down there smoke'n marijuana!!" I had remembered the lad and knew he was nine years old, about Troy's age. I asked Troy where he got it and he said Ronnie's mom grew it at their trailer.

How sad fer children when their parents have such little concern fer the little ones. It breaks your heart. This sort of thing was very widespread in southeast Alaska, probably some people's way to cope with the constant rain. But everywhere you go these days, ya see kids runnin' amuck fer lack of guidance and love. It would take thousands of ranches fer abused children to take care of the need.

Jesus said, "Woe to them who cause the little one to go astray. It would be better for him to have a large millstone hung around his neck and to be drowned in the depths of the sea." There are hundreds of thousands of children out there today liv'n in fear and despair. Adults ought to be ashamed at the very least, and at the most, fearful of falling into the hands of an angry God.

Get'n on with my journey, we were cut'n a lot of timber. Huge flats of virgin forests fell to the snarl

THE NITTY GRITTY

of power saws. A lot of money was changing hands since Congress passed this public land into Native Corporations. Yes, a few Indians were get'n some money, but what a terrible price the land was pay'n. These millions and millions of board feet of logs were shipped to Japan and China and who knows where. It was a disgrace, and no one ever tried to stop it. Many hands were get'n greased.

Coop and Butch and me rode together every day to cut down on expenses. Once the easy ground was cut off, we got stuck on some broken-up terrain. The timber was mostly hemlock, and some big ones. Hemlock, of course, is very heavy. A big three-footer on my strip had broken off about thirty-five feet up and looked like an easy couple of bucks. I faced it up and never saw it had a five-inch hole dead center. The sawdust never showed any change of color as I cut the backside. The inside, of course, was like a stovepipe filled with rotten wood. When the tree started to fall, all that rot shot down with tremendous force. It split the tree in half quicker than you could say, "Help"!! I tripped and fell just as that tons of slab fell on me, right across my chest. By all rights, it should have been the end of the trail fer me. But another miracle had preserved me—a cleft in the rock; fer the ground on both sides of me were higher than where I'd fell.

I laid there expecting the worst. The log was barely touch'n my chest, and I feared it would settle. Call'n fer Coop who was closest wouldn't help till he shut his saw off. It's a time such as this a man tends to review his life.

JOURNEY TO THE BACKWOODS

Embedded there in the moss, my nerves finally quieted down. I began to wiggle and push with my heels. Inch by inch I groaned and crawled till I was free. I couldn't stand right away 'cause of my rubbery knees. Sit'n there on that log I figured I'd cut no more logs this day. When Coop shut his saw off, I yelled I was head'n to the pickup. There I sat the last hour till quit'n time.

Those barber-chaired-widow makers tend to sharpen a feller's skills. The trouble was, every day was different trees, dangerous trees and a flirt with death. I was well aware better men than me had started their saw fer the last time. But the job and the challenge and the need took ya back every day. I sometimes think back to some of those dangersome days and wonder how we made it till quit'n time.

Like I said before, we were cut'n a lot of timber, too much, too fast. Leave it to a logger to work himself out of a job. Butch, Coop, and me were the last hired, so one of us had to go. I volunteered, as I was mighty tired of the rain and that diesel generator. I put an ad up at the pay window to sell the trailer. That very night a nice young man, newly wed, came and bought it. We said our good-byes and headed back fer Montana. On the way we enjoyed a couple of stops at some museums.

He reached down from on high and took hold of me: He drew me out of deep waters.

—Ps. 18:16

CHAPTER FORTY-EIGHT

END OF THE OLD JOURNEY
Circa 1981

The homestead cabin never looked better, bare floor and all, but not fer long. We'd been walk'n on that particleboard fer four years. With the money we'd made on the trailer, new carpet was on the way. Everyone enjoyed their own beds again and Mickey dog went about remark'n his territory. Pine branches waved hello in the mountain breeze. Swallows darted fer bugs and were busy cleaning their houses. Sunshiny days shined down upon us.

The housesitters hated to leave and filled us in on all the valley happenings. The kids returned to school as they had a few weeks left. Friendships were renewed. We dug in like a badger spruce'n up after the long winter and long absence.

I fired up the old stock truck and went over to old Mormon Sam's to pick up the horses. Sam was

END OF THE OLD JOURNEY

Ready to fly and cut logs. Idaho in the late '70s.

always a joy to see and visit with. We heard some stories, some were true and some truer than others. The ponies were in nice shape and rare'n to go somewhere. Before I left, Sam showed me his pig litters, peacocks, pheasants, and oddball chickens. The farm was like a zoo.

As of this writing Old Sam had a stroke, lost a leg to diabetes, and is in a nursing home near Great Falls. Most days he don't remember anybody. Sad to see a man reduced to that. We really miss his colorful personality. He treated us right and always shared his

JOURNEY TO THE BACKWOODS

bounty. His faithful wife fed us good farm fare; they knew the meaning of hospitality. As of this editing in the year 2003, Sam passed away this fall. His wife had gone every single day to see him at the nursing home. It was a long drive and her health isn't good either, but she took her marriage vows seriously. If only lots of our young people would use their marriage as an example.

They say life goes on. I guess it does, but not always as full as it once was.

The carpet layers arrived, and we were now almost liv'n like blue-collared folks. Whatever that means. Geraldine needed a new vacuum and boots had to be checked fer mud and other particles that clung from the corrals.

Somewhere down in my soul I knew in the near future I'd be off on another timber tramp. I wanted to enjoy my time with the kids so decided to take 'em fish'n. Kids make great fishermen. They may not catch much, but they have the best time. And what dad wouldn't smile when he hears the shriek of a child when he get's a bite. And when they finally catch one, they whoop and chatter and proudly hold up the prize: "Hey Dad, look at this one!!" It takes a guy back to Trout Pond and Uncle Vinny.

Pierce Lake, right behind the house, usually had a few stocked trout about kid's size. The summer homers there kept it near fished out, but I decided to give it a try.

Both ends of the lake gave way to marshes. Cattails and muskrat houses laid claim to several feet

END OF THE OLD JOURNEY

of muck. Golden eye ducks jealousy guarded their territory. Everyone was hav'n a great time in the great outdoors.

All the high ground where access was available held a cabin every hundred feet or so. Not see'n any activity, we marched on down to the water's edge. We picked one of several dilapidated small docks and went to fish'n. The kids spent as much time with tangled line in the alders behind them as they did fish'n. And Dad spent all his time bait'n hooks and get'n out the tangles. The fish'n hit a fever pitch once Troy caught one. It's perty hard to instruct excited kids to enjoy themselves in subdued tones. Across the pond, I noticed many adults suddenly appearing in front of a camp. Most headed around our way. It wasn't what I expected.

They showed up with blood in their eyes. "You can't fish here. This is private property!!" Taken back a bit from their evil greeting, I could see this bunch was bad to the core. "Not by a long shot," sez I, "this here land is National Forest and we have a right to fish here, and ain't hurt'n no one!!" Be'n retired folks, I thought they'd be old enough to know better than to act this way in front of children. The oldest one and crankiest of the lot sezs, "This is our lease and our dock, you can't fish here." I knew fer a fact that taxpayers stocked this pond and I told him so.

Then he lied and said they didn't, and to add credibility to his false words he yells, "We'll get the law." By then my dander was up. My milk of human kindness was turn'n into curds and whey. I

JOURNEY TO THE BACKWOODS

answered him, "I'll be right here fish'n when they show up." Geraldine, by now, was fit to be tied and kept whisper'n, "Let's go home." I didn't want to go home. I wanted to toss this bunch of killjoys into the pond. But that wouldn't be a good example to the young-uns. So begrudgingly I left.

Mother used to say, "Careful how you treat others 'cause it will come back to you whether good or bad." And mothers are seldom wrong.

Many years later some hoodlum or group of hoodlums raided their cabins. A nabor of ours said considerable damage was done. Most everyone was taken back by such deviltry. I considered what the Almighty said in the Good Book: "Vengeance is mine saith the Lord, I will repay." And God is NEVER wrong.

Before I knew it, our paper money had dwindled to a concern. A quick scour of the area showed the usual scarcity of jobs with wages to match. And somehow by way of the backwoods telegraph, Butch and Coop got in touch. They'd got the ax up in Klawock also shortly after I left. Now they were in Lowman, Idaho cut'n fer the helicopter. "Terrillion!" sez Butch, "Come on over." So I did.

The timber was generally big and the ground steep. When I sometimes fell a big pine it would roll and roll a long way down. Then you chased it to buck it into logs so the helicopter could fly it. Some days ya got so tired ya could hardly put one foot ahead of the other. And when yer overtired ya get careless.

END OF THE OLD JOURNEY

It was one close call after another. Fly'n limbs, dangerous cuts on the steep ground, roll'n logs cascading with a crash.

At night I was often awakened by the fear of be'n killed on the mountain. Night after night the fear grew worse till it turned to thoughts of eternal hell. I didn't realize it then, but it was the Spirit of God calling me. In other words, my life of high jinks was up. God was say'n, "Whoa, you will stop here and consider your eternal destiny?" Well, a quick check of my inventory told me where I was headed. And I wouldn't need no Zippo lighter where I was go'n.

Fer days and nights I was overwhelmed with grief, and guilt, and remorse. Fer the first time in my life, I saw myself as a great sinner instead of the good ol' boy. My soul was so downcast. "Oh where would I go seeking a refuge for my soul?" That's what the old hymn sez.

There was a Gideon Bible in the nightstand. Surely here was my answer. Fer that was what the old Bensons in Oregon had said. One night I opened it somewhere in the Old Testament. The great I Am was let'n the children of Israel have it fer all their disobedience and rebellion. They were suffer'n greatly and would suffer even worse. And I closed the book feel'n bad. Had I read the recommended places in the front fer comfort I'd have found hope. But I never did figure I needed to read instructions.

Next morning the helicopter left me off on top of the mountain, the sun was just peek'n over the Sawtooth range. The mountains were serene, majestic, and grand, and the valleys below were a picture of peace. But I had no peace. The tall Ponderosa pine stood like giants and their fragrance clung to my soul. The trees that always was my joy did nuthin' this day to lift a heavy heart. I stood look'n east at that bursting sunrise and was suddenly overwhelmed with the greatness of God.

Overcome by my guilt, I couldn't stand before a holy God. I fell on my face and cried out, "Oh, God what would you have me do?" His Spirit lay upon me as to convict me and console me. Within my being I heard Him say, "Build my church."

Just how long I knelt there with my face stuck in the pine needles I don't remember. When I was finally able to stand I still was under terrible conviction. And like so many other sinners who had come to the end of their journey of sin, change must start now. Peace, however, would not come fer another year and a half when I realized Jesus had walked that road to Calvary and died fer me, taking my place so I could be set free from the law of sin and death.

This new journey to help build His church—the body of Christ—was so clear according to the Scriptures, but I would find a church seriously divided among denominations to the point that no sincere fellowship could be found. I could find a limited fellowship as long as I didn't hang around with a different denomination than where I was attending. I became lonely for sincere fellowship. Centuries of discord, envy, and jealousy had allowed Satan a firm foothold and kept the saints from interfellowship.

END OF THE OLD JOURNEY

Therefore, we could not become fully mature, attaining to the whole measure of the fullness of Christ.

An outpouring of the Spirit of God upon His church similar to Pentecost is needed to bring out the remnant of His people from denominational bondage. Our Father in heaven will bring it about—through repentance and peaceful prayer gathering at each other's churches or through great trouble. The choice is ours. Either way, He will pour out His Spirit in these last days. It will be a pillar of fire to lead us to the great revival and beyond, enabling us to be faithful and ready for Christ to receive His Bride.

Hallelujah!!!!!

JOURNEY TO THE BACKWOODS

Flat ground, big timber, Northeastern Oregon

END OF THE OLD JOURNEY

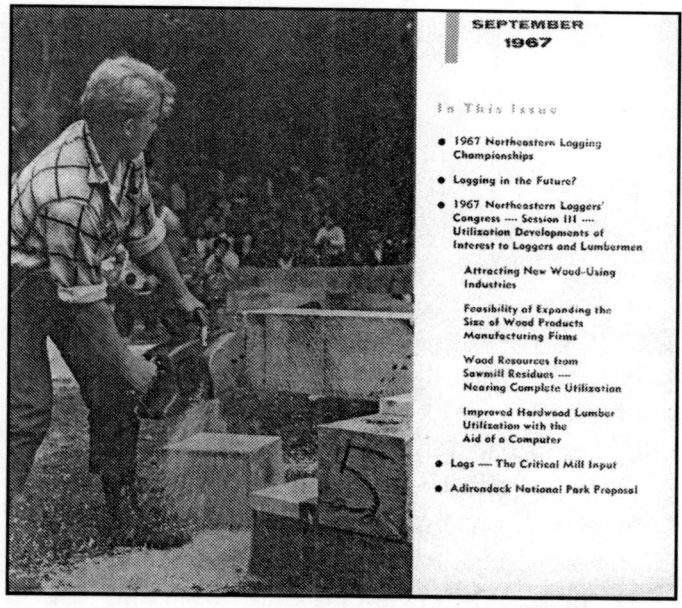

Yours truly making precision cuts at the Northeastern Logging Championships. Old Forge, New York, 1967.

EPILOGUE

Since the end of the journey in 1981, Dale continued to cut timber and live the life of the great outdoors. He and Geraldine improved their Montana homestead and seeing their children all grown up, one by one they all left home. They always remember the young 'uns coming up the driveway after school chattering at the dogs as they ran to meet them. Winters they raced down the hill on their sleds shrieking with delight. In the summers they entertained themselves with their bicycles and horses. There were no computer games to rob them of their childhood.

For several years Dale attended many churches and tried in vain to get church leaders to drop their pride and repent for the divisions in the body

EPILOGUE

of Christ. These divisions are tools of Satan. The Father's waiting that the great revival might come.

Dale spends much of his winter writing tracts on spiritual matters, camped on the desert in Arizona whenever he and Geraldine can get down there. The tracts and writings will be a book called *Passages*. Dale also has been working on a collection of stories, "Out'n the Woods Again" rewritten from his column in the weekly newspaper, *The Pathfinder*.

In about the middle 90s Dale had to quit the physically demanding timber cutting. They sold the homestead and built a cabin near Flathead Lake. He and Geraldine spend their time helping children and grandchildren. Dale loves his horses and when he isn't riding them, makes "Backwoods" furniture of heirloom quality.

REFERENCES

1. Volwiler, A.T., *George Croghan* Printed in the U.S.A. Publishing Company, Crowell-Collier Educational Corporation, 1968. Vol 7, pg. 491.
2. *The Autobiography of Ben Franklin,* Edited by; Leonard W. Labaree, Ralph L. Ketcham, Helen C. Boalfield, and Helene H. Fineman. Printed by Bookcrafters Inc., Chelsea, Michigan, U.S.A. Yale University Press, 1964, New Haven and London, pg. 223-225.
3. George Croghan, *Pennsylvania Magazine of History and Biography* Vol. LXXI Center Street Philadelphia Pennsylvania; Pennsylvania Magazine of History and Biography, Copyright date), 444.
4. *The Autobiography of Ben Franklin,* p. 13.

To order additional copies of this title:
Please visit our Web site at
www.pleasantwordbooks.com

If you enjoyed this quality custom published book,
drop by our Web site for more books and information.

www.winepressgroup.com
"Your partner in custom publishing."

For more information contact:
Dale Terrillion
51068 Lake Mary Ronan Rd
Proctor, MT 59929
Phone: 1-406-250-1275